THE SHIP OF FOOLS

By SEBASTIAN BRANT

TRANSLATED INTO RHYMING COUPLETS
WITH INTRODUCTION AND COMMENTARY

By EDWIN H. ZEYDEL

with reproductions of the original woodcuts

DOVER PUBLICATIONS, INC.
NEW YORK

International Standard Book Number: 486-20266-6

Manufactured in the United States of America
Dover Publications, Inc.
180 Varick Street
New York, N. Y. 10014

PREFACE

THE REASONS prompting the writer to make this translation of Sebastian Brant's fifteenth-century *Narrenschiff*, or Ship of Fools, in modern English in the verse form and rhyme scheme of the original may be summed up briefly.

This is actually the first English translation of Brant's masterpiece ever to appear. The two sixteenth-century versions of Barclay and Watson, both published in 1509, are not translations of Brant in any sense, but very free adaptations based upon Latin and French editions.

Brant's work was the most famous book of its time and exercised a tremendous influence in England as well as on the Continent, appearing between 1497 and 1548 in Latin, Low German, French, English, Flemish, and Dutch. With the *Narrenschiff* German literature entered for the first time into the stream of European letters and, indeed, helped to give that stream a new direction.

The *Narrenschiff* expresses the views of a noted forerunner of German humanism, but one who, not in sympathy with the ideas which were paving the way for the Reformation, wanted to conserve and strengthen the *status quo* throughout the Christian world. This phase of European thought at the dawn of the sixteenth century must be appreciated too if we desire a comprehensive picture of that all-important age.

Finally, the *Narrenschiff* is a work of truly popular appeal—aphoristic, quotable, humorous—and contains authentic comments and illuminating sidelights on the customs, activities, follies, and foibles of its day, with the earliest reference in literature to the discovery of America by Columbus.

This edition reproduces the approximately one hundred woodcuts of the original edition—among them some of the finest of their kind ever made. The work cannot be fully understood or appreciated without this integral component.

The translation is based upon the first edition, which appeared in Basel in 1494; the Franz Schultz facsimile of 1913 was used. It was felt that the material added by Brant to the second and third editions contributes nothing essentially new or necessary to an understanding of the work. The Introduction aims to supply the necessary background, and the Commentary strives to explain such difficulties as a work now almost four and a half centuries old is bound to present. Both Introduction and Commentary are based upon independent research.

For many courtesies received, the writer would express his gratitude to the staffs of the various libraries which he has used, especially those of the University of Cincinnati, of Cornell University, and of the New York Public Library. He is indebted to the Charles Phelps Taft Memorial Fund of the University of Cincinnati for substantial financial aid in making his research possible and in publishing this handsome volume. He is deeply grateful to Professor Bayard Quincy Morgan of Stanford University for reading the translation with great care, giving it the benefit of his expert criticism, and making numerous suggestions for its improvement. He would also thank Professor Austin P. Evans, the general editor of the series in which this volume appears, Miss Elizabeth J. Sherwood, managing editor of the Columbia University Press, and Professor Robert Herndon Fife of Columbia University for trenchant criticism of the entire manuscript, and the Columbia University Press for undertaking its publication.

It is hoped that the friends of Brant everywhere will see in the present undertaking a modest tribute to his memory on the approaching four hundred and fiftieth anniversary of the first appearance of his epoch-making masterpiece.

EDWIN H. ZEYDEL

Cincinnati, Ohio,
January 1, 1944

CONTENTS

INTRODUCTION   1

  I. THE LIFE AND WORKS OF BRANT   1

 II. THE ANTECEDENTS AND GENESIS OF THE "NARRENSCHIFF"   8

III. A CHARACTERIZATION AND LITERARY HISTORY OF THE "NARRENSCHIFF"   15

    (1) Contents and Style.—(2) The Woodcuts.—(3) The Editions and Reprints.—(4) The Translations and Adaptations

 IV. THE "NARRENSCHIFF" AS A FORCE IN LITERATURE   31

  V. BIBLIOGRAPHY   45

TEXT   55

COMMENTARY   367

INDEX   393

INTRODUCTION

THE LIFE AND WORKS OF BRANT

THE AGE in which Sebastian Brant lived marks a period of imminent revolutionary changes in Germany as well as in Europe generally. It is the era immediately preceding and ushering in sixteenth-century German humanism and the Protestant Reformation. The date of the famous letter of the Mainz chancellor Martin Meyer to Aeneas Sylvius (1457) coincides almost exactly with that of Brant's birth. At the same time the first important books were coming from the printing press, and there had long been signs of the influence of Greek fugitives in Italy in favor of the Greek classical writers. When Brant was thirty-four, Columbus made his first crossing of the Atlantic and discovered the New World. When he was forty-four, Zwingli came to Basel. Five years later Martin Waldseemüller, in his *Cosmographiae Introductio* (1507), suggested the name "America" for the newly found continent. Ten years after this, in 1517, Martin Luther posted his ninety-five theses on the portals of the Wittenberg Schlosskirche. In 1519 Zwingli began spreading the doctrine of the Reformation from his pulpit in Zürich, and in the same year Luther engaged in the famous Leipzig disputations with Eck and Karlstadt, questioning the infallibility of the Council of Constance. A year later Luther's pamphlet, *An den christlichen Adel deutscher Nation*, spread through the German-speaking countries like wildfire. In 1521 Luther refused to recant at Worms, and on May 4 of that year —six days before Brant's death—Luther was spirited away to the Wartburg.

Brant did not take an active part in any of these momentous events, although he warned urgently against religious differences and possessed reliable information about the first voyage of Columbus. All the available evidence concerning the date of his birth points to the year 1458, except his gravestone preserved in the municipal library of his native Strassburg. It records his death as occurring on May 10, 1521, but states that he lived to be sixty-four. This may be an error or may mean that he was in his sixty-fourth year; at any rate it has prompted some scholars to assign his birth to 1457. The Brant family was not prosperous, and when the father, an innkeeper, died in 1468, the mother, born Barbara Picker, struggled hard to maintain her home and educate her young children. She must have been a resolute and able but also a tender woman. Taking personal charge of young Sebastian's education, which she determined should be the best they could afford, she impressed her character indelibly upon him and influenced him to a marked degree. If Brant always revealed a tender, almost effeminate nature and the sensitivity of a mother's pet, this was a part of his heritage from his mother. This influence explains, too, his deep respect for good women, a trait which sets him apart from his contemporaries.

The schools in Strassburg were still inferior, and Barbara may have decided to send her eldest away to school. Possibly he had some of his preparatory education under the then noted educator Dringenberg in Schlettstadt in Lower Alsace, where Erasmus also studied not long after.

At any rate, by the autumn of 1475 he was ready for the university. He matriculated in the philosophical faculty of the recently founded University of Basel. This city, already famous as the seat of the great Council (1431–1448), was an important center of the young humanistic movement. Here Brant cultivated the friendship of the Realist Johann Heynlin von Stein, known as "a Lapide." [1] He was also on good terms with

1 See Zeydel in *Modern Language Quarterly*, IV (1943), 209 ff.

Reuchlin, who took his baccalaureate degree in Basel the year of Brant's arrival and his master's degree two years later, when Brant was awarded the lower degree.

During his first two years at Basel Brant studied Aristotelian philosophy, logic, the rudiments of what was then styled physics, as well as rhetoric and a very little Greek. By the time he secured his baccalaureate he must have done considerable writing in the Latin language. Now he decided to transfer to the faculty of law. At this time Basel occupied a unique position in the field of legal studies, for unlike the average German university it offered not only canon but also civil law, the latter taught by Italian professors. In 1484 Brant secured his license to practice and teach canon law. He appears to have taken up teaching at the university immediately—not only law, but also humanities—and perhaps practiced also, for within a year he felt economically secure enough to marry Elisabeth Burg.

Once having become a licentiate, Brant was required by law to take the doctorate at the same university. He did so in 1489, becoming Doctor Utriusque Juris. His inclination was toward civil, or Roman, law and is explained in part by his enthusiasm for the Holy Roman Empire. The most important of his works *law* at this time is the original historico-political pamphlet *De origine et conversatione bonorum regum et laude civitatis Hierosolymae.* The latter part of this has much in common with Chapter 99 of the *Narrenschiff.*

During the late eighties Brant became interested in another kind of literary activity, that of publication expert and adviser for the Basel book printers. Probably a Lapide recommended him for this work. It consisted of advising printers, editing manuscripts, reading proof, writing introductions or prefaces and what we would call "blurbs," in the form of dedicatory or epilogic Latin verse soliciting the readers' interest in newly published books. At least one-third of all the volumes printed in

Basel before 1490 show signs of his collaboration, whether they mention his name or not. Soon he became very skillful at turning out Latin verse, and he indulged this flair ever more freely, producing religious, political, and didactic poems, mostly of an occasional nature, which express the conservative views of a Lapide and his circle.

At first he had difficulty in finding appropriate subjects for his worldly poems. For Brant represents a comparatively new type of poetry in German literature, that of the bourgeoisie, or the upper middle class. This new poetry, in its infancy in Brant's time, knew little of, and cared less for, the medieval folk and chivalric literature of the thirteenth century. It was therefore forced to cast about for novel subjects of contemporaneous interest. When Maximilian became Roman king in 1486, this problem was solved for Brant. He became the unofficial panegyrist of the monarch of the Holy Roman Empire, lauding him to the skies in well-rounded Latin hexameters or elegiac distichs.

Brant wanted to coöperate with the Pope in effecting reforms in the Church, pleaded for a revival of the Empire in the East and action against the Turks, and prayed God to guide the ship of state well and to bring unity to the dismembered and impotent body politic. The collection of his Latin poems was issued three times in 1498 under the title *Varia carmina*.[2]

Believing that not only the scholars who could read Latin, but also the more intelligent burghers who knew the vernacular, should be reached and influenced by his verse, he began translating his own and others' Latin poetry into German. While many of these translations have been lost, some have come down to us. The first efforts are written in a stiff, almost

---

[2] The writer has examined the copy in the Cornell University Library, Petrarch Collection. Prior to this, Brant had already published a shorter collection of his Latin verse.

unintelligible German. But as Brant became more adept in using his native tongue, his verse technique improved. By way of
a severe schooling in Latin, Brant gradually acquired the ability
to write a German which for that day was remarkable for its
purity and neatness of form.

Many of Brant's earlier writings are satiric broadsides or
lampoons published as popular pamphlets or "fliegende Blätter," often in journalistic fashion, describing some recent event,
but always espousing Brant's own philosophy of life.[3] Here he
delighted in exploiting natural phenomena and in attaching to
them political significance favorable to Maximilian's cause.

One of Brant's closest friends in Basel was his former fellow
student, Johann Bergmann von Olpe of Westphalia, who had
become an archdeacon in Switzerland. Early in the nineties
Bergmann spent much of his time in Basel. Interested in the new
trade of printing, he took it up as an avocation in order more
readily to disseminate the ideas of his circle of friends. A well-
to-do Maecenas, he was not impelled by motives of gain. He
learned the trade in the shop of Michael Furter and in 1493 as-
sisted him in publishing the *Ritter vom Turn* (a collection of
moralizing tales translated and adapted by Marquart vom Stein
from the original French of the Chevalier de la Tour Landry),
one of the most beautiful volumes of Basel craftsmanship, illustrated with exquisite woodcuts. Then Bergmann established a
press of his own, and Brant's *Narrenschiff*, the *editio princeps*
of which came out in 1494, was perhaps the first product of
his shop—a magnificent piece of bookmaking. In publishing
Brant's masterpiece and providing it with some of the finest
woodcuts of the fifteenth century, Bergmann identified himself
with one of the truly remarkable books of the age.

In addition to the works already mentioned, Brant published
an illustrated redaction of Freidank's *Bescheidenheit* (1508),

[3] See P. Heitz (ed.), *Des Sebastian Brant Flugblätter* (Strassburg, 1915).

the first edition and expansion of this work to appear in print and the only edition before Wilhelm Grimm's (1834), and practically the sole evidence of Brant's later interest in early German literature. This, together with German versions of the jest book *Facetus* (1496) and of *Moretus* (1499), bears some kinship to the *Narrenschiff*.[4]

Practically all of Brant's more important writings, characterized throughout by stern religious conservatism, appeared during his Basel period. In Strassburg, whither he returned early in 1501 as municipal syndic, official duties prevented him from devoting much time to literary pursuits. Two years later he secured the key position of "Stadtschreiber," or chancellor, and as such played a very distinguished role in the public life of the Alsatian capital for the rest of his days. He became a prominent member of the Strassburg literary society, which had been founded by Wimpheling. When in 1514 Erasmus, on his journey from England to Basel, stopped at Strassburg, he was tendered a dinner by the society and was received like a prince. Deeply impressed, the great Dutch humanist praised the "incomparable Brant" and expressed his satisfaction at having got to know and embrace him; [5] in a subsequent poem he honored Brant, saying that while others bask in the glory of their environment, Brant has added new luster to his native town. Later Erasmus himself founded a similar society in Basel.

Brant headed several missions to the Emperor Maximilian and was honored when the Pope sided with him in a controversy. Because of its disparaging remarks about the Emperor Maximilian, Brant prevented the publication in Strassburg of *Gäuchmatt* by Thomas Murner, the opponent of Luther and the imitator of the *Narrenschiff*. After the death of his beloved

[4] F. W. Chandler in *The Literature of Roguery* (Boston and New York, 1907), I, 27, goes so far as to say that the jest books gave birth to satirical fool literature.
[5] In a letter to Wimpheling of October, 1514.

emperor in 1519 Brant headed an official Strassburg mission to Ghent, to do homage to Charles V, by whom he was graciously received. In Antwerp he may have met Erasmus a second time. Here, too, Dürer made a portrait of him.[6]

Brant's last years were clouded by ill health and evil forebodings. Recognizing abuses and vicious practices which had become rife in the Church, sensing the threat of rising Lutheranism and Zwinglianism against the hierarchy, and convinced that the bonds of the Empire were loosening because of internal disunity and the alarming progress of the Turkish invaders—a conviction which he had already expressed in Chapter 99 of the *Narrenschiff* almost thirty years before—Brant feared a dreadful catastrophe for the Holy Roman Empire and could see no way of averting it.

Brant was a man of deep religious convictions and of stern morality, even to the point of prudishness. His motives were of the highest. He wanted to elevate his generation, and dreamed too of improving its political condition through moral regeneration. He was a typical fifteenth-century savant, a typical South German, and a typical upper-class burgher, proud of his civic rights. He admired the common people, though chiding the peasants severely for many excesses, and acquired the ability to express himself in the vernacular so popularly and sententiously that even the humblest could understand him.

Yet he was also nervous and irritable, positive and dogmatic, a carping satirist of the very follies of which he himself may often have been guilty. His tendency to seek weaknesses and flaws in others was congenital. His morality was philistine. What was bad, in his eyes, was not bad *per se*, but because the authorities—the Bible, the canonical writers, the ancients—said so. And sins like adultery seemed to him to be on the same level

[6] See J. Janitsch, *Das Bildnis Sebastian Brants von Albrecht Dürer* (Strassburg, 1906).

with vices like drinking, or even with foibles like slavery to fashion. While Luther, Zwingli, Erasmus, Reuchlin, and Hutten sought to dethrone existing authority and to establish new standards, Brant revered and defended the accepted traditions.

If Brant encouraged and promoted humanism, he did so unwittingly by setting certain examples—through his pure, clear Latin style; his not infrequent references to Homer, Xenophon, and Plutarch (whom he probably could not read in the original), to Terence, Catullus, Ovid, Vergil, Juvenal, and Seneca; his interest in old manuscripts; his friendship with the Basel printers; his concern for the fate of the individual; and his skill as a metricist. But he kept aloof from most of the controversies of the day. His interest in literature, whether ancient or modern, was not a poet's; it was always colored and conditioned by his concern for morality or for Church dogma. He regarded the sale of indulgences as proper and deemed absolution good for the soul. Lacking historical perspective, he had no notion of the development and progress of civilization. In his philosophy, which may be summed up in the thought that it is foolish to sacrifice eternal salvation for the sake of passing pleasures, he considered himself a preacher in the wilderness.

ANTECEDENTS AND GENESIS OF THE ''NARRENSCHIFF''

It is possible that separate chapters of the *Narrenschiff* came out at first as separate handbills, or at least were initially planned for individual publication. Originality was not Brant's forte, and his book may be called a compilation of "fliegende Blätter" and a piecing together of authorities—the Bible, the *Corpus juris canonici*, and ancient writers. In literature the distinction between fools and wise men is at least as old as the Bible and can be found in ancient Greek and Roman literatures as well. In the German, as early as the twelfth century, the erring are referred to as fools. In Hans Vintler's *Pluemen der Tugend* (1411), translated and adapted from the fourteenth-century Italian of Tomaso Leoni and printed in Basel in 1486, could be found portraits of fools considered from a moralizing point of view. The words *narr, tore, affe, esel, gouch* were all in everyday use to refer to those who comported themselves as fools. The idea was a commonplace in the later Middle Ages and the usual means of venting wrath and scorn, in France [7] as well as in Germany. Various types of fatuous persons were subjects for popular amusement in the "Fastnachtspiele" (Shrovetide plays) before Brant (though not the Brantian idea that all sins are reducible to forms of folly); also in the tractate *Doctoratus in stultitia* of the Zürich writer Felix Hemmerlin (which Brant edited toward the end of the century) and in the anonymous satire of about 1450, *Die acht Schalkheiten*, consisting of eight handbill woodcuts with rhymes.[8] The notion of a utopia of ruined revelers was well known throughout the Continent and in England too long before Sir Thomas More, who derived it anew from Lucian; in France in the *Fabliaux de Coquaigne*, in Holland in *Van det edele lant van Cockaenghen*, in Germany in the tales of the *Schlaraffenland*, and in England as the *Land of Cockayne*.

In England, indeed, Brant had two important forerunners in Nigel Wireker (*Speculum stultorum*, twelfth century) and John Lydgate (*Order of Fools*, fifteenth century). But unlike Brant, each of these starts with the idea of a religious fraternity.

[7] As early as 1450 "la sottie" was a peculiar and popular species of literature in France, whence it was taken to Holland and Denmark.

[8] That at least one other such handbill containing a series of eight cartoons, each showing a fool with a couplet in a scroll, was in circulation as early as the seventies or eighties of the fifteenth century, and that (unless one assumes Brant himself to be its author) it influenced him in writing his *Narrenschiff* was proved by Zarncke when he described such a series in two articles, *Zur Vorgeschichte des Narrenschiffes*, the first in Naumann's *Serapeum* (1868), the second as a pamphlet (Leipzig, 1871). The Cornell University Library possesses copies in the Zarncke collection.

Wireker's work, a satire on the clergy, is the livelier of the two and is built on the fiction of the ass looking for a longer tail, going to foreign lands to study, and forming a new order in which he may do as he pleases.[9] Lydgate's work is a catalogue of isolated traits of dangerously foolish persons, similar to Brant's, but without presenting the fools in person in a sort of rudimentary drama supported by woodcuts, as Brant does. In his catalogue of sins Lydgate stresses deceit and duplicity, while Brant emphasizes riotous sensuality. This difference of emphasis is interesting if one agrees with the Englishman Herford,[10] who sees in these cardinal vices the outstanding national vices of the two respective countries at the time. But it is certain that Brant had no direct knowledge of either Wireker or Lydgate.

Gradually there was born in Brant's mind the idea of writing a series of chapters, each depicting some type of fool. Bergmann must have encouraged him in this, and the *Narrenschiff* was, as has been indicated, one of the very first products of the Bergmann printing establishment.[11] Having at his disposal apparently a whole corps of artists and woodcarvers, Bergmann had each of these chapters illustrated, no doubt under Brant's personal supervision. In this way about one half of the entire work, or the first sixty-one or sixty-two chapters, was planned, with the possible exception of Chapter 48.

There are several indications of this. Each of the earlier chapters begins at the top of the left-hand page with a three-line motto, followed by the cut and by four lines of text. Then thirty more lines of text appear on the opposite right-hand

---

9 Chaucer in the "Nun's Priest's Tale" quotes from the *Speculum stultorum*.
10 *Studies in the Literary Relations of England and Germany in the Sixteenth Century* (Cambridge, 1886).
11 The fact that the first edition of the *Narrenschiff* is set up in a planless mixture of Roman and Gothic types, either style being used apparently as it was momentarily available, would indicate that the shop was very new and had not yet been supplied with a sufficient number of letters of each font.

page, the entire chapter, therefore, consisting of thirty-four lines. Some chapters, however, consist of three plus ninety-four lines. In such cases two more full pages of text followed, so that the next chapter might again begin on the left-hand page. Apart from Chapter 48, which has a full-page cut and which fits into the scheme of the latter half of the work, and the *Vorred* (Prologue), only Chapter 58 deviates slightly from this scheme in having one extra line, making three plus thirty-five in all. In the second half, this plan is no longer strictly adhered to; the cuts are either on the left or the right-hand page, and the length of the chapters runs from three plus thirty-four to over two hundred lines. Another distinguishing characteristic of the first half of the work is that it is, on the whole, more carefully done metrically. But the most striking difference between the two halves is that while the fiction of a *ship* of fools plays practically no part in the first half (in Chapters 1, 8, 16 and 36 a *narren schiff* is referred to, but more usually Brant speaks of a *narren dantz* or *spil* or *schlitt* or *seil* or *bri* or of the traditional fool's bagpipes or of a court of fools), the allegory of the ship becomes much more common in the second half and in the Prologue, which was probably written last.[12] The notion of a ship, then, predominated by the time the work was completed but not in its earlier stages of composition, and was used in the title.

Where did Brant derive this allegorical idea of a ship? Some early critics, relying upon what is no doubt a false etymology of the word "carnival," which they would derive from *car* and *naval* (a "cart-ship"), link the fools' ship with the floats still used during carnival time. These floats, some resembling vessels, others wagons, were laden with various types of comical or fantastic characters. The practice, said to go back to pagan

---

[12] In the *Prologue* Brant comments upon the finished work in general and speaks of having burned midnight oil in writing it.

tradition and cult, is supposed to have been a part of the worship of Isis and Nerthus, goddesses of spring, who bring peace and fertility to earth and mankind. These divinities were then impersonated by masked figures, represented at first by priests, then by the populace.

However authentic or not these conjectures may be, it is true that the idea of placing careless livers, rakes, drinkers, and the like together upon a ship was widespread from Holland to Austria before Brant's time. The most famous of such ships was actually said to have started on a cross-country journey from Aachen (Aix-la-Chapelle). This notion is the basis of a poem entitled *Das schif der flust* (*ca.* 1360) by Heinrich Teichner, an Austrian,[13] and of some Shrovetide verse, *Die blauwe schute* (1413), by a Dutch writer, Jacob van Oestvoren; it is suggested also in the French *Renart le Nouvel* of Giélée (1288). But of more direct and immediate significance for Brant's *Narrenschiff* is a humorous academic oration, delivered in Latin from a platform built in the style of a ship, by Jodocus Gallus in Heidelberg some time in the late 1480's at a meeting presided over by Brant's friend Wimpheling. This oration, entitled *Monopolium et societas vulgo des Liechtschiffs*, was published by Attendorn in Strassburg, probably at Wimpheling's behest, in 1489.[14] It seems to derive from both Teichner and van Oestvoren, for, as in *Das schif der flust*, the ship waits on land for the passengers, and, as in *Die blauwe schute*, a privileged guild of ne'er-do-wells boards it.[15] It travels across country and is

[13] See Zarncke's edition, p. lxv.

[14] Modern critics all believe that it was Zarncke who discovered the oration of Gallus. As a matter of fact, a Chemnitz publication of 1760, *Altes aus allen Theilen der Geschichte* (Stösselische Buchhandlung, 2. Stück, pp. 235 ff.) proves that as early as that date it was known to have influenced Brant.

[15] The idea of an order or a guild (but not a ship) of worthless persons was found also in Wireker and Lydgate, so that this notion must have been common literary property on the Continent and in England as early as 1450. Probably the idea of a shipful of such people was also common property on the Continent long before Brant. On the oration of Jodocus Gallus, see

followed by a second vessel. A woodcut accompanying the oration shows a ship laden with passengers sailing through the air. One man cries out: "hie har zum liecht schiff zu." [16] Another shouts: "fiensche companie, fiensche." Below is a man hurrying to catch up with the ship, crying: "beita, beita," while in the distance we see a wine keg drawn by two horses.

In view of Brant's usual dependence upon sources and his close personal relationship to Wimpheling it is more than likely that the *Monopolium* of Jodocus Gallus, published in his native town five years before the appearance of the *Narrenschiff*, is one of the sources for his idea of a ship. The recent discovery by Adolf Spamer of a sermon on the subject of a fools' ship, entitled *Disz ist ein hubsche predig gethon uff S. Ursula tag, sagt von dem geistlichen narrenschiff*, etc., [17] seems to prove beyond a doubt that even the conceit of a fools' ship was no innovation of Brant.[18] Internal evidence indicates that this sermon dates from the sixties or seventies of the fifteenth century; besides, the anonymous preacher boasts that with a ship of fools he is offering something *new*, although admitting that allegorical interpretations of St. Ursula's ship have occurred before. In his sermon this preacher describes twenty-one fools of the "Narrenschiff" and, as the twenty-second character, Christ, who, followed by St. Ursula's ship, crosses the sea dry and exhorts the fools to leave their vessel and board Christ's St. Ur-

---

besides Zarncke, Riegger, *Amoenitates literariae Friburgenses* (Ulm, 1776), and P. von Wiskowatoff, *Jacob Wimpheling, sein Leben und seine Schriften* (Berlin, 1867), p. 74.

[16] These words are in a scroll. Cf. the second prefatory cut to the *Narrenschiff*, where one fool on the ship shouts to others rowing toward it: "har noch." Cf. also the words directly under the *Narrenschiff* cut: "zu schyff zu schyff bruder: Esz gat, esz gat."

[17] Adolf Spamer, "Eine Narrenschiffspredigt aus der Zeit Sebastian Brants," in *Otto Glauning zum 60. Geburtstag. Festgabe aus Wissenschaft und Bibliothek*, II (Leipzig, 1938), 113–30.

[18] Spamer's important discovery refutes the conjecture of Pompen, *The English Versions of the Ship of Fools*, p. 299, that Brant may have derived the idea of a ship from one of the *Narrenschiff* woodcuts.

sula's ship, which is described as a ship of penitence. This sermon is remarkable not only in anticipating Brant's notion; it
must also be the source for Geiler's *Schiff der Penitentz und
Busswirkung.* It clearly foreshadows the *St. Ursulä Schifflein*
compiled by the Carthusian monks of Strassburg in 1497 on the
basis of Brant's *Narrenschiff;* it suggests Chapter 103 of Brant's
Narrenschiff, which contrasts the ship of fools with St. Peter's
ship; and finally it vindicates Lessing (after almost two hundred years) in assuming a relationship between the fools' ship
and St. Ursula's ship.[19]

Given Brant's original notion of a series of chapters depicting
various fools and the subsequent influence of Jodocus Gallus
and of the *Predig,* the development of the new conceit is natural
enough. That it is not carried out better in the *Narrenschiff* is
due, probably, to the gradual and casual development of the
idea in his own mind and to his inability to elaborate the concept to a logical, imaginative, and consistent conclusion. In the
Prologue he speaks of a ship and of an entire fleet traveling on
land and sea. This is not taken up again (except for Chapter 48)
before the second half of the work. In Chapters 103 and 108
(the latter of which takes up the conceit of the prefatory cuts
and is the last integral chapter) the fate of the fleet is discussed.

[19] *Zur Geschichte der deutschen Sprache und Literatur von den Minne-
sängern bis auf Luthern,* in Lessing's *Schriften,* Lachmann-Muncker edition,
XVI, 364. See Zarncke's edition of the *Narrenschiff,* p. lix. The story of
St. Ursula is told most completely in accordance with the revelations made
to the German nun Helentrude, who lived in the eleventh century. Ursula,
a beautiful British maiden, demanded in marriage by a pagan king, asked
for three years' respite and during that time collected a host of eleven thousand virgins, whom she trained in vigorous physical exercises. Carried off by
a sudden breeze in eleven triremes to Thill on the Waal in Gelderland,
Ursula and her spiritual Amazons proceeded in their vessels up the Rhine
to Köln and thence to Basel. Here they moored their ships and continued on
foot to Rome, to do homage to their bridegroom Christ. But on their return homeward by ship from Basel, they were slaughtered by the Huns at
Köln. St. Ursula's day is October 21. Lessing, in the place noted above,
records the existence of a brotherhood called "St. Ursulä Schifflein" as early
as 1470.

It is destined to be destroyed, and all the fools will drown, thus atoning for their thoughtless, foolish lives. This notion is expressed by Brant himself in his introduction to Locher's Latin translation. It is also indicated by Geiler in his sermons, and is in harmony with a favorite medieval thought, also found in a Spanish morality—that a fool's aimless life is comparable to a fool's sea voyage, undertaken without rudder and compass. But that this idea should have been so widely popularized by Brant only two years after the first voyage of Columbus to the New World, of which Brant had knowledge [20]—that is one of those singular quirks of fate with which the pages of history are dotted.

It should be borne in mind, however, that Chapter 108 is not intended to describe the fate of the entire fools' company but merely of the *Schluraffen*—the lazy, carefree carousers of the Land of Cockayne. The purpose of the trip has been interpreted variously—as a deportation, a trip to a fool's utopia, a journey to a madhouse or to a Horatian Anticyra. Murner believed that Brant meant to colonize the world with fools, which explains why there are so many everywhere! The starting point, Narbonne, and the destination of the voyage of *all* the fools, the land of Narragonia (an imaginary country meant to suggest Aragon and the German word "Narr"), are inventions of Brant.

A CHARACTERIZATION AND LITERARY HISTORY OF THE ''NARRENSCHIFF''

CONTENTS AND STYLE

It has been noted that the *Narrenschiff* is in a sense a compilation. In the introductory prose at the beginning and in the closing remarks at the end Brant notes that his work is "gesamlet."

[20] See Zeydel in *Journal of English and Germanic Philology* (July, 1943), pp. 410–11.

This does not mean that he has plagiarized any work in the usual way. But true to the spirit of the *bispel* collections—examples and guides for good moral conduct—Brant requires authorities for every point he makes. Whether discussing book collecting or education or dishonest servants or usury or any one of the numerous subjects considered in the 112 chapters of the first edition, he deems it necessary to quote numerous instances from the Bible,[21] from the *Corpus juris canonici*, from the Church Fathers, and from the ancients, usually in that order, to support his argument. So systematic is he that he sometimes cites his authorities in alphabetical order, but in the sequence noted—the Bible first, then the *Corpus*, and so forth. The Book of Proverbs and Ecclesiastes are his favorites in the Old Testament, and this is much more frequently used than the New Testament. He invariably employs the Latin Vulgate and does not shun the Apocrypha. Of Greek writers, Plutarch's *Paidagogia*, Xenophon, and Homer are used, but probably in Latin translations. Latin writers, especially Ovid, Vergil (but only pseudo-Vergilian works or the commentaries of Servius), Juvenal, and Seneca, and to a lesser degree Catullus, Cicero, Persius, and Boethius, are more often used. To make the identification of references easier, some of them are given in the margin of Locher's Latin translation. Later writers are mostly ignored; Freidank (whose work Brant later edited) is not mentioned, and the pranks of the Pfaffe von Kalenberg and Monk Islan, popular predecessors of Till Eulenspiegel, and the Moringen folk song are scorned as vulgar and obscene. In some cases an entire chapter is based upon a single source, for instance the Book of Proverbs. Chapter 112 is for the most part merely a free translation of the pseudo-Vergilian poem *Vir bonus*.

---

[21] Originally Brant may have intended to restrict his examples altogether to the Bible. The biblical quotation below the third prefatory cut would indicate this.

The *Narrenschiff* is unique, however, because of its conception, without perspective, of the sins, faults, and foibles of its own day as exemplifications of folly—"Narrheit"; [22] its humble, quotable sententiousness; [23] its broad scope of types; its suggestive but never exhaustive treatment of subjects; its skillful versification; and the fact that it treats all estates alike, from the highest to the lowest, including even Brant himself, who delights—compare Chapter 111—in referring to his own folly. Another very important reason, no doubt, for the success of the work is the fact that it is a picture book, that each fool is depicted in an interesting woodcut, alone or in a group, the blocks measuring 3½ by 4½, and in a few cases 4 by 6½, inches, some of them being outstanding masterpieces. They will be discussed below.

Nor is it necessary to read the book from beginning to end to understand it. Its biting satire, its humor, its popular language can be enjoyed just as much by random samplings. Even the occasional long lists of stock examples from Brant's favorite sources are not tiresome. For the naïve and casual manner in which they are introduced, their pertinence or lack of it, the systematic way in which they are marshaled, their rich variety, and occasionally Brant's complete failure to understand the point of his source [24]—all these things are more apt to hold the modern reader's attention, and even to amuse or delight him, than to arouse boredom.

[22] The *Narrenschiff* contributed much toward giving the word "narr" precedence over the other words for "fool"—"tore," "affe," "esel," "gouch," which were previously all about equally popular.

[23] Brant also had a rare gift for coining pithy compound words, striking phrases, and whimsical names. The *Narrenschiff* abounds in such gems, some of which immediately became part of the language. A few examples: 76, 7: vater macht bumble bum; 81, 34: der zapf macht glunk, glunk; 91, 15: klapperbenkly; 73, 91: klosterkatz; 93, 24: Kristen-Juden; 72, 1: Grobian; 76, 83: Hans Mist; 85, 27: Hansachtsinnit.

[24] Cf. Archer Taylor, *Problems in German Literary History of the Fifteenth and Sixteenth Centuries* (New York, London, 1939), p. 71.

Mention has been made of the fact that the second half shows
more evidence of haste and carelessness. It reveals the author
off his guard more frequently and, since he is here not impeded
by mechanical requirements of space, gives him a better oppor-
tunity to express his opinion less formally and more candidly.
Chapters 99 and 108 are examples of his best work.

Both content and style of the *Narrenschiff* as a whole bear
the stamp of Brant's individuality. In no other German work
of the fifteenth century are grave seriousness and heavy moral
didacticism, schooled in the accepted authorities, so completely
fused with ribald, teasing humor.[25] The style is always clear,
always animated and buoyant, and often balladesque. Although
Brant lacked the deep insight and broad horizon of Erasmus
and was given far more to moralizing than to sustained plot, yet
his work shows more loyalty to an ideal and more consistency
than the *Moriae encomium.*

It is not difficult to boil Brant's criticism down to its essen-
tials. The subjects of his preachment may be classed under six
general headings, namely: (1) vicious or criminal offenses, (2)
insolence, (3) riotousness, (4) sloth, (5) presumptuousness,
and (6) perversities. Herford has appropriately styled the
Narrenschiff a telling picture of the infirmities of German society in 1494. Isaac Disraeli writes in his *Amenities of Literature:* [26]

The Ship of Fools is, indeed, cumbrous, rude, and inartificial, and
was not constructed on the principles which regulate our fast-
sailing vessels; yet it may be prized for something more than its
curiosity. It is an ancient satire, of that age of simplicity which
must precede an age of refinement . . . he who turns over the
volume of the learned civilian of Germany will find detailed those

[25] There is some relationship between the *Narrenschiff* and the popular jest
books of the time. Cf. p. 6, above.
[26] New edition edited by his son, Benjamin Disraeli, I (London, New York,
1859), 286 f.

great moral effects in life which, if the modern moralist may invest with more dignity, he could not have discovered with more truth. We have outgrown the counsels, but we never shall elude the vexatious consequences of his experience; and many a chapter in the Ship of Fools will point many an argument *ad hominem*.

Professor Henry Charles Lea in his article "The Eve of the Reformation," in the *Cambridge Modern History*, claims for Brant's work a powerful influence on the course of historical events, calling it a "singularly instructive document for the intellectual and moral history of the period" and a notable embodiment of humanistic teaching, establishing a personal relationship between God and man.

THE WOODCUTS

The splendid woodcuts which accompanied the contemporaneous editions of Brant's work go far in explaining its success at the time, for with certain changes and additions they were used again and again for over a generation and were even copied in most foreign translations. They appeared in 1520 in the German edition of the sermons which Geiler von Kaisersberg derived from the *Narrenschiff*,[27] but the later sixteenth-century editions of the *Narrenschiff* no longer carried them.[28] Zarncke, in his monumental edition of the work, published in 1854, reproduced only a few of them in the back of his volume. They were not published again in their entirety until Simrock reproduced them excellently in his modern German translation in 1872, and Bobertag included them, in their original size but on poor paper, in his edition seventeen years later. They have come into their own again in the splendid facsimiles of the

---

[27] They had also been used in one of Murner's books. See also *More Books: a Bulletin of the Boston Public Library*, XVI (1941), 19, and XVII (1942), 183 ff.

[28] Some of the later translations, however, contained copies of them and in some cases new cuts.

original edition of 1494 published by Schultz in 1913 and in the same year by H. Koegler.

The subject of the *Narrenschiff* cuts is a difficult one to approach, for one must be schooled in iconography, the history of art, general history, literary research, philology, and folklore in order to do them justice. A controversy was aroused when Daniel Burckhardt in 1892 ascribed at least some of the better *Narrenschiff* cuts to young Dürer, who stopped in Basel between 1492 and 1494 when he was between twenty-two and twenty-four years of age. Some noted critics, among them Max Friedländer and Jaro Springer, supported this belief, while others, among them Wölfflin, were more skeptical. Certainly Wölfflin's moderate view deserves consideration. Perhaps the resemblance of some of the cuts to Dürer's work, he remarks, was due to the influence of his presence; perhaps occasionally he looked over the artist's shoulder or made suggestions to him, or even took the stylus into his own hand now and then. At any rate it is possible that Brant met Dürer in Basel, and it is certain that they met in Antwerp in 1520, when Dürer sketched his excellent portrait of Brant.

But whether Dürer participated in making the *Narrenschiff* blocks or not, internal evidence indicates that at least five or six artists were involved, that some of these were mere tyros and that the principal artist, or the master of the Bergmann shop, as he has been called since Weisbach's study of 1896, was responsible for about seventy-five, or practically two thirds of all the cuts.

The question what role Brant himself played in the preparation of the cuts has also been frequently discussed. The present writer feels that "har gemacht" in line 25 of the *Vorred* means not "hergestellt"—produced—but merely "hergesetzt"— placed or inserted here. The present generation of scholars believes—and it seems rightly so—that Brant had no ability whatsoever as an artist, that the cuts are usually superior to his verse, that they exemplify widely varying types and styles of illustration, and that while Brant may have given the artists an occasional suggestion, he could not have taken a prominent part in their work.

One can study and admire the better *Narrenschiff* cuts a long time and still discover new beauties and allurements. These cuts are delicate and yet sure of touch. The artist reveals a deftness, a pronounced talent for the figurative, great virtuosity, yet also refreshing simplicity and naturalness.

THE EDITIONS AND REPRINTS

Six authorized editions of the *Narrenschiff* came out during Brant's life. The best extant copy of the first (quarto) edition (Basel, 1494, Bergmann von Olpe) is that from the Meusebach collection, now in the Preussische Staatsbibliothek, Berlin. It forms the basis, through the Schultz facsimile edition of 1913, for the present translation. Brant himself did the proofreading, yet the edition contains at least twenty-five misprints which he must have overlooked. The second edition (Basel, 1495, Bergmann von Olpe) contains two new chapters, inserted between 110 and 111 and now usually referred to as No. 110 a (with the same cut as No. 16 and dealing with bad manners in eating and drinking, 3 plus 216 lines) and No. 110 b (no cut, no motto, and dealing with those who practice excesses at Shrovetide and carry them over into the holy period of fasting and praying, 115 lines). The third edition (Basel, 1499, same printer) adds a so-called "Protestation" of forty lines, now often numbered Chapter 113, written to protect Brant against the unauthorized additions and mutilations of pirated editions, which will be discussed below. The fourth edition (Basel, 1506) still contains the name of Bergmann as the printer, but probably his successor Nicolaus Lamparter was already in charge. The fifth edition

(Basel, 1509) gives Lamparter as the printer, while the sixth (Strassburg, 1512) was printed by Matthys Hüpfuff.

While these are the only *authorized* editions to appear during Brant's lifetime, at least six unauthorized editions came out in various cities of South Germany, supplying the entire region liberally with copies. Three of these are faithful copies of the first edition—with alterations only of dialect—and came out in Reutlingen, Nürnberg, and Augsburg, all in 1494. Three others (Strassburg, 1494 and 1497; Augsburg, 1495; Augsburg, 1498) are arbitrarily altered and expanded. Perhaps the Strassburg printer Grieninger (or Grüninger) was responsible for many of the changes.

The later editions and reprints of the sixteenth and seventeenth centuries appeared after Brant's death and lack the cuts. The following octavo editions were all published for the Frankfurt fairs in that city: 1553, Hermann Gülfferich; 1555, same publisher; 1560, Weygand Han; 1566, also 1567 (?) Georg Raben and heirs of Weygand Han; 1574, Nicolaus Höniger; and 1625, Jakob de Zetter. A Basel reprint of 1574 published by Sebastian Heinric Petri is also to be noted. But many of these contain arbitrary alterations in language and content and are often obviously meant for Protestant readers. Other unauthentic, grossly mutilated editions, some even under new author's names, are numerous: Augsburg, 1531 (a shamelessly plagiarized edition); Strassburg, 1540 (by Jacob Cammerlander of Mainz), 1545, 1549 (Rihel), and 1564 (Rihel); Zürich, 1563; a reprint by J. Flitner containing also a work of Murner, 1625; Hasleben (probably Frankfurt is the real place of publication), 1629 (Brant's work is here used as an appendix to another poem, *Hasen Jacht*, and the hare takes the place of the fool); and Freystadt (probably Augsburg), no date, but probably about 1670.

Twenty-nine more or less faithful editions or reprints of the original text of this famous book, mostly appearing within a period of about one hundred twenty-five years, have been noted. No doubt the Protestant Reformation hindered its progress seriously, for German readers, Protestant and Catholic alike, were flooded with other often less entertaining but more timely reading from 1520 on. Soon after the outbreak of the Thirty Years' War the book all but disappeared, and no new edition of it came out until 1839,[29] when Adam Walther Strobel, professor in the Strassburg Gymnasium, got out the first modern edition, based upon the first Basel edition of 1494. His text is generally accurate, and his successors have relied upon him heavily.[30] His biographical sketch of Brant is also admirable. But Strobel's notes reveal inaccuracies galore. In 1845 a new edition came out in Volume I of Scheible's *Kloster*. It is worse than useless, being based upon the garbled, emasculated, and adulterated Frankfurt Höniger edition of 1574. Zarncke's monumental edition of 1854 is a masterpiece of philological assiduity and acumen and a mine, though not a well-ordered one, of useful information. Goedeke, in his edition of 1872, made the grave error of normalizing the text, thus robbing his work of all authenticity, despite the helpfulness of his notes. Bobertag's edition in the Kürschner *Deutsche Nationalliteratur* (1889) has a good introduction, a text not as reliable as Zarncke's, and sparse notes of indifferent value. Probably more students have read the work in this edition than in any other. The more recent edition of Franz Schultz (1913) has been referred to several times. Since it is a facsimile of the first Basel edition, contains a

[29] In 1826 Jakob Grimm confessed that he had not read the work.
[30] It is indeed a curious fact, never before noted, that Zarncke, Goedeke, and Bobertag all copy an error which Strobel committed. In Chapter 103, line 85, the first edition has "sie lügen," but Strobel prints "die lügen." This is copied by all three, although Zarncke speaks, p. 265, of "ein buchstäblich genauer Abdruck der Originalausgabe." Bobertag sins even more gravely when he copies other errors of Zarncke, ignoring the latter's list of errata, P 474.

useful epilogue with the best extant discussion of the wood-cuts, a list of misprints overlooked by Brant himself, all the cuts (including even the new ones found in Locher's Latin version), and a correction of the position of cuts 38 and 55, which were erroneously interchanged in Brant's first edition, Schultz's work may be placed beside Zarncke's as one of the two most valuable contributions to the subject. Finally, H. Koegler published another facsimile of the first edition for the Weimar Society of Bibliophiles, Basel, 1913.

THE TRANSLATIONS AND ADAPTATIONS

The thirty-six editions and reprints of the text of the *Narrenschiff* to appear between 1494 and 1913 are indication enough of the popularity of the work up to 1650 and again from 1830 on. But the many translations and adaptations, which began appearing as early as 1497, in Latin, Low German, French, Dutch, Flemish, English, and modern German and which number an even dozen (published in a total of over forty editions) furnish still more eloquent testimony of the dissemination of what Schultz calls "this secular Bible which nourished an entire age." Including the present work, the total number of editions of the *Narrenschiff*, in the original language or in translation, makes an average of one edition every six years over a period of about four hundred fifty years—a remarkable record, considering the almost total eclipse of the book for a period of nearly two hundred years.

The first, and the most significant translation of the *Narrenschiff* is the Latin rendering of Jacob Locher (Philomusus Suevus), Brant's own pupil and protégé. This translation, published in Basel in 1497, was done with the direct collaboration of Brant himself on the basis of the second authorized edition. In fact, Brant personally made important contributions to this work. As indicated above, it contains some new woodcuts.

A very important point regarding this rendering becomes clear right at the outset. While Brant, in the body of his work, does not make much of the fiction of the *ship* until the second half, Locher stresses it at the very start and carries it through consistently. This influenced the later translations to a considerable extent.

A literal Latin translation, in a classical meter, of a work so popular and informal in tone, would of course be a physical impossibility, and one must agree with the view of Pompen, expressed in his excellent monograph, *The English Versions of the Ship of Fools*, that Locher scarcely reproduces more than one-third of the ideas and one-tenth of the wit and irony of Brant's original poem. Based upon the general idea of the German version, usually but not always following the approximate course of the thought in development and sequence, and offering the attractive woodcuts (with certain changes), Locher's *stultifera navis* is a very free adaptation of Brant's *Narrenschiff*, not a translation, made however, it should be noted again, with the warm approval and active collaboration of the author himself. Being in Latin, it strives to appear more learned. It contains far more classical allusions than did Brant's original and frequently shifts the emphasis. Many of the chapters are considerably shortened. Chapter 66, for instance, is cut from 154 to 34 lines.

The Low German (that is, Low Saxon) translation, *Dat narren schyp*, read in practically all northern—especially northwestern—Germany, may have appeared even before Locher's work. The first edition, of which but two copies seem to be extant (one in the British Museum, one in the Royal Library of Stockholm), came out of Lübeck in 1497 and is said to be by Hans van Ghetelen; a second revised edition is dated Rostock, 1519. Van Ghetelen's work is based chiefly upon the unauthorized but reliable Nürnberg edition of 1494 and to a

Locher's version is extremely important, not o[
was in the international language of its day, bu[
practically all the other translations of the fifte[
teenth centuries, except the Low German versio[
or partially upon it. A second authorized edition[
in 1497, a third in 1498, a Paris edition, publishe[
in 1498 (based, it seems, upon the second Basel[
a Lyons edition, published by Zachoni, in 1498.[
appeared in Strassburg, Augsburg, and Nürnbe[
at least eight printings—and, according to the[
catalogue of the British Museum, that institution[
a Basel edition of 1572.

Locher's arrangement of the chapters does [
faithfully to that of the original. Chapters 36, 74[
totally lacking in the first edition. No. 46 follow[
Nos. 48, 108, and 111 are interspersed among [
Each motto is resolved into two elegiac distic[
chapters proper are in dactylic hexameters or ele[
Chapter 111, however, is done in Sapphic strophe[
from the first chapter:

> Inter precipuos pars est mihi reddita stultos
> Prima: rego docili vastaque vela manu.
> En ego possideo multos, quos raro libellos
> Perlego: tum lectos negligo; nec sapio.
>
> Primus in excelsa teneo quod nave rudentes
> Stultivagosque sequor comites per flumina vas[
> Non ratione vacat certa: sensuque latenti:
> Congestis etenim stultus confido libellis
> Spem quoque nec parvam collecta volumina pr[
> Calleo nec verbum: nec libri sentio mentem.

[81] In the second Locher edition Chapter 75 is added, but in th[
medieval Goliards: Si non vultis indignari/ Et poetam c[
sagitarii/ Io Io, etc.

lesser extent upon the Strassburg edition of the same year, mentioned above. Far more faithful and reliable than Locher, it served its mission well in helping to make the *Narrenschiff* a truly universal German classic. It shows a definite effort on the part of the translator to propagandize Brant's ideas. He introduces a great deal of independent moralizing and polemics for this purpose. It is generally believed that the same author translated *Reinke de Vos* into Low German. Herman Brandes published a new edition of the Lübeck original of 1497 (Halle, 1914), while Carl Schröder got out a facsimile of the Rostock, 1519, edition (Schwerin, 1892).

Three separate French translations, or rather paraphrases, appeared between 1497 and 1499. The first, done anonymously by Pierre Rivière (Paris, 1497—copies are in the British Museum and the Dresden Landesbibliothek), is based upon the first edition of Locher. Though a conscientious attempt to adhere faithfully to its source, the handicap of being a translation of a free adaptation proves insurmountable. A few lines, again from the first chapter:

> Le premier fol de la nef suis
> Les voiles regis de ma main
> A livres avoir me deduys
> Lesquelz ie ne voy soir ne main
> De ceulx que iay leuz faiz dedain
> Ou ne les entendz, somme toute
> Tel cuyde bien scavoir qui doubte.
>
> Le premier suis en la navire
> Les cordes ie tourne ie vire
> Je suis des compaignons vagans
> Je suis des grans folz navigans
> Sur la mer du monde parfonde.

An abridgement came out about 1535.

The second French rendering, by Jehan Drouyn (Lyons,

1498), is an abbreviated prose version based upon Rivière, but relying also apparently upon the Paris edition of Locher. Some passages are in verse, copied word for word from Rivière. A reprint appeared in 1499 and a third in 1579. The third and last French translation, by an anonymous writer, appeared in Paris, published by Marnef in 1499 and usually called the Marnef translation. It was popular for a long time and is an independent prose rendering of Locher. There are also Paris and Lyons editions (1529 and 1530).

A Flemish version, which was published at Paris in 1500 by G. Marchand, is recorded in Van Praet, *Catalogue des livres imprimés sur velin de la bibliothèque du roi*, IV, 233, and mentioned by Pompen. Having been made in Paris, it was probably based upon Locher. It is referred to again below in discussion of the later Dutch version.

A second Latin version, by the Paris book dealer Iodocus Badius Ascensius (Paris, 1505, Marnef and Badius), based upon the Paris, 1498, edition of Locher, is even further removed from the original than is Locher's, and not as good. Chapters 48 and 108 have been boiled down to five lines! A second edition appeared in Basel in 1506, and according to the new printed catalogue of the British Museum, at least four reprints appeared later (1507–1515). This *Navis stultifera* has little in common with Brant or Locher except the title and the woodcuts.[32]

Early in 1509, or perhaps late in 1508, the English priest Alexander Barclay, probably of Scottish origin, got out the first English adaptation in stiff, uninspired Chaucerian stanzas under the title *The Shyp of folys of the worlde . . . translated . . . out of Laten, Frenche, and Doche into Englysse*

[32] Already, in 1500, Badius had written a Latin imitation of the *Narrenschiff*, partly in prose and partly in verse, on the follies of women. It was published in Paris early in 1501. In 1502 Wimpheling published a new edition of this imitation in Strassburg.

tonge. It was published by Richard Pynson. In 1570 a second edition, published by Cawood, appeared, and in 1590 another. Barclay's rendering, based upon one of the two 1497 editions of Locher, with some transpositions and considerable additions,[33] contains also the Basel woodcuts, recut in England to the same size. Barclay, in his introduction, mentions having used both Brant and Locher, but refers also to Locher's Latin verse as though it were the original. As a matter of fact, he did not consult Brant's original at all. But he did use Rivière's French adaptation to a considerable degree, and became acquainted with the Ship of Fools through Rivière. Barclay's work, an illustration of early French Renaissance influence in England, is discussed in greater detail by F. Fraustadt in a Breslau dissertation (1894) and, more recently, by Pompen.

Suffice it to say that Barclay writes a pure, natural English, which attempts to bridge the gap between the language of scholarship and the vernacular; that he introduces many new references and allusions, while omitting others found in Brant or Locher; that he is a very subjective moralizer, especially in his *Envoys;* that he usually expands Locher's text, using a seven-line strophe for two, three, or four lines of Locher; that when he employs the French text of Rivière, as he often does, he usually copies that writer's errors. Barclay's *Shyp* is a ship of fools of sixteenth-century England, rather than a translation of Brant. A brief passage from the first chapter:

> I am the firste fole of all the hole navy,
> To kepe the pompe, the helme and eke the sayle:
> For this is my minde, this one pleasure have I,
> Of bokes to have grete plenty and aparayle.
> I take no wysdome by them, nor yet avayle,
> Nor them perceyve nat, and then I them despyse;
> Thus am I a fole, and all that sewe that guyse.

[33] The chapter "Of Foles that are Overworldly," for instance, is based upon a Latin poem of Robert Gaguinus, used by Badius in his Latin translation.

That in this shyp the chefe place I governe,
By this wyde see with folys wanderynge,
The cause is playne and easy to dyscerne,
Styll am I besy, bokes assemblynge,
For to have plenty it is a plesaunt thynge
In my conceyt, and to have them ay in honde:
But what they mene do I nat understonde.

Barclay's work was reprinted in the nineteenth century in two volumes (Edinburgh and London, 1874, also New York), and even that edition, with a good introduction by T. H. Jamieson, is now a rare-book item. Selections from the work are also to be found in Warner's *Library of the World's Best Literature* (various editions from 1896 on), J. C. Ridpath's *Library of Universal Literature* (New York, 1899), and Julian Hawthorne's *The Masterpieces and the History of Literature*, Vol. 6 (New York, 1906).

Inferior to Barclay is Henry Watson's competitive English prose version, *The Shyppe of Fooles* (Wynkyn de Worde, London, 1509), of which only a single copy, in Paris, is now extant. A second edition, now almost as rare as the first, appeared in 1517. Watson's work seems to be a literal translation of the second, not the first, edition of Drouyn's French prose version. The mottos are done in verse, as is seen in the following excerpt from Chapter 1:

The fyrste foole of the shyppe I am certayne
That with my handes dresse the sayles all
For to have bookes I do all my besy payne
Whiche I love not to rede in specyall
Nor them to se also in generall
Wherefore it is a proverbe all aboute
Suche thynketh to knowe that standeth in doute.

Yonge folkes that entende for to knowe dyvers thynges approche you unto this doctryne and it revolve in your myndes organykes to the ende that ye maye comprehende and understande

the substaunce of it, and that ye be not of the nombre of the fooles
that vageth in this tempesteous flode of the worlde.

A Dutch version by Jan van Ghelen is based chiefly upon
Locher but, since Chapters 34 and 74 are also included, it
probably goes back to the original German as well. It seems to
have been published first in Brussels in 1548.³⁴ Three later editions—Antwerp, 1584 (Cornell University Library has a
copy), Leyden, 1610, and Amsterdam, 1635, have been noted.

Reference has been made to the 1874 reprint of Barclay's
Shyp. Two years before this Karl Simrock published his
modern German "renewal" (Erneuerung) of the *Narrenschiff*
in an attractive quarto volume, with the woodcuts of the original. When in the same year Karl Goedeke, in his edition of
Brant's work, criticized Simrock's rendering rather severely,
accusing him of gross inaccuracies and of failure to reproduce
the nuances of Brant's language, Simrock wrote a heated reply,
defending his translation.³⁵

A second modern German resuscitation of the *Narrenschiff*,
by H. A. Junghans, has been published in the popular Reclam
series (1877). The new edition available to the writer is dated
1930.

THE "NARRENSCHIFF" AS A FORCE
IN LITERATURE

The far-reaching influence of Brant's *Narrenschiff* in Germany and abroad is a subject which has not yet been exhaus-
tively studied. Not even for Germany has the question been
fully answered, although Zarncke made a cursory examination
of it in the introduction to his edition. Curiously enough the
situation is somewhat better with regard to England, although

³⁴ Whether this version is related to, or perhaps identical with, the Flemish
version of 1500 which Van Praet mentions, is not clear. It is also not clear
whether it depends upon the Low German version.
³⁵ Published in *Alemannia*, I, 3.

C. H. Herford (1886; see Bibliography) has treated only partially and misleadingly the remarkable hold that Brant exercised upon English literature for about a hundred years. In the
following paragraphs an attempt has been made to sketch
briefly the part which Brant's masterpiece has played in German, French, and English literatures, with some attention also
to Dutch and Italian literatures.

The earliest trace of such influence in Germany seems to be
in *St. Ursulä Schifflein* (Strassburg, 1497),[36] a book of excerpts
from the *Narrenschiff* compiled by Carthusian monks of Alsace when they were in search of a compendium of maxims for
righteous Christian living. Already at this early date Brant's
work was widely recognized as Germany's most brilliant book
for good Christians since the invention of printing and as a sort
of layman's Bible destined to guide the coming generation of
conformists. This mission of the *Narrenschiff* became patent
when Brant's friend Geiler von Kaisersberg delivered his one
hundred forty-two sermons in the vernacular on the book, from
his pulpit in the Strassburg Cathedral in 1498–99, and thereby
exercised a profound influence upon his contemporaries. Geiler
used Brant's original, the Strassburg revision and interpolations,
and the Locher translation, quoting from them liberally, but he
treated Brant's text very freely and added a good deal of original material. Soon after his death in 1510, these sermons were
published in Latin, with the original woodcuts, under the title
*Navicula seu speculum fatuorum praestantissimi sacrarum lite-
rarum doctoris Joannis Geiler Keisersbergii concionatoris Ar-
gentinensis a Jac. Otthero collecta* (Strassburg, 1510). Other
editions of this important work followed, among them a severely abbreviated German redaction, published by Johann
Grieninger and edited by Johann Pauli (Strassburg, 1520); this
is the last contemporaneous edition to contain the woodcuts.

[36] See above, pp. 13–14.

Hyperbolic praise of the *Narrenschiff* among Brant's friends was a commonplace during its first decade. Hutten lauded its "classical" prosody and form, Tritheim remarked that it was doubtful if a more timely book had ever been written, Wimpheling, Locher, and Geiler were just as outspoken in their encomium. The *Epistolae obscurorum virorum* referred to it prominently (Part II, Epistle 9).

In the generation of Brant and in those immediately succeeding him, it was Murner, Sachs, Fischart, and Gengenbach especially, and later Abraham a Santa Clara, who followed in his footsteps or even moved entirely in the field which had been opened by him. The vociferous itinerant Franciscan Thomas Murner, about seventeen years Brant's junior and like him a native of Alsace, who helped prepare for the Reformation, and then turned against it, came so strongly under the influence of the *Narrenschiff* that his earlier works, especially the *Narrenbeschwörung* (1512), may be called direct copies of Brant. Murner takes verse after verse, also woodcuts, over bodily, and about one-third of the *Narrenbeschwörung* is merely a rehash of the *Narrenschiff*. Almost as much can be said of the *Schelmenzunft*. It is not so much the case in Murner's later works, but even in *Gäuchmatt* (1519, which, as we have seen, Brant kept from being published in Strassburg for other reasons) and in *Von dem grossen Lutherischen Narren* (1522) the imprint of the *Narrenschiff* is clearly evident. Indeed, from Brant on the "Narr" as a type became a commonplace in German literature. He was put through every conceivable form of grotesque test and torture, exorcised, poured like lead, bathed, devoured, and what not, as the many popular terms such as "Narrenbeschwörung," "Narrengiessen," "Narrenschneider," "Narrenbad," "Narrenfresser," found in profusion in sixteenth-century German letters, attest.

Although Brant's influence upon Hans Sachs and Johann.

Fischart is not quite as palpable as it is on Murner, yet it is strong. Both have made Brant their intellectual property, and their works teem with reminiscences of the *Narrenschiff*. Sachs frequently draws his examples from Brant, derives entire passages from him, and expands upon them. He is particularly fond of Brantian aphorisms and saws. Fischart, too, often refers to Brant. Both Fischart and Sachs learned from Brant the practice of combining the bizarre middle-class humor of the earlier "Fastnachtspiele" with Brant's grave, awe-inspiring role of wise teacher-preacher.

Pamphilus Gengenbach, in poems and dramas, schooled himself on Brant's style and language. On every page of his earlier works one can find expressions, entire lines, and expanded themes which reveal this influence. Brant's famous "Rotwelsch" chapter (No. 63) on thieves' and beggars' slang was amplified by Gengenbach in his *Liber vagatorum*. Much later —at the end of the seventeenth century, when Brant was no longer in the public eye—Abraham a Santa Clara, the Billy Sunday of his age, still used the same device as Brant for castigating fools.

The notion of a *ship* of fools, quite alive in Brant's own generation, died out soon after in Germany, but the "Narr" himself as a type lived on, later to be metamorphosed into a dove, a bee, a hare, a worm, and even the Protestant devil. In his introduction Zarncke quotes a host of sixteenth-century writers, besides those already mentioned, who (1) took long passages from Brant, (2) interlarded their own verse with passages from him, or (3) made fools and types of fools the center of their interest. This influence is manifest even in the "Volksfeste," with their pantomimes, which have survived to this day. The only phase of Brant's work, regrettably enough, by which its progeny did not profit is its style. German literature of the sixteenth century would be superior in its prosody, clearer and more precise in its style and treatment, and less fantastic in its allegorical conceits if it had followed Brant in these respects, too.

As late as 1840 a *Neues Narrenschiff* appeared in Germany from the pen of Felix Weickert,[37] prompted perhaps by the publication of Strobel's first nineteenth-century edition of Brant's masterpiece a year before.

As for France, the imitation of the *Narrenschiff* by Badius (1501) has already been noted.[38] About the same time Symphorien Champier, the physician of Duke Antoine of Lorraine, published *La Nef des princes et des battailes de noblesse avec aultres enseignments utilz et profitables à toutes manières de gens pour congnoistre à bien vivre et mourir* (Lyons, 1502). This is the work of his friend Robert de Balsac (also called Balsat and Barsat), a royal (and, it seems, boisterous) counselor, chamberlain, and seneschal in Gascogne and the region of Agen, and a noted warrior. In this publication there was included another work of Balsac entitled *Sensuit le droit chemin de l'hôpital et les gens qui le trouvent par leurs œuvres et manière de vivre* (there are also editions of 1505, 1525, one appearing at Troyes without date, and 1635).

While the *Nef des princes et des batailles* interests us only because, probably by way of the Drouyn translation which appeared in Lyons, it has taken over the Brantian idea of a ship (but not of fools!), *Le Droit Chemin* is of greater importance. In the manner of Brant it describes as fools various types of people who by virtue of their stupid ways go "a lospital." The

[37] Felix Weickert, *Neues Narrenschiff und Freud und Leid zu lustiger Kurzweil* (Stuttgart, Scheible, 1840). Lieblingsbücher in alten und neuen Geschichten, Sagen, und Schwänken . . . mit dienlichen Bildern geziert durch Willibald Cornelius, Teil 7.
[38] It is entitled *Stultiferae naves sensus animosque trahentes mortis in exitium* (Paris, Thielmann Kerver). Wimpheling's 1502 edition bears the title *Jodoci Badii Ascensii stultiferae naviculae seu scaphae fatuarum mulierum: circa sensus quinque exteriores fraude navigantium.*

work [39] begins: "Gens qui ont petit et despendent beaucoup. Gens qui jouent voulontiers et perdent souvent. Gens qui ont petite prise et rents qui portent draps de soye et chiers habillemens." In this vein it goes on repetitiously for seven pages: "Gens qui . . . gens qui . . . ," often followed by the exclamation "a lospital!" Many, though not all, of the malefactors are clearly old Brantian friends: merchants who sell on credit, men seeking vengeance, those who lose what their masters gave them, who are guided by the advice of fools, who delight in ostentation, who cheat their masters, gourmands, those whose servants carouse at night and sleep during the day, who clothe their wives beyond their means, who always sing *gaudeamus* but never *requiem,* who are ungrateful to God, who covet legacies, who invite lawsuits only to lose, who put things off, who give away their master's best wine.

The great and prolonged success of Balsac's little work, due partially perhaps to the foreign origin of its underlying idea,[40] is seen from the five editions (besides two free imitations) through which it went between 1502 and 1635. It is extremely important in the history of Brant's influence in Europe. In France it helped determine the nature of Gringoire's satire *Les Abus du monde,* and Gringoire in turn influenced Desmoulins's *Le Catholicon des maladvisez, autrement dit le cymetière des malheureux.* Then the *Catholicon* pointed the way to free imitations of Balsac's catalogue of follies and explains such works as Jacques d'Adonville's two versified warnings against sins leading to beggary, namely *Les Moyens d'éviter meren-*

[39] It is reprinted in P. Allut, *Étude biographique et bibliographique sur Symphorien Champier* (Lyons, 1859), pp. 119-26. See the same work for the bibliographical description of *La Nef des princes et des battailes,* pp. 109 ff. Another reprint, by Tanizey de Laroque in *Revue des langues romanes,* 1886, pp. 276 ff., is less accurate. C. Schmidt, *Histoire littéraire de l'Alsace,* I, 315, merely refers to these works and erroneously ascribes the *Nef* to Champier.
[40] Cf. also the "Ellend Herberg" in Strassburg, for which Geiler framed a constitution in 1501: *Geilers älteste Schriften,* ed. by Dacheux, pp. 26 ff. and G. Kalff, *Westeuropäische Letterkunde* (Groningen, 1923), I, 123 and note.

*colie, soy conduire et enricher en tous estatz par l'ordonnance
de raison* (1530, a second edition 1540) and the more dramatic
Regretz et peines des mal advisez.

But the influence of Balsac's *Le Droit Chemin* extended
much further even than this. The singular work forms the
basis, apparently, for the Englishman Robert Copland's *Hye
Way to the Spyttel House*, written about 1535, which will be
discussed below.[41] More striking still, there is also a Dutch version of Balsac's conceit, published at Antwerp but written
probably in the middle of the sixteenth century. It is found in
a collection called *Veelderhande geneuchlijcke Dichten, Tafel
spelen ende Refereynen* and bears a title which suggests the
influence of Balsac: *Den rechten weg nae t Gaesthuys met die
by weghen ende toe paden die daer leyden tot den Broodt-
sack.*[42] Parts of this work are taken directly from Balsac, while
other parts are altered or amplified. Like the other imitators
of Balsac, this anonymous Dutch writer introduces distinctly
new features, although like Gringoire, Desmoulins, and
d'Adonville he buries the pith and core of Balsac's terse and
pointed satire under a mass of verbiage.

As W. G. Moore in his article in the Kastner volume suggests, it is not at all impossible that Rabelais, when a printer's
reader in Lyons, was familiar with the literary tradition of
Balsac and his train and more or less unwittingly crowned
their second-rate satires with his great masterpiece.

[41] On the popularity of Balsac's *Le Droit Chemin* as an offshoot of Brant's
Narrenschiff, see the work of a British scholar, W. G. Moore, *La Réforme
allemande et la littérature française* (Strassburg, 1930), pp. 204–23. As for the
influence of Balsac upon Copland, the present writer, sensing this French-
British relationship keenly after reading both writers, was gratified to find his
conviction confirmed in two articles by Moore, "Robert Copland and His
Hye Way," in the *Review of English Studies*, VII (October, 1931), 406 ff.,
and "The Evolution of a Sixteenth Century Satire," in *A Miscellany of Studies
in Romance Languages and Literatures Presented to Leon E. Kastner.* Edited
by Mary Williams and James A. de Rothschild (Cambridge, 1932), pp. 351–60.
[42] Attention was called to this work by Pompen in *The English Versions of
the Ship of Fools*, p. 194, note.

But even this does not exhaust the widely ramified influence of Brant in and through France. About 1503 P. Le Dru published for A. Vérard in Paris the anonymous *Les Regnars traversant les perilleuses voyes des folles fiances du monde, composées par Sebastian Brand.* The real authorship of this satire, which censures with severity the manners of the period, and ridicules the transgressions and follies of all classes of society, and which, by the use of Brant's name again reveals his extreme popularity in France at that time, is disclosed by an "Exhortacion ou par les premiers lettres des lignes trouverez le nom de lacteur de ce present livre et le lieu de sa nativite." These initials spell the name of Jean Bouchet, historian and poet of Poitiers. Four editions of *Les Regnars* appeared within two years, two others in 1510 and 1522.

Finally a work by Balsac's friend Champier, *La Nef des dames vertueuses* (1503) [43] also deserves mention. Like Balsac's *Nef,* it utilizes the notion of a ship, but not a ship of fools. The curious woodcut which accompanies it is more interesting than the text. It depicts a ship at sea bearing the Holy Virgin, the child Jesus, St. Catherine, St. Barbara, and two gowned doctors.

In Italy the *Narrenschiff* was mentioned at a rather late date in Lilo Giraldi's *Dialogi duo de poetis nostrorum temporum* (Florence, 1551).[44] So far as is known, it led to no imitations of Brant.

Wireker and Lydgate have been noted as predecessors of Brant in England. The influence of Brant's work itself in that

---

[43] For a bibliographical description, see Allut, *op. cit.,* pp. 131 ff.

[44] Lilius Gregorius Gyraldus, *De poetis nostrorum temporum,* herausgegeben von Karl Wotke (Berlin, 1894, Lateinische Literaturdenkmäler herausgegeben von Max Herrmann, 10), p. 65: "Fuit et Sebastianus Ticio [Brant's Latin name] Germanus ex Argentorato [i.e., Strassburg], qui paene infinita poemata apud suos scripsit, quorum quaedam in Italiam advecta ut Rosarium divae virginis matris sapphicum [found in the *Varia carmina*] et Navis, quae stultifera vocatur."

country, ascribable wholly to Barclay's and Watson's translations and to French imitations of Brant, and lasting well into the seventeenth century, parallels its influence in France and may be called one of the most remarkable examples of the infiltration of a foreign literary work into the pattern of English letters. In a long list of writings from *Cock Lorell's Bote* and the satirical poems of Skelton to Tarlton, Rowlands, and Dekker the imprint of the *Narrenschiff* is patent.[45] Indeed, Brant's masterpiece held its ground in England more persistently than in Germany, despite stronger competition—not as a German work, however, but through the English and French adaptations. And it did English literature, as it did French literature, too, a great service in giving a fresh stimulus and a new form to vernacular satire, and in helping to bridge the gap between the literature of personified abstractions and that of social types, of modern satirical portraiture. It played an important role in outmoding medieval allegory and morality and in directing literature into the channels of the drama, the essay and the novel of character.[46]

The anonymous fragmentary poem *Cock Lorell's Bote* (ca. 1510), a serious portrait of vagrant life but not as bitter a one as Brant's *Narrenschiff*, derives its main ideas from the English adaptations of Brant's Prologue; and from his Chapter 48 ("Gesellenschiff"); and, most of all, from Chapter 108 (Schluraffenschiff"), especially the cut accompanying it in the Watson edition. These conceits are superimposed upon that of a new religious order, derived from Wireker and Lydgate. But the *Bote* is far from being merely a copy of Brantian ideas, for it is typically English; it shows more imagination yet also a realistic, distinct, and vigorous treatment, and a much better

---

[45] Sir Thomas More wrote an epigram in which he referred to the *Ship of Fools*. Cf. Pompen, *op. cit.*, p. 297.
[46] Cf. A. W. Ward on Barclay in the *Dictionary of National Biography* (London, 1921), I, 1076 ff.

sustained plot. The inmates of the *Bote* are all merry Londoners interested in commercial ventures; they travel the length and breadth of England in their fools' ship. As illustrations the author uses four cuts made for the Watson translation.

Skelton's *Boke of Three Fooles* reverts clearly to three chapters of the *Narrenschiff* as presented by Barclay, namely, Chapters 50, 52, and 53. His *The Bowge of Court* (ca. 1520), an allegorical picture of the follies and perils of court life, although it is more dependent on Langland, again borrows the Brantian conceit of a ship and, by way of Barclay (Jamieson edition, II, 210), derives ideas from Brant's chapter on courtiers (Chapter 100). Skelton's *Colyn Cloute,* finally, bears kinship with Chapter 73 of Brant. Copland's *Hye Way to the Spyttel House* (about 1535) deals with beggars and with the economic aspects of folly. A brief visit to the "Spyttel House" affords the writer an excuse for a description of those classes which are on the road to ruin, usually through their own stupid conduct. Again, as in the *Bote* and in the *Bowge,* the satire is narrowed down to one particular class (cf. *Narrenschiff,* Chap. 63) but is carried out less discursively and with more attention to realistic detail and plot, and also with more artistry than Brant could muster. As noted above, Copland's work is strikingly similar in conception to the French work of Balsac, *Le Droit Chemin,* mentioned above. Copland, who knew Barclay and who probably became familiar with Balsac's satire by way of d'Adonville's *Moyens,* gave it a new lease on life, more body, and a fresh and original turn. For a further discussion of the remarkable three-cornered literary relationship of the German Brant, the French Balsac, and the English Copland—a clear example of French Renaissance influence in England—see the two articles of W. G. Moore mentioned in footnote 41, above.

During the first quarter of the sixteenth century the Orders of Knaves were being organized in England. It is with them that Awdelay deals in his *Fraternity of Vagabonds*. In his *Quartern of Serving Men*, however, he broadens this into a satirical classification of social types. The *Quartern* is clearly linked to Brant-Rivière-Barclay-Watson through the *Bote* and represents another step away from morality and toward literary realism. Copland's *Gyl of Brentford's Testament* should be mentioned in this connection too and also the ballad of *The Twenty-Five Orders of Fools*, which follows Brantian procedure chapter for chapter, ousting the English fools of Lydgate and the *Bote* and replacing them, by way of Rivière-Barclay, with Brant's German exemplars. Here for the first time the full scope of Brant's satire as interpreted by his adapters came to be appreciated in England, not only as a piece of humorous imagery, but as a collection of satiric types.

Undoubtedly the woodcuts which, as has been noted, Barclay reproduced had much to do with the sustained popularity of the *Narrenschiff* in England. For these cuts, though based on proverbs rather than on ancient fables, were genuine "emblems," introduced by Barclay in England a generation before Alciati founded emblem literature.[47] In this connection it is also of great interest to note that the first English emblem book, Van der Noot's *Theatre for Voluptuous Worldlings*, was followed almost immediately by a new edition of Barclay's *Shyp*, accompanied by Locher's Latin version.

Queen Elizabeth's jester Tarlton must be mentioned also as coming indirectly under the spell of Brant. The fools in his *Horseload of Fools*, who cavort through Fleet Street in a pony cart to be exhibited in a puppet show, are a merry lot, depicted according to their various callings. Here moral satire has disappeared entirely and made way for more modern satire of

---

[47] On Brant as a forerunner of emblem literature, cf. Wilhelm Fraenger, *Altdeutsches Bilderbuch: Hans Weiditz und Sebastian Brant*, Leipzig, 1930. Hans Weiditz, the Younger, who lived in the early sixteenth century, was the artist of the Augsburg and Strassburg woodcarvers.

manners. The situation is similar in Armin's *Nest of Ninnies* (1608), which grew out of anecdotes about six well-known court jesters, represented as symbolizing human frailties in general and serving as a means of universal satire on the age.

Dekker's *Gul's Hornbooke*, too, can be traced back to the *Narrenschiff*, though by a devious course, as can two works of Rowlands, *A Foole's Bolt Is Sone Shot* and *Sixteen Knaves Marching in Order*. And even in the heyday of the drama, we can still find references to the ubiquitous *Shyp* in Nash's *Summer's Last Will and Testament*, Greene's *Friar Bacon*, and other plays. Two later English imitations of Brant are only of passing interest. They are mentioned by Jamieson in his modern edition of Barclay, pp. ci-cii. The first is a four-leaf quarto tract, *The Ship of Fools Fully Fraught and Richly Laden with Asses, Fools, Jack-daws, Ninnihammers*, etc. etc. It appeared in London about 1650, is entirely in prose, and, except for the general idea, has nothing in common with Barclay. The other is a 295-page *Stultifera navis . . . The modern Ship of Fools* (London, 1807), a wretched production in verse in imitation of Barclay's *Shyp*, published anonymously by W. H. Ireland, the Shakespearean forger. Of more significance are the references to the *Narrenschiff* and to Barclay in Robert Burton's early seventeenth-century *Anatomy of Melancholy*. Burton speaks of fools "who sail along to the Anticyrae in the ship of fools for company together" [48] and, later, he mentions among those who "tax vice" Barclay, Erasmus, and "Fishcart" (*sic* for Fischart!).[49]

It is clear, then, that even after the first decade of the seventeenth century the "Shyp" can still be found in some English ports, although to the new age the old device of a parade of fools seemed rather insipid and was gradually replaced by a

[48] *The Anatomy of Melancholy*, edited by Floyd Dell and Paul Jordan-Smith (New York, 1941), p. 59.
[49] *Ibid.*, p. 293.

more dramatic and psychological approach to the ever-present thought which prompted Puck's ejaculation, "What fools these mortals be."

It remains to say a word about the most famous of all books on folly, the *Moriae encomium* (1509) of Erasmus, with the illustrations which Holbein furnished in 1514. Erasmus, only eight years younger than Brant, was certainly familiar with the *Narrenschiff* before 1509, for Badius, one of its earlier translators and imitators, was a friend of his. As has been seen, Erasmus met Brant in Strassburg in 1514, and probably again in Antwerp in 1520 and admired him greatly. To trace the delicate threads which connect Erasmus' masterpiece (written for scholars) with Brant's (addressed to the upper middle class generally) and which biographers of Erasmus have consistently overlooked or slighted, not because they were unaware of them but rather because too little research has ever been devoted to the subject,[50] would require a monograph in itself. It should be pointed out that while Erasmus, the humanist *par excellence*, unlike Brant, the scholasticist at the threshold of humanism, is loud in his criticism of the abuses prevalent in ecclesiastical circles, while he rarely quotes the Bible (except toward the end of his work), and is much more outspoken, more bitter and telling in his satire, and far superior to Brant in carrying out his theme artistically, he follows Brant in a very great number of his subjects and uses him as a source without mentioning him.

[50] Cf. the following two studies: Max Radlkofer, *Brants Narrenschiff, Murners Narrenbeschwörung, Erasmi Stultitiae laus, literarisch-historische Parallele*, Programm (Burghausen, 1877), and Hermann Schönfeld, "Die kirchliche Satire und religiöse Weltanschauung in Brants Narrenschiff und Erasmus' Narrenlob. resp. in den Colloquia," *Modern Language Notes*, VII (1892), No. 2, pp. 78–92, and No. 3, pp. 137–49, and No. 6, p. 345. This is a subject for further research which might well have been mentioned in Archer Taylor's *Problems in German Literary History* as a problem which could feasibly be undertaken in America. It is incomprehensible how Pompen, *op. cit.*, p. 298, could make the categorical statement that Erasmus did not know Brant's *Narrenschiff*.

In the introductory verse he complains, as Brant did, that the writers commit the very sins they would impugn. Throughout the early part of the work, which is, of course, in prose, Folly speaks much like Venus in Brant, and her child Cupid, too, is described as the stupid blind boy who never grows up. Other themes which Erasmus has in common with Brant are: the parade of learning; folly nourished by drunkenness and ignorance and attended by self-love, flattery, forgetfulness, sloth, pleasure, sensuality, madness, intemperance, and sleepiness; old men acting like children but cursed with infirmities; contempt for Bacchus; women as fashion slaves; feasting and drinking; husbands winking at their wives' forwardness and allowing strange eggs to be laid in their nests; ill-founded jealousy and suspicion of wives; folly governing cities, appointing magistrates, and supporting judges; nobility of character as superior to nobility of birth, and virtue as the greatest consideration in heraldry; quack doctors and ignorant lawyers; men who build without planning; dicing and gaming; hoping to get to heaven through lip service; concern for the place and manner of burial; tracing ancestors; flattery; idolatry; dishonest merchants; endless lawsuits for little gain, merely to enrich dilatory judges or knavish advocates; long pilgrimages to no good purpose; begging as a trade. Many verbal parallelisms could be pointed out in the treatment of these subjects by the two writers.

It should be noted, too, that when Erasmus does quote from the Bible he, like Brant, is very fond of the Book of Ecclesiastes. While Erasmus attacks the clergy in all its ranks, Brant says more about the humble priests and monks and only mildly censures the bishops. It is significant also that a few of Holbein's cuts, for example, Nos. 107 and 131,[51] are strongly reminiscent of *Narrenschiff* cuts. So much is certain, that Erasmus could

---

[51] They are opposite pages 106 and 130 in the London, 1876, English translation.

and did find far more numerous and direct suggestions in Brant than in Pasquin, and that he did so freely but never slavishly; that Brant was parochial but patriotic, Erasmus a cosmopolite; that Brant was more sternly religious than Erasmus; that Erasmus was more volatile and fickle than Brant, even flippant in serious matters; that while Brant lacked the enlightenment, rich ideas, perspective, subtle judgment, and brilliant style of Erasmus, he possessed a more steady character. The *Moriae encomium*, under the influence of Lucian and the Italian Renaissance, is surely much more sparkling than the *Narrenschiff*, but the latter is superior in its nobility of purpose and grave steadfastness of ideals.

Incidentally, it is of interest to note that upon the appearance of Erasmus' *Moriae encomium* Brant penned a six-line Latin poem on it.[52]

BIBLIOGRAPHY

The following Bibliography, while not aiming to be complete, gives a selected chronological list, with critical comments, of works pertaining to Brant's *Narrenschiff* or to Brant himself. It does not revert to the editions, translations, and adaptations of the fifteenth, sixteenth, and seventeenth centuries, which were dealt with above.

Wenker, Jacob, Article in *Apparatus et instructus archivorum* (Argentorati [i.e., Strassburg], 1713), pp. 15 ff.
The first known reference to Brant and his *Narrenschiff* in the eighteenth century, giving valuable information on his life, used by Strobel and his successors. Curiously, it is not mentioned by G. O. Arlt in his Chicago thesis, *Acquaintance with Older German Literature in the Eighteenth Century* (1931).
Altes aus allen Theilen der Geschichte, oder alte Urkunden, alte Briefe und Nachrichten von alten Büchern mit Anmerkungen.

---

[52] C. Schmidt, *Histoire littéraire de l'Alsace*, I, 315, discusses the relationship of Brant and Erasmus in general terms.

2. Stück (Chemnitz, Stösselische Buchhandlung, 1760), pp. 235–251.

This important work, too, is completely overlooked by Arlt. A copy is in the Cornell University Library, Zarncke collection. It mentions one of the 1494 editions of the *Narrenschiff* on the authority of Schottel's *Ausführliche Arbeit von der deutschen Hauptsprache*, V, 1171, also referred to in *Das Neueste aus der anmuthigen Gelehrsamkeit* (1755), p. 99. It alludes to the French, English, and Locher Latin translations (dating the latter 1496) and to the Badius translation, quoting from both Badius and Locher. It lists the other works of Locher and refers to Geiler. Remarkably enough, it also mentions Jodocus Gallus and his oration, without however making it clear that this is a forerunner of the *Narrenschiff*.

Meister, Leonhard, "Sebastian Brants Narrenschiff," in *Beyträge zur Geschichte der teutschen Sprache und Litteratur* (London, 1777), I, 252 ff.; also in *Charakteristiken teutscher Dichter* (Zurich, 1785), I, 360 ff.

This work was occasioned by a biographical sketch of Brant, with brief selections from the *Narrenschiff*, in Wieland's *Teutscher Merkur vom Jahre 1776*, 1. Vierteljahr, pp. 168 ff. For Lessing's reference to the *Narrenschiff* see above, p. 14.

Strobel, Adam W., "Einige Nachrichten über Sebastian Brants Lebensumstände und Schriften," in *Beiträge zur deutschen Litteratur und Litterärgeschichte* (Paris and Strassburg, 1827).

Contains valuable data on Brant's life.

―― *Das Narrenschiff von Dr. Sebastian Brant, nebst dessen Freiheitstafel.* Neue Ausgabe, nach der Original-Ausgabe besorgt und mit Anmerkungen versehen (Quedlinburg und Leipzig, 1839). Bibliothek der gesammten National-Litteratur, Band 17.

The first edition since about 1670. It contains none of the woodcuts. The text is reliable and the introduction, on Brant's life, good, but the notes are poor and philologically unreliable.

Scheible, J., *Das Kloster; Weltlich und Geistlich*, Vol. I (Stuttgart, 1845): Volksprediger, Moralisten und frommer Unsinn; Sebastian Brants Narrenschiff mit Geilers von Kaisersberg Predigten darüber und Thomas Murners Schelmenzunft.

The text of the *Narrenschiff* published by Scheible is based upon a worthless sixteenth-century adaptation. The cuts that Scheible uses are not those of the *Narrenschiff*.

Fischer, F., Article in Friedrich Eggers's *Deutsches Kunstblatt*, Nos. 28–29 (1851).

A pioneer article on the woodcuts, uncritical.

Zarncke, F. (editor), *Sebastian Brant, Das Narrenschiff* (Leipzig, 1854).

Still by far the best critical edition, although Zarncke's text is superseded by more recent facsimile editions of the first Basel edition of 1494. Zarncke's introduction on the historical background, antecedents, and influence in Germany, even his remarks on philology and metrics are still valuable. He also prints generous excerpts from other writings of Brant, both German and Latin, and from the various *Narrenschiff* translations. His notes are good but a bit dogmatic and unduly hostile to Strobel. He is little concerned about iconography and publishes only a few of the woodcuts in the back. Brant's biography is not stressed. The Cornell University Library, which possesses the Zarncke collection, has Zarncke's own copy. A pocket contains interesting and valuable manuscript and other material, viz.: (1) the printed review of Zarncke's work by Rudolf von Raumer published in *Gelehrte Anzeigen der kgl. bayerischen Akademie der Wissenschaften*, III, Nos. 16–19 (December, 1854); (2) a Latin poem by Brant in Zarncke's hand; (3) a letter from Charles Schmidt to Zarncke (Strassburg, April 11, 1856; see Schmidt's article of 1874 and book of 1879) calling attention to some works of Brant overlooked by Zarncke; (4) a letter by Greist to Zarncke (Augsburg, June 19, 1856), calling attention to the Leipzig copy of the Augsburg, 1494 (Schönsperger), edition; (5) an unsigned manuscript review of Zarncke's book, dated November, 1854; (6) a facsimile of the title of Brant's doctoral oration, 1489; (7) a copy of a German poem by Brant; (8) a printed review of Zarncke's book by August Stöber published in *St. Galler Blätter*, No. 15, 1855 (practically identical with the same writer's review in *Revue de l'Alsace*, Sept., 1854, p. 425 ff.); and (9) Zarncke's notes on the British Museum copy of the Low German translation of the *Narrenschiff* (Lübeck, 1497), together with a list of all the *Narrenschiff* editions then in the British Museum.

—— *Zur Vorgeschichte des Narrenschiffes.* 1. (abgedruckt aus Naumanns Serapeum, Band 29) und 2. Mittheilung (Leipzig, 1868, 1871).

Describes an eight-cut cartoon of fools with accompanying verse dated 1470–1480.

Simrock, Karl, *Sebastian Brants Narrenschiff; ein Hausschatz zur Ergetzung und Erbauung erneuert.* Berlin, 1872.

This translation, with all the woodcuts of the first edition, has been sufficiently discussed above, p. 31. See Junghans (1930), below.

Goedeke, Karl, *Das Narrenschiff Sebastian Brants herausgegeben* (Leipzig, 1872). Deutsche Dichter des 16. Jahrhunderts, herausgegeben von Karl Goedeke und Julius Tittmann, Band 7.

This edition, without any cuts, has also been sufficiently discussed.

Brant, Sebastian. *The Ship of Fools; translated by Alexander Barclay.* Edited by T. H. Jamieson, with a life of Barclay and a bibliography (Edinburgh and London [also New York], 1874). A new edition of Barclay's classic, with much valuable supplementary material.

Schmidt, Charles, "Notice sur Sébastian Brant," in *Revue de l'Alsace*, III (1874).

Contains valuable information and bibliography.

Allgemeine Deutsche Biographie: Articles on Brant, by Steinmeyer, III (1876), 256 ff.; on Bergmann von Olpe, by Steiff, XXIV (1887), 314 ff.

Especially is the latter article useful.

Radlkofer, Max, *Brants Narrenschiff, Murners Narrenbeschwörung, Erasmi Stultitiae laus, literarisch-historische Parallele* (Programm, Burghausen, 1877).

A general discussion, not going into detail.

Schmidt, Charles, *Histoire littéraire de l'Alsace à la fin du XVe et au commencement du XVIe siècle* (Paris, 1879), I, 189 ff., and II, 340 ff.

Contains a better bibliography than Goedeke's *Grundriss*. In spite of its rather unfavorable attitude toward Brant, the work is extremely valuable in presenting a mass of facts.

Seifert, Julius, *Alexander Barclays Ship of Fools* (Programm, Brünn, 1884).

Builds upon unsubstantiated hypotheses.

Goedeke, Karl, *Grundriss zur Geschichte der deutschen Dichtung*, 2. Auflage. I (Dresden, 1884), 381 ff.

Adds nothing of importance to Zarncke's contribution of 1854 and to Schmidt's two works.

Herford, Charles H., *Studies in the Literary Relations of England and Germany in the Sixteenth Century*. Cambridge, 1886.

The chapter on the "Ship of Fools," p. 323 ff., is an able but incomplete treatment of Brant's influence in England, a subject about which Zarncke could say nothing. Herford's greatest weakness is that he quite overlooks that not only Barclay and Watson but also the French imitators of Brant influenced the English writers—that Brant did not do so directly.

Bobertag, Franz (editor), *Sebastian Brants Narrenschiff* (Berlin and Stuttgart [1889]). Kürschners Deutsche Nationalliteratur, Band 16.

This edition, with all the woodcuts of the first edition, has been discussed above, p. 23.

Singer, L., *Die wirtschaftlichen und politischen Tendenzen des Narrenschiffs und einiger anderen Dichtungen des Sebastian Brant* (Programm, Prague, 1890).

Besson, P., *De Sebastiani Brant sermone* (Argentorati [i.e., Strassburg], 1890).

Unsatisfactory.

Schröder, Carl (editor), *Dat nye schip van Narragonien*. Die jüngere niederdeutsche Bearbeitung von Sebastian Brants Narrenschiff (Rostock, 1519) herausgegeben (Schwerin, 1892).

A modern facsimile of the second edition of the important Low German translation. See the Brandes edition of 1914.

Schönfeld, Hermann, "Die kirchliche Satire und religiöse Weltanschauung in Brant's Narrenschiff und Erasmus' Narrenlob, resp. in den Colloquia," in *Modern Language Notes*, VII (1892), 78–92; 137–149; and 345.

Helpful as far as it goes.

Burckhardt, Daniel, *Dürers Aufenthalt in Basel 1492–94* (München, 1892).

Here the theory that Dürer may have had a hand in making the woodcuts was expressed for the first time.

Schreiber, W. L., *Manuel de l'amateur de la gravure*, Vol. II (Berlin, 1892).
A good account, now superseded, of how Brant came by the idea of treating folly.

Fraustadt, Fedor, *Ueber das Verhältnis von Barclays Ship of Fools zur lateinischen, französischen und deutschen Quelle* (Dissertation, Breslau, 1894).
A useful work, now superseded in some respects by Pompen's work of 1925.

Weisbach, W., *Der Meister der Bergmannschen Offizin und Albrecht Dürers Beziehungen zur Baseler Buchillustration* (Strassburg, 1896). Studien zur deutschen Kunstgeschichte, Heft 6.
—— *Die Baseler Buchillustration des XV. Jahrhunderts* (Strassburg, 1896).
This and the foregoing are indispensable for the student of the *Narrenschiff* cuts.

Friedländer, Max, Article in *Repertorium für Kunstwissenschaft*, XIX (1896), 383 ff.

Rey, A., *Skelton's Satirical Poems in Their Relation to Lydgate's Order of Fools, Cock Lorell's Bote, and Barclay's Ship of Fools* (Dissertation, Bern, 1899).
Supplements Herford's work of 1886 in details.

Kautzsch, R., *Die Holzschnitte des Ritters vom Turn (Basel, 1493)* (Strassburg, 1903). Studien zur deutschen Kunstgeschichte, Heft 44.
Kautzsch proves that these blocks are by the artist who became Bergmann's master-artist soon after.

Wölfflin, F., *Die Kunst Albrecht Dürers* (München, 1905).
While not convinced that Dürer took a hand in the woodcuts, Wölfflin believes he may have influenced them by his presence.

Janitsch, J., *Das Bildnis Sebastian Brants von Albrecht Dürer* (Strassburg, 1906). Studien zur deutschen Kunstgeschichte, Heft 74.

Springer, Jaro, *Sebastian Brants Bildnisse* (Strassburg, 1907). Studien zur deutschen Kunstgeschichte, Heft 87.
A standard work on the subject.

Koegler, H., Article in *Repertorium für Kunstwissenschaft*, XXX (1907).

This article on the cuts must be used with caution. It contains many bold assertions.

Claus, P., *Rhythmik und Metrik in Sebastian Brants Narrenschiff* (Strassburg, 1911). Quellen und Forschungen, No. 112.
The best study on the subject, adding to Zarncke's remarks.

Schroeder, Carl, *Der deutsche Facetus* (Berlin, 1911). Palaestra, No. 86.

Schultz, F., *Sebastian Brant, Das Narrenschiff*. Faksimile der Erstausgabe von 1494 mit einem Anhang enthaltend die Holzschnitte der folgenden Originalausgaben und solche der Locherschen Uebersetzung und einem Nachwort (Strassburg, 1913). Jahresgaben der Gesellschaft für elsässische Literatur, I.
This work has been sufficiently discussed above, pp. 23–24. It is excellent.

Koegler, H. (editor), *Sebastian Brant, Das Narrenschiff*. Faksimiledruck für die Gesellschaft der Bibliophilen herausgegeben (Basel, 1913).

Ghetelen, Hans van (editor), *Dat Narrenschyp*, herausgegeben von H. Brandes, Halle, 1914.
A new edition of the Low German translation of the *editio princeps*, Lübeck, 1497. See the Schröder edition of 1892.

Heitz, P. (editor), *Des Sebastian Brant Flugblätter*, herausgegeben, mit Nachwort von F. Schultz (Strassburg, 1915).
Contains fifteen "flying sheets" of Brant.

Maus, T., *Brant, Geiler und Murner* (Dissertation, Marburg, 1915).
Murner treated Brant's text very freely. Geiler probably did not influence Murner strongly.

Learned, Henry D., *The Syntax of Brant's Narrenschiff* (Philadelphia, 1917).
Shows that Brant was very conservative in his language.

Wolters, Maria, *Beziehungen zwischen Holzschnitt und Text bei Sebastian Brant und Thomas Murner* (Dissertation, Strassburg. Baden-Baden, 1917).
In Murner's case text and illustrations are by the same person, in Brant's case not.

Kärntner, J., *Des Jakob Locher Philomusus Stultifera navis und ihr Verhältnis zum Narrenschiff des Sebastian Brant* (Dissertation, Frankfurt, 1924). Typewritten.

Rauck, J., *Das Strassburger Plagiat von Sebastian Brants Narren-schiff verglichen mit dem Baseler Original.* Ein Beitrag zur Verskunst des ausgehenden 15. Jahrhunderts (Dissertation, Frankfurt, 1924). Typewritten.

Pompen, Aurelius, *The English Versions of the Ship of Fools, a Contribution to the History of the Early French Renaissance in England* (London, 1925).
The best study of the subject. Completely explodes the idea that Brant influenced English literature directly.

Stammler, W., *Epochen der deutschen Literatur*, Vol. II, Part 1 (Stuttgart, 1927).

Junghans, H. A., *Sebastian Brants Narrenschiff.* Erneuert; Neu-druck (Leipzig, 1930).
Improves upon Simrock to some extent. The first edition appeared in 1877. See the Simrock version of 1872.

Moore, W. G., *La Réforme allemande et la littérature française* (Strassburg, 1930).
Discusses the popularity of Balsac's *Le Droit Chemin* as an offshoot of Brant's *Narrenschiff*. See Moore's article of 1932.

Fraenger, W., *Altdeutsches Bilderbuch: Hans Weiditz und Sebastian Brant* (Leipzig, 1930).
Brant as a forerunner of emblem literature.

Moore, W. G., "The Evolution of a Sixteenth-Century Satire," in *A Miscellany of Studies in Romance Languages and Literatures.* Presented to Leon E. Kastner. Edited by Mary Williams and A. de Rothschild (Cambridge, 1932), pp. 351-60.

Baucke, L., "Das mittelniederdeutsche Narrenschiff und seine handschriftliche Vorlage," in *Niederdeutsches Jahrbuch*, LVIII-LIX (1933), 115-64.
The author of the Low German version wanted to influence the populace, hence he introduced many moralizing and polemical passages. Baucke agrees with Brandes that the *Narrenschyp* and *Reinke de Vos* were translated by the same person, probably a cleric who had some academic training and literary experience.

Eberth, H. H., *Die Sprichwörter in Sebastian Brants Narrenschiff.* Dissertation, Greifswald (Bamberg, 1933).

Westermann, Ruth, "Sebastian Brant," in *Die deutsche Literatur des Mittelalters. Verfasserlexikon.* Edited by W. Stammler, Vol. I (Berlin and Leipzig, 1933), columns 276-89.

Genschmer, F., *The Treatment of the Social Classes in the Satires of Brant, Murner, and Fischart* (University of Illinois *Abstract of Thesis*, Urbana, 1934).

Stresses Brant's ultra-conservatism and fundamentalism.

Spamer, Adolf, "Eine Narrenschiffspredigt aus der Zeit Sebastian Brants," in *Otto Glauning zum 60. Geburtstag.* Festgabe aus Wissenschaft und Bibliothek, II (Leipzig, 1938), 113–30.

Publishes and comments on a sermon in manuscript found in the Germanisches Museum, Nürnberg, which anticipates Brant's use of the idea of a ship of fools, reveals an early connection between St. Ursula's ship and Brant's ship and also anticipates Geiler's *Schiff der Penitentz.*

Legner, W. K., *The Strong Verb in Sebastian Brant's Narrenschiff* (Dissertation, University of Pennsylvania, 1936).

Bond, E. Warwick, *Studia Otiosa, Some Attempts in Criticism* (London, 1938).

Chapter 2 on Brant's *Narrenschiff*, pp. 18–42, is the best essay on Brant in English, with translations of selected but brief passages, some in prose, some in verse.

Gilbert, W., *The Culture of Basel in the Fifteenth Century; a Study in Christian Humanism* (Dissertation, Cornell, 1941). Typewritten.

Includes a scholarly study of all of Brant's works; the appraisal of the man and his work, however, seems unduly harsh.

Zeydel, Edwin H., "Notes on Sebastian Brant's *Narrenschiff*," in *Modern Language Notes*, LVIII (1943), 340–346.

—— "Johannes a Lapide and Sebastian Brant," in *Modern Language Quarterly*, IV (1943), 209–212.

—— "Sebastian Brant and the Discovery of America," in *Journal of English and Germanic Philology*, XLII (1943), 410–11.

NOTE. Only with great caution should the student of Brant use the encyclopedias written in English.

The *Encyclopaedia Britannica*, 14th edition, contains a good brief account of Brant's life and importance but fails entirely to note that the English writers influenced by the *Narrenschiff* were so influenced by way of France. The writer of the article still relies entirely upon Herford (1886) and knows nothing about more recent researches of Pompen, Moore, etc. Besides, he con-

sistently writes "Lovell" when referring to *Cock Lorell's Bote*.
The *New International Encyclopaedia*, 2d edition, contains no less
than five errors in its brief article: (1) Brant's father was not a
wealthy burgher; (2) Brant received no pension from Maximilian, only a promise of one; (3) Brant took no part in any
negotiations with the Holy See; (4) the author of the Latin
translation was Locher, not Locker; and (5) Watson's translation first appeared in 1509, not in 1517.
The *Encyclopedia Americana*, 1941 edition, adds four new errors:
(1) Brant did not become state councilor in 1501; (2) he did
not translate Vergil, Terence, and other Latin writers; (3) his
influence on the literature of Germany and other Germanic
countries *was very* considerable; (4) Watson's translation was
not reproduced in 1874; Barclay's version was. A reference to
Brant's allusion to Columbus would have been in place.

Two brief articles by Mary O'Connor in *Modern Language Review*, XX, 64 ff., and *Revue* de littérature comparée, VIII, 309 ff.,
on the influence of Brant in France, add nothing of importance to
the findings of Pompen and Moore.

Das Narren schyff

Ad Narra goniā Gaudeumus oe

har nod

Zů schyff Zů schyff Brůder. Eß gat/ eß gat

Das Narren Schyff.

Gen Narragonien.

Hi sunt qui descendunt mare in nauibus
faciétes opationem in aquis multis.
Ascendūt vscz ad cęlos / & descēdunt vscz
ad abyssos. aia eorū in malis tabescebat
Turbati sunt & moti sunt sicut ebrius: &
omnis sapientia eorū deuorata est.
Psalmo .Cvi.

A PROLOGUE TO THE SHIP
OF FOOLS*

*For profit and salutary instruction, admonition
and pursuit of wisdom, reason and good manners:
also for contempt and punishment of folly, blindness, error, and stupidity of all stations and kinds
of men: with special zeal, earnestness, and labor
compiled at Basel by Sebastian Brant, doctor in
both laws.*

All lands in Holy Writ abound
And works to save the soul are found,
The Bible, Holy Fathers' lore
And other such in goodly store,
So many that I feel surprise
To find men growing not more wise
But holding writ and lore in spite.
The whole world lives in darksome night,
In blinded sinfulness persisting,
While every street sees fools existing
Who know but folly, to their shame,
Yet will not own to folly's name.
Hence I have pondered how a ship
Of fools I'd suitably equip—
A galley, brig, bark, skiff, or float,
A carack, scow, dredge, racing-boat,
A sled, cart, barrow, carryall [1]—

*The superior figures refer throughout to the Commentary, pages 367-91.

One vessel would be far too small
To carry all the fools I know.
Some persons have no way to go
And like the bees they come a-skimming,
While many to the ship are swimming,
And each one wants to be the first,
A mighty throng with folly curst,
Whose pictures I have given here.
They who at writings like to sneer
Or are with reading not afflicted
May see themselves herewith depicted
And thus discover who they are,
Their faults, to whom they're similar.
For fools a mirror shall it be,
Where each his counterfeit may see.
His proper value each would know,
The glass of fools the truth may show.
Who sees his image on the page
May learn to deem himself no sage,
Nor shrink his nothingness to see,
Since none who lives from fault is free;
And who would honestly have sworn
That cap and bells he's never worn?
Whoe'er his foolishness decries
Alone deserves to rank as wise,
Whoever wisdom's airs rehearses
May stand godfather to my verses! ²
He'd injure me and have no gain
If he would not this book retain.
Here you will find of fools no dearth
And everything you wish on earth,

The reasons why you're here are listed,
Why many fools have ay existed,
What joy and honor wisdom bears
And why a fool in danger fares,
The world's whole course in one brief look—
Are reasons why to buy this book.
In jest and earnest evermore
You will encounter fools galore.
The wise man's pleasure I will win,
While fools speak oft of kith and kin,
Fools poor and rich, high-bred and tyke,
Yes, everyman will find his like,
I cut a cap for every chap,
But none of them will care a rap,
And if I'd named and then apprized him,
He'd say I had not recognized him.
I hope, though, men who're really wise
Will find a deal to praise and prize,
And out of knowledge say forsooth
That I have spoken but the truth.
If I were sure that they'd approve
I'd care not what the fools reprove.
Naught else but truth the fool must hear,
Although it pleases not his ear.
Terence asserts that truth can breed
Deep hate, and he is right, indeed,[3]
And he who blows his nose too long
Will have a nosebleed hard and strong,
And he whom evil tempers pall
Will often agitate his gall,
And so not deeply am I riled

When I by rabble am reviled,
Because my teachings seem too good.
Fools ever have misunderstood
And spurned and laughed at wisdom's touch,
Of simpletons this book tells much.
But pay more heed, I beg you do,
To common sense and honor's due
Than e'er to this poor verse or me,
In truth I've slaved laboriously
That 'mongst these leaves these idiots might
Foregather; I have worked at night
While snug in bed they slumbered tight
Or gambled, freely drinking wine,
And never thought of me and mine.
Some rode about in sleds on snow
With frozen ear or frost-bit toe,
Some pranced like love-sick calves elated,
And others losses estimated
That they had undergone that day,
And how themselves they would repay,
Or how tomorrow they would ply
Their falsehoods, sell, deceive, and buy.
In pondering these many pranks,
The pranks of countless stupid cranks,
'Tis wonder not that anxious fear
Lest rhyming bring me hate and jeer
Has robbed of sleep my nights so drear.
Both men and women, all mankind
Their image in this glass will find,
That both I mean will follow soon,
For man is not the only loon,

'Mongst women fools are hardly fewer,
I'll deck their heads and veils demure
With fool's cap, though I'm sure it hurts,
For girls, too, have on idiot's skirts.
Some clothes they wear would put to shame
Full many a man's unblemished name,
Shoes pointed, bodice cut too low,
So that their breasts might almost show,
And rags they wrap into their braids,
And build huge horns upon their heads,
The giant oxen mocking they
Parade about as beasts of prey.
But honorable women should
Forgive me what I say, I would
Not wish to injure their good name,
I'd stress the bad ones' evil fame,
Full scores of whom deserve a trip
Aboard our crowded idiot's ship.
With caution everyone should look
To see if he's in this my book,
And who thinks not will say that he
Of wand and fool's cap may be free.
Who thinks that he is not affected
To wise men's doors be he directed,
There let him wait until mayhap
From Frankfurt I can fetch a cap.[4]

moralizing about clothing

In dunce's dance I take the lead,
Books useless, numerous my creed,
Which I can't understand or read.[1]

1. OF USELESS BOOKS

If on this ship I'm number one
For special reasons that was done,
Yes, I'm the first one here you see
Because I like my library.
Of splendid books I own no end,
But few that I can comprehend;

I cherish books of various ages
And keep the flies from off the pages.
Where art and science be professed
I say: At home I'm happiest,
I'm never better satisfied
Than when my books are by my side.
King Ptolemy did once decree
That he have all the books there be,
And thought he owned a treasure-trove,
But oh, he needed Christian love,
Could not profess the proper creed.
I, too, have many books indeed
But don't peruse them very much;
Why should I plague myself with such?
My head in booklore I'll not bury,
Who studies hard grows visionary;
A Dominie I well could be
And pay someone to learn for me;
Though I may be a vulgar lout
I can when scholars walk about
Say 'ita' when I might say 'yes.'
The man of German tongue I bless;
Although my Latin isn't fine
I know that 'vinum' stands for wine,
'Gucklus' [3] a cuckold, 'stultus' fool,
And I am 'doctor,' that's my rule;
My ears are covered up for me,
If they were not, an ass I'd be.

[handwritten margin note:] respect for wisdom of the ancients but they do lack Christianity

[handwritten margin note:] fools who use Latin without really knowing it also a plug for the vulgar vernacular?

[handwritten note at bottom:] people following the trend of owning books and muttering Latin because it is "the thing to do" rather really knowing what they're doing

Who heeds what mighty men have said
And e'er by fickleness is led
Drives sows to vats before they're dead.[1]

2. OF GOOD COUNCILORS

Full many exercise their wit
That soon in council they may sit,
Not knowing right or wrong at all
They blindly grope along the wall.
Hushai, alas, has long been dead,
Ahithophel has got ahead! [2]

Wouldst others with advice delight,
Then counsel but what's fair and right,
So you will not be like a slat
That drives the sow into the vat.
I truly say it is not fair,
Let judgment be a lesser care,
For it alone does not make right,
One must be searching, must be quite
Inquisitive of evidence,
Else right is wrong and bare of sense,
Else God will not accept your plea;
I give the warning earnestly.
If we could see the future clear
We'd not be rash with judgment here.
The standard every man's applied
In life, by that he too is tried,
As you judge me and I judge you
Our heavenly Father judges too.[3]
When he is dead a man will find
The judgment he once gave his kind;
Whose judgment injures others may
Expect his own grim Judgment Day.
The judgments spoke by cruel men
Will some fine day rebound on them;
Who does not render justice well
Will meet harsh justice down in hell;
No godless counsel God will praise,
No violent, sly, or crafty ways.[4]

mans judgement should be in accordance w God's fairness

is God active in the affairs of the world, to Brant?

young, inexperienced counselmen who have no opinion & become tools of older colleagues

Who sets his heart on earthly ware
And seeks his joy and comfort there,
Inveterate foolishness his share.

3. OF GREED

A fool who gathers earthly ware
And finds no joy or comfort there
And hardly knows for whom to save
When once he finds his dark, cool grave;
More foolish still is he who spends
To frivolous and wasteful ends

What God once gave for him to own,
What he should husband all alone.
Some day accounting he must make,
Where more than limb will be at stake.
A fool gives liberally to friends,
His own salvation never tends
And dreads the lack of earthly wares,
But ne'er for things eternal cares.
O silly fool, how blind you are,
You fear the mange, invite a scar.
The man who wrongful riches wins
Will burn in hell for all his sins;
To that his heirs pay little heed,
They'd not assist in time of need,
They'd not redeem him for a sou
When once in hell he needs must stew.
For God's sake, give the while you may,
When you've died other men hold sway;
No wise man ever deemed it worth
His while to garner wealth on earth,
He'd rather learn to know himself.
Who's wise has more than trifling pelf;
Crassus did drink the gold, they say,
For which he craved and thirsted ay;
Crates his gold tossed out to sea,
So that for studies he'd be free.
Who piles up goods that evanesce
Inters his soul in filthiness.

Who everywhere would innovate
Arouses scandal, wrath, and hate,
A dunce's stupid traveling mate.

4. OF INNOVATIONS

(vanities)

An erstwhile quite disgraceful thing
Now has a plain, familiar ring:
An honor 'twas a beard to grow,
Effeminate dandies now say no!
Smear apish grease on face and hair
And leave the neck entirely bare,

With rings and many a heavy chain,
As though they were in Lienhart's train; [1] *patron St. of prisoners*
Vile sulphur, resin curl their hair,
An egg white's added too with care,
That curls may form in basket-pan, [2]
The curls amid the breeze they fan,
Or bleach them white in sun and heat,
For lice no ordinary treat;
Their number now would wax untold,
Since modern clothes have many a fold,
Coat, bodice, slipper, also skirts,
Boots, pants, and shoes and even shirts,
Fur hoods, cloaks, trimmings not a few,
The Jewish style seems smart and new.
The styles change oft, are various,
It proves that we are frivolous.
Shameless and fickle I do brand
Style slaves who live in every land;
Their coats are short and shorter grow,
So that their navels almost show.
Shame, German nation, be decried!
What nature would conceal and hide,
You bare it, make a public show,
'Twill lead to evil, lead to woe,
And then grow worse and harm your name;
Woe's every man who rouses shame,
Woe's him too who condones such sin,
His wages will be paid to him.

My name is on the Reaper's list,
Nor has the knife my buttocks missed,
And yet in folly I persist.

5. OF OLD FOOLS

My foolish conduct mocks my age,
I'm very old but am not sage,
A naughty child of hundred years,
A youthful dunce cap o'er my ears;
The children I would regiment
And write myself a testament

That after death I well may rue.
Example bad and counsel too ⟩
I give that in my youth I learned
And think that praise I've thereby earned,
And dare to boast of my disgrace,
That I've deceived in many a place;
Clear water I have turned to slime
And practiced evil every time.
That I'm no longer quite as bad
As once I was, that makes me sad;
But pranks that I must leave undone ⟩
I'll teach to Henry, he's my son,
He'll carry on my evil stock,
For he's a chip from off this block;
Such conduct suits him perfectly,
And if he lives, a man he'll be.
'Tmust be confessed that he's my son
If justice would to him be done,
His talents never stinting, sparing,
We'll find him in the fool's ship faring.
When I am dead 'twill give me cheer,
I've left some good successors here;
Old age has such a recompense,
Old age today is bare of sense.
Susanna's judges [1] showed us why
On older men we can't rely;
An oldish fool spares not his soul,
A sinner cannot change his goal.

Whoe'er his children's mischief bears
Indulgently and always spares
The rod, will later suffer cares.

6. OF THE TEACHING
OF CHILDREN

A fool is he and blind indeed
Who ne'er to children pays much heed
That properly they may be reared
And in the right direction steered;
He must not suffer them to err

Like sheep that have no shepherd's care,
And if to mischief they're addicted
Chastisement due must be inflicted.
That they are young is no excuse,
They should be taught that for abuse
There's punishment discreet, severe.
O fool, I beg you, lend your ear,
Since youth has ready memory
The child can learn quite easily.
The liquid poured in brand-new tubs
Will leave a smell howe'er one scrubs;
A youthful shoot can well be bent,
But old shoots curved with such intent
Will very often snap or shatter;
Fit punishment's no grievous matter,
The rod will drive without a smart
All folly from your youngster's heart.
He seldom learns who's never cuffed,
And evils grow when not rebuffed.
Eli [1] was righteous, never bad,
But since he punished not his lad,
God punished him and did destroy
In wrath the father with the boy;
Since children are not reared betimes
We now have many Catilines.
Our children too'd be better trained
If they had teachers like the famed
Phoenix [2] whom Peléus admired
And for his son Achilles hired,
And Philip scoured Greece till he'd won
The ablest teacher for his son;

The greatest king that ever reigned,
By Aristotle was he trained,
And he did sit at Plato's knees,
While Plato learned from Socrates.
But fathers, oh, of nowaday,
When greed and stinginess hold sway,
Engage such teachers for a son
Who'd make a fool of anyone
And send him home again (for shame!)
More foolish now than when he came.
It's little wonder that a fool
Has foolish children as a rule.
Old Crates said, if 'twere allowed
And proper he would loudly shout:
You fools, who think of getting rich
And have this constant burning itch
And ne'er to children pay much heed,
Since riches are your only need!
But retribution hastens then
When once your sons are councilmen
And strive for honor, high renown,
Then each will play the stupid clown
As he had learned in early youth.
Their father soon will hear the truth
And eat his very heart and rue
That he has reared a bugaboo.[3]
Some join a brutal ruffian's horde,
Blaspheming they malign our Lord,
Some go about with slattern whores,
Some gamble, losing shirt and horse,
Others carouse by day and night,

That, mark you, that's our children's plight
If once in youth they've been neglected,
By teachers never well directed.
From start to finish honor's prize
Derives alone from precepts wise.
A noble mind's a precious stone,
Your sacred trust, but not your own,
For from your parents it doth flow,
And riches also blessings show,
But that depends on fortune's call,
And fortune bounces like a ball;
An asset too is worldly fame,
But gross inconstancy's its name;
But beauty too's a great delight,
Enduring scarcely over night;
Good health is also very lief,
But it escapes like any thief;
Great strength of body too doth please,
With age and illness though it flees.
But one thing's constant, never dies }
In this wide world: Good precepts wise. }
Gorgias asked: "Does happiness
The mighty Persian monarch bless?"
Spake Socrates: "The answer's yes,
If wisdom, virtue he confess."
He meant that power and gold are vain }
If virtue does not guide the twain. }

Who 'twixt two millstones puts his frame
And many people would defame
Will suffer hurt, will suffer shame.

7. OF CAUSING DISCORD

Full many a man takes great delight
In causing other men to fight
And pitting neighbor 'gainst his neighbor,
So that in hate and spite they labor;
With slander too and many lies
His neighbor's fortitude he tries,

Who only later finds it out;
He treats his friends as would a lout,
And that his proof the better be,
He magnifies indignity
And treats it like a church confession
That no one blame his indiscretion,
Pretending that to you alone
His whispered secret now is known.
'Tis thus they'd curry friends and please,
The world is full of feuds like these.
Tongues carry tales to every place
Much faster than a coach could race.
Thus Absalom [1] and Korah [2] did
When for adherents once they bid,
But only grief resulted thus.
In every land an Alcimus [3]
Who'd cheat his friends with discord sore
And jam his fingers in the door,
And often doth his fingers maim
Like him who riches hoped to claim
When old King Saul he put to death,[4]
Like those who murdered Ish-bosheth,[5]
Like him who 'twixt two millstones pines
And causes discord oftentimes.
Just watch him act and soon you'll see
Of what base quality he be.
Conceal a fool behind the door,
His ears are salient as before.

Who cannot answer no or yes
And spurns advice as valueless
Must bear his own unhappiness.

8. OF NOT FOLLOWING
GOOD ADVICE

A fool who with the wise would go
Yet reason, measure cannot show,
And e'en when speaking wisdom's word
A cuckoo is his fowling bird.
Some men are wise in what they say

But hitched to folly's plow they stay;
The reason is that they rely
Upon their shrewdness keen and sly
And heed to no one's counsel pay
Until misfortune comes their way.
Thus Tobit always taught his son [1]
That sage advice he should not shun;
Because Lot's wife good counsel spurned
And looked in back of her and turned,[2]
The Lord chastised this grievous fault
And changed her instantly to salt.
When Rehoboam once declined [3]
Wise teachings, caring more to mind
The idiots, ten tribes he lost
And stayed a fool at any cost.
If Nebuchadnezzar had not ceased
Obeying, he'd not be a beast,[4]
And Maccabeus, hero bold,
Of whom great deeds are often told,
If he had done what Joram said,
He would not have been stricken dead.[5]
The man of stubborn, willful mind
To prudent counsel's ever blind,
Of gracious fortune he is void
And prematurely is destroyed.
Friends' counsel value every hour,
Good counsel oft spells fortune, power.
Ahithophel soon after died
When his advice King Saul [6] decried.

Who's crude and rude from skin to core
And plays the fool's part evermore,
He drags his cap along the floor.

9. OF BAD MANNERS

Who wears full robes with haughty stare,
Who struts with head held high in air,
To this side, then to tother side,
Now back again in circles wide,
Now moving fast, now ambling slow,
To me his conduct oft will show

This man doth sport frivolity,
And that avoided it should be.
The man who brains and breeding shares
Will never feign affected airs,
And what he does or what he tries
Seems good to people truly wise.
Real wisdom starts with modesty,
It's decorous, acts peaceably,
It is a friend of goodness too,
Which brings God's blessing unto you;
The man whose breeding knows no dearth
Owns more than riches here on earth.
Good breeding seen in men of parts
Reveals their nature, shows their hearts;
The man whose manners seem but poor
Shows he was trained to be a boor,
Ill-bred, uncouth the arrant knave,
That like a cow he doth behave.
The noblest, finest traits there be
Are breeding, manners, modesty;
Good breeding Noah'd always prize,
But Ham, his son, was otherwise.
If you've a prudent, well-bred son,
Who sense and wisdom would not shun,
Then saying thanks to God is meet
For showing you the mercy seat.
His father's nose Albinus ate
For rearing him in shameful state.[1]

Who cuffs and beats his human brother
That nothing did to harm or bother
Offends the sense of many another.

10. TRUE FRIENDSHIP

A fool is he, a derelict,
If wrongs on others he'd inflict,
Because it's thus he'll win a foe
Who'll later triumph o'er his woe.
If you do wrong or hurt a friend
Who trusted you to every end

And now finds evil recompense,
A fool you are devoid of sense.
Such friends today are very rare
As Jonathan and David were,
Or as Patroclus, Achilles,
Orestes, also Pylades,
As Demades [1] and Pythias,
Or as the squire of Saul once was,[2]
Or Laelius and Scipio.
When money lacks, your friendships go,
For none his neighbor loves so well
As God's commandment would impel.[3]
Self-love expels whate'er is just,
All friendship, family, and trust;
Where might today that Moses be [4]
Who loves his neighbors honestly?
Is Nehemiah anywhere,
God-fearing Tobit, is he there?
Who common welfare would despise
And only craves for personal prize,
I deem him foolish and inane.
What's public good is each man's gain,
But Cains there are in every state
Who Abel's joy begrudge and hate.
Friendships, alas, when woes are many
Are four-and-twenty to the penny,
And men who deem themselves so fine:
A mite will purchase ninety-nine.

A man who's ready fools to hear
When Holy Writ is always near:
The dunce's game will cost him dear.

11. CONTEMPT OF
HOLY WRIT

A fool is he who has forsook
His faith in Writ and Holy Book
And thinks that he can live as well
Without a God, without a hell,
Despising preachment with a sneer

As though he could not see or hear.
If someone from the dead should hie,
A hundred miles or more we'd fly
To meet him and to hear him tell
The news that he has brought from hell,
If many live in hell's confines
And if they drink young, heady wines,
And other mischief bare of wit.
There is so much of Holy Writ,
Of Testament both Old and New,
That everything's been proved to you.
We'll not require assurance queer
From Niklashausen's shepherd-seer.[1]
The Lord doth verily proclaim:
Who sins on earth, in hell finds shame,
And who on earth in prudence lives,
To him eternal praise God gives.
'Twas God who fashioned verity,
The ear can hear, the eye can see,
Therefore an idiot he and blind [2]
Who wisdom will not hear or mind,
Or who would hark to teachings new.
I fear the day is near when you
Will hear new teachings, new belief,
Far more than pleasing, more than lief.[3]
Old Jeremiah warned aloud,
But those in earshot were not bowed,
And others too gave admonition,
But no one could arrest perdition.

Who never girds before he'd ride,
And shows no care in proper tide,
Is scorned when falling off the side.

12. OF HEEDLESS FOOLS

In him is folly oft detected
Who says: "Ah, that was unexpected!"
For who shows care in proper tide,
He seeks a saddle ere he ride.
Whoe'er with thought and plan would wait
Will find their plans are often late,

But those who plan the while they act
Must have experience in fact,
Or must have watched the other sex,
Who're very shrewd in these respects.
Had Adam used a little wit
Before into the fruit he bit,
He'd never for a tiny slice
Have been expelled from Paradise.
If Jonathan had been apprised,
The gifts he'd surely have despised
That Tryphon brought, the faithless man,
Before he slew poor Jonathan.[1]
Sagacious plans were ever rife
When Emperor Julius joined in strife,
But once while peace prevailed unchecked
He erred in only one respect
And friendly letters did not read
That prophesied a heinous deed.
Nicanor's scheming came to naught,[2]
He sold the game he had not caught;[3]
His plot failed signally, instead
He lost his tongue, his hand, his head.
Good plans are always fine, no doubt,
If but in time they're carried out.
Some hurry, yet arrive too late,
Excess of zeal may break your pate.
If Asahel had never sped
Abner would not have stabbed him dead.[4]

My rope pulls many fools about,
Ape, cuckold, ass, and silly lout,
Whom I seduce, deceive, and flout.

13. OF AMOURS

Dame Venus I, with rump of straw,[1]
Fools do regard me oft with awe,
I draw them toward me with a thrill
And make a fool of whom I will,
My clients, who could name them all?
Whoever's heard of Circe's stall,

Calypso, famous sirens' bower,
He knows my skill and knows my power.
Whoever thinks he's very shrewd
In idiot's broth will soon be stewed,
Whom I decide to wound by stealth
Through herbs will not regain his health.
My little son stark blind is he
Since love-sick swains can never see;
My son's a child, he never grew,
For lovers act like children too.
They seldom speak a serious word,
Their speech like children's is absurd.
My son goes naked every day,
Love can't be hid and tucked away;
Since evil loves are flighty things
My offspring wears a pair of wings;
Amours are changeful, fickle e'er,
There's naught more fitful anywhere;
And Cupid brings along his bow,[2]
While round his waist two quivers show.
In one, barbed arrows he doth bear,
To shoot the fools who have no care.
Whom once these sharp gilt barbs do hit,
Deprived are they of sense and wit,
They dance about like fools insane.
The other pouch doth bolts contain,
They're dull and leaded, hardly light,
One causes wounds, the other flight.
Whom Cupid strikes, Amor ignites,
So that the fire his vitals bites
And he cannot put out the flame

That killed Dido of ancient fame
And caused Medea, cruel mother,
To burn one child and slay another.[3]
Tereus would not have been a bird,
Pasiphaë the steer'd avoid,
Phaedra would Theseus not pursue
And passion for her stepson shew,
For Nessus death would not have loomed
And Troy would never have been doomed,
Scylla would leave her father's hair,
Hyacinth be a flower fair,
Leander would not swim the sea,
Messalina pure and chaste would be,
And Mars in chains would never lie,
Procris from thickets green would shy,
Sappho would not fall off the cliff,
Sirens would not upset a skiff,
Circe no vessel would impede,
Pan, Cyclops play no plaintive reed,
Leucothoë would incense spare,
Myrrha would no Adonis bear,
And Byblis would her brother leave,
Through gold would Danaë not conceive,
In night Nyctimine not rejoice,
And Echo would not mock our voice,
Thisbe would dye no berries red,
Atalanta be no lion dread,
The Levite's wife none would disgrace,[4]
Causing the death of one whole race;
David would not take Bersabë,[5]
Samson would not trust Dalitë,[6]

Solomon would not to idols pray,[7]
Amnon his sister not betray,[8]
And Joseph would not be undone [9]
Nor Hippolytus, Bellerophon;
As horse the wise man would not fare,[10]
And Vergil would not hang in air,[11]
Ovid the emperor's friend would be,
Had he not learned love's artistry,
And more to wisdom's fount would go
If smitten not with lover's woe.
Who sees too much of woman's charms
His morals and his conscience harms;
He cannot worship God aright
Who finds in women great delight.
Clandestine love in every race
Is foolish, sinful, black disgrace;
Such love is still more foolish when
It seizes older wives and men.
Fool who from love takes inspiration
And means to practice moderation,
For wisdom's treasure rich and pure
Cannot be mingled with amour;
A lover's oft so blind indeed,
He thinks no one his loves will heed.
Such folly I can but deride,
This dunce cap's pasted to his hide.

Who says: No pity God avows,
And that no justice He doth house,
Is ignorant as geese and sows.

14. OF INSOLENCE
TOWARD GOD

He smears himself with donkey's fat
And has the grease pot 'neath his hat
Who dares assert that heaven hath
Much mercy and but little wrath
Against a man committing wrong

And would condone it for a song,
Since these are only human faults.
God did not fashion heaven's vaults
To be a paradise for geese,
And sins have never been a piece
Of human life, and nothing new.
Some know the Bible through and through
And other books that others wrote,
But nowhere do they seem to note
That punishment is always stated
And retribution's unabated,
And God will evermore rebuff
A human giving Him a cuff.
God's joined no Czech or gypsy band,
Their tongues though He can understand,
Although the mercy He doth send
To men is boundless, has no end,
His justice e'er stays grand and free,
Chastising sin eternally.
Vengeance nine generations long
Greets all of those who would do wrong;
God's mercy too would fail and must
If He should ever grow unjust.
Heaven was meant nor then nor now
For geese, nor will a fool or cow
Or ape or grunting swine or ass
To heaven's timeless kingdom pass.
The soul the devil has enslaved
Can never be redeemed or saved.

By those who build it should be heeded
What sums of money will be needed,
Or else the task will not be speeded.

15. OF FOOLISH PLANS[1]

A fool is he who has not paused
When building to compute the cost
And see if with his funds he can
Complete the work as he did plan.
The buildings blindly undertaken
Must later often be forsaken:

Nebuchadnezzar boasted loudly [2]
And claimed with arrogance and proudly
That through his might the great and feared
City of Babylon had been reared,
And yet the Bible tells us how
He stayed afield quite like a cow.
Nimrod would build on high a tower,
A buttress 'gainst the water's power,[3]
But since no careful plans he heeded
His work to no good end was speeded.
Not many build as much today
As when Lucullus had his way.
Whoe'er would build without regret
Should plan before the stones are set.
Regret in many a man commences
When losses in his purse he senses.
If you would venture something bold,
Reserves are needed, cash and gold,
To reach your distant destination
Of which you dream without cessation,
So never mishap comes to mock
And make of you a laughing stock.
'Tis better never to attempt
Than end with losses, with contempt.
A pyramid's a costly pile
And labyrinths at River Nile,[4]
But they decay and lose their worth,
No building can endure on earth.

He merits future poverty
Who always lives in luxury
And joins the spendthrift's revelry.

16. OF GLUTTONY AND FEASTING

He shoes a fool in every wise
Who day and night forever hies
From feast to feast to fill his paunch
And make his figure round and staunch,
As though his mission he were filling

By drinking too much wine and swilling
And bringing hoar-frost o'er the grape.
Into the fool's ship toss the ape,
He kills all reason, is not sage,
And will regret it in old age.
His head and hands will ever shake,
His life a speedy end may take,
For wine's a very harmful thing,
A man shows no sound reasoning
Who only drinks for sordid ends,
A drunken man neglects his friends
And knows no prudent moderation,
And drinking leads to fornication;
It oft induces grave offense,
A wise man drinks with common sense.
For wine old Noah cared no whit,[1]
Although he found and planted it;
By wine Loth twice to sin was led,[2]
Through wine the Baptist lost his head,[3]
Through wine a wise man comes to prate
And set a fool's cap on his pate;
When Israelites were drunk with wine
And glutted full like silly swine,[4]
They gamboled then in highest glee
And had to dance in revelry.
To Aaron's sons did God decree
That abstinent and chaste they be
And that to wine they should not turn,
But this decree the priests would spurn.[5]
King Holofernes too when drunk,
He had his head cut off his trunk;

To feasts Tomyris had recourse
When old King Cyrus she would force; [6]
Wine caused the fall of Ben-hadad, [7]
Deprived was he of all he had;
When Alexander played the sot
His honor, virtue he forgot [8]
And practiced deeds in drunkenness
That presently brought sad distress.
The rich man reveled once so well
That on the morn he ate in hell. [9]
Man would not be a slave, in fine,
If he disowned the demon wine:
Are wine and sumptuous food your itch?
You'll not be happy, not get rich.
Woe's him and woe's his father too,
He'll have misfortunes not a few
Who always gorges like a beast
Proposing toasts at every feast,
And would with others glasses clink;
The man whose joy is endless drink
Is like a man who falls asleep [10]
Defenseless on the ocean deep;
Thus they who drink and e'er are gay,
Carousing, toping night and day:
If he's their friend, the generous host
Brings veal galore, a cow almost,
And gives them almonds, figs, and rice,
The bill, alas, is writ on ice.
Some men would be intelligent
From wine if wisdom e'er it lent,
Who cool their throats with rich libation.

Friend drinks to friend without cessation:
"I drink to you." "Here's happy days!"
"This cup for you." "This yours!" he says;
"I'll toast you till we both are filled!"
Thus speak the men of folly's guild.
Upset the glass, the drinker too,
A rope around his neck would do
Him better far than wild carousing
And naught but foolishness arousing,
That ancient Seneca did flay
In books that still are read today,
Which say one pays a drunken man
More heed than many a sober man,
And how an honor high 'tis rated
By wine to be intoxicated;
I censure those who tipple beer,
A keg of it per man, I hear,
Becoming so inebriate
That with them one could ope a gate.
A fool shows no consideration,
A wise man drinks with moderation,
Feels better, illness too defies,
Than one imbibing bucketwise.
The wine, 'tis true, our thirst will slake [11]
But later stabs one like a snake,
And poison through the veins will pour,
As Basiliscus found of yore.

The wealthy man of foolish creed
Who nevermore would beggars heed
Will be denied when he's in need.

17. OF USELESS RICHES

The greatest folly ever told
Is honoring wisdom less than gold,
With such beliefs one only rears
Rich men with bells on asses' ears.
Such councilmen one fain would choose
As have the greatest wealth to lose;

The world believes a man as much
As he has funds inside his pouch.
Lord Lucre leads the greedy on:
If still alive were Solomon,
The council he would have to shun
If but a simple weaver he,
Or if his purse of gold were free.
To rich men dinners we will proffer,
And game, fowl, fish to them we offer,
The scraping host cajoles and flatters
The while the beggar waits in tatters
And from the cold his jawbone chatters.
The wealthy guest is greeted: "Sir,
Please eat!" Yes, riches cause a stir;
You force all men to scrape and bend.
Who has the coin has many a friend,
He's called a chum on every side,
And if a man would take a bride,
The first thing is: How rich is he?
No one inspects his honesty
Or asks if wisdom in him rules;
He's chosen from the guild of fools,
Who can afford some bread with milk,
Though he be rowdyish of ilk.
Nor wisdom, honor have much backing
Wherever shining gold is lacking.
Who from the poor his treasure locks
Will find God deaf whene'er he knocks.

Two hares at once would he waylay
Who'd serve two masters well for ay,
Performing more than one man may.

18. OF SERVING TWO MASTERS

Fool he who thinks he can afford
To serve both world and eke the Lord,
 For where two masters one must serve
No one gets all he would deserve.
Whoe'er to many trades would run

Will master ne'er a single one.
The hunter who with single hound
Would catch two hares as off they bound
Will very often lose them both
And may return annoyed and wroth;
The man who shoots with many a bow,
His arrows past all targets go;
The man whose posts are too diverse
Will often do what all men curse.
Who must be here and also there
Will often not get anywhere;
The man who'd please both young and old,
His breath must be both warm and cold,
He eats what ne'er he could digest,
Must take what may not be the best,
'Neath each man's elbow he must squeeze
A cushion soft to soothe and please,
And wheedle him with clever lies
And flattery, lest choler rise.
But many offices bring pride
And furnish coal for fireside,
Who samples many kinds of wine
Will find some brands not quite so fine.
One quickly buys plain jewelry,
The wise man likes simplicity.
Who serves but one without ado
Is called a servant good and true.
The donkey died for want of hay
Who changed his master every day.

Both religious & secular meanings.

Who guards his speech and holds his tongue
By anguish ne'er his soul is stung;
Woodpeckers' screech betrays their young.

19. OF IDLE TALK

That man's a fool who'd criticize
When they keep silent who are wise,
And he will harvest needless hate
When silence were appropriate;
Who speaks his mind when silence pays
Is arrant fool in many ways,

Who answers long before there's need,[1]
That person is a fool indeed.
To many talking much is lief,
But often ends in bitter grief.
We're so persuasive, they will say,
We'd wheedle nuts from any jay.
Their words are oft so eloquent
They'd poke holes in a document,
For glib speech is their great obsession,
But when they come to take confession
And for salvation they should pray,
Their tongue has not a word to say.
E'en now the Nabals are not few,[2]
They prate what they must often rue.
We'd credit many a man with wit
If he had not confuted it.
Woodpeckers tell us by their tongue
Where they have nested broods of young.
By silence one can say a lot,
'Tis bad to be a talking sot.
The tongue is very short and small
Yet causes many a man a fall,
It can besmirch th' entire body
And causes quarrels mean and shoddy.
I'm oft surprised, to say the least,
That we can tame full many a beast
However treacherous it may be,
But tongues defy our mastery.
The tongue's a quite uncertain tool,
It's dangerous to many a fool.
The tongue it is that oft blasphemes,

The tongue insults our neighbors, schemes
And curses him and does upbraid
Whom God in His own image made.
Our tongues bring on our ruination,
Leave naught to our imagination;
Through talk some men such lives have led
That they need buy nor wine nor bread;
The tongue is used in litigation
To give a scamp sanctification,
Through it the needy lose their suit
So that they're rendered destitute;
Praters can always prate their fill,
Tickling themselves, they laugh at will,
Good things to say they never know
Of anybody high or low.
Who make a noise and great ado
Are roundly praised and honored too,
Above all, those who strut around
Studded with rings and richly gowned,
They seem to please our worthies well,
Thin gowns now cast no magic spell.
If we still had Demosthenes
Or Tullius or Eschines,
No one their wisdom would acclaim
Unless they knew the men of fame
And spoke the words they like to hear,
The flowery words a fool holds dear.
Who talks will talk what ne'er he should
To make impression fine and good,
Plays shrewd at games without cessation
And schemes and plots in emulation.

'Tis bad to prate without an end,
A lying person has no friend.
Who would revile a mighty lord
Will find his slander noised abroad.
Indeed, no matter where you are
The birds will carry it afar,
And in the end 'twill do you harm.
His lordship has a long, strong arm.
Who wields his axe and lets chips fly
Will get a chip into his eye
And who his mouth in heaven sets
His own chastisement often gets.
Whate'er he knows a fool will prate,[3]
The wise men keep their peace and wait,
For idle talk's of little use,
It only nurtures harm, abuse,
And so to hush is surely better
Than talking, prating, useless chatter.
Sotades few words spoke in vain,[4]
Yet got to jail as though he'd slain;
This only spoke Theocritus:
That one-eyed was Antigonus,
And died anon in his own house
Like Demosthenes and Tullius.
Silence is good, I always teach,
But better still is rightful speech.

Who makes a find and takes it home
And thinks that God His favor's shown,
The devil loves him as his own.

20. OF FINDING TREASURES

A fool is he who makes a find
And in his mind is so purblind
That he believes: "God gave me this,
It makes no difference whose it is."
The seeds that you have never sown,
When harvest comes, are not your own.

It's clear to all as 'tis to me
That that's another's property
If from another man you have it.
It matters not how much you crave it
And found it but by accident,
To its true owner be it sent,
If it is known what man is he
Or who the owner's heirs may be.
If them one cannot ascertain
Then let thereby some poor man gain,
Or give it else to charity,
But keep it not, whate'er it be.
Such goods are not acquired well
And often he's consigned to hell
Who keeps them for himself and frets
And gets a rubbing ere he sweats.
Achor [1] did keep unlawful gain
And caused the people grievous pain
Until his sin he had atoned,
When mercilessly he was stoned.
The man who takes a little loot
Would willingly take more to boot:
To find, to steal—of selfsame hue
To God when He examines you.
'Tis better not to find, you'll learn,
Than finding things you don't return;
If you put findings in your sack
You'll never want to give them back.

Who might to highways broad repair
But rather in the mud would fare,
Of sense and wisdom he is bare.

21. OF CHIDING, AND ERRING ONESELF

A fool is he who chides in you
What he himself would often do;
A fool he worth dishonoring,
Who sees the worst in everything,
Who'd play the critic, who'd deride,

⟨But senses not his seamy side.⟩
A hand that's to the crossroads tied
Points out a path it's never tried.
Who has a beam in his own eye [1]
Should take it out ere he say: "I,
O brother, in your eye do see
A mote that quite displeases me."
A teacher too is quite unwise
Who fellow men can oft chastise,
But his own vices will not chide
And other people will deride.
They'll tell him: "Doctor, if you please,
Why don't you cure your own disease?"
Some counsel others when in need,
But their own words they never heed.
Both Gentilis and Mesuë
By fever were they snatched away [2]
For which they had prescribed a cure,
As in their books they did assure.
Consider vices as you would,
If they do seem alluring, good,
To men of lofty reputation,
Then they're a truly great sensation; [3]
First do the work, then theorize
If you want men to call you wise.
Israel's tribe, themselves in sin,
Attacked the sons of Benjamin,
But their attack was all in vain
Because their God they did disdain. [4]

Who harks to wisdom e'er and learns
And every day to wisdom turns
Eternal honor richly earns.

her *wisdom*
is a woman!

22. THE TEACHING OF WISDOM[1]

In piercing accents Wisdom says:
"Perceive my words, O human race,
You must be prudent, wise, and shrewd,
Hear me in all your folly crude,
Seek teachings ever, never gold,

Wisdom holds preciousness untold,
'Tis better than mundane delight,
Pursue it ever, day and night.
There's nothing like it here on earth,
In councils it's of sterling worth.
"All strength and man's most prudent care
I give you," Wisdom does declare.
"Through me the king can wear his crown,
Laws give I meaning, wide renown,
Through me the princes hold their land,
I give all powers their sanction grand,
Who loves me dearly's loved by me,
Who seeks me early him I see.
Through me are wealth and honor stored,
I am possessed by God, the Lord,
Forever, in eternity,
And God created all through me.
Without me nothing holdeth sway,
Blest he who loves me every day.
Therefore, my sons, be not too slow,
He's happy who my path can know.
Who finds me, also finds salvation,
Who hates me, suffers harsh damnation."
A fool will be in sorry state,
For Wisdom he will contemplate,
And that reward that flows so free
And lasts until eternity,
The while with bleeding heart he'll sigh:
O what a piteous fool am I!

Who thinks that he has everything,
That Lady Fortune's on his string,
Will some day feel Fate's mallet swing.

23. OF VAUNTING LUCK

He is a fool who dares to say
That fortune always comes his way
And that it never stands aloof,
He'll feel the mallet on his roof.
For kindly fortune's nothing less
Than proof that things will evanesce,

That God will leave to tears and sighs
The person He does not chastise.
A well-known proverb doth contend
That often friend will visit friend.
A father punishes his son,
That fear he learn and evil shun.
The doctor gives a potion bitter,
To make the patient feel the fitter,
A surgeon oft will lance the wound
That soon the patient will be sound;
Forlorn those patients are indeed
To whom no doctor says: "Take heed,
This, mark you, you should not have done,
But this 'twere meet that you'd begun."
No doctor tells a man who's ill
That he may have whate'er he will!
The man the devil wants to pluck
Is given wealth and ample luck;
Far better suffer poverty
Than have all wealth and luck there be.
Let no one boast: My luck is good,
For God could take it if He would.
He is a fool who's prone to say:
"O fortune, leave me not, I pray,
And give me so much, I implore,
That I may play the fool some more."
No greater fool was ever made
Than one whose luck has never strayed.

If all men's cares you fain would borrow
And you neglect your joy and sorrow
You'll get a fool's bath on the morrow.

24. OF TOO MUCH CARE

A fool is he who fain would bear
What's heavier than mortal share,
And who alone would do what three
Could not do with impunity;
Who takes the world upon his back
Will soon succumb beneath his pack.

They say 'twas Alexander's whim:
The world was far too small for him,
He sweated in it, I assume,
Because he had too little room,
Yet finally this monarch grand
Got only seven feet of land.
For death alone can show a man
How much of earth he needs may span;
A greater, mightier man than that,
Diogenes, had but a vat,
And nothing else he e'er possessed,
By no desire was he oppressed,
Had but the king not kept the sun
From lighting up his humble tun.
Who has ambitions bold and high
Must take a chance to do or die.
What profits it to win the earth
And yet to suffer want and dearth?
Why let the body ride on high,
While into hell the soul must fly?
Who'd furnish shoes for geese's feet
And sweep all alleys, every street,
And level mountain off and vale,
He'll have no peace in any dale.
Nor care nor worries aught avail,
They make men haggard, lean, and pale,
And those are fools who fret and falter
Because of things they cannot alter.

Who in his borrowing's too free
The payment date—the wolf—will see,
Meanwhile the ass will kick his knee.

25. OF BORROWING
TOO MUCH

A prominent, outstanding fool
Who must make borrowing a rule
And credits not the man who quotes:
"Wolves eat no promissory notes." [1]
Thus also he whose wrongs and sin

God overlooks, to chasten him,
While daily he commits more ill
And God in heaven waits until
The final hour will come around
When he will pay the final pound.
The women, beasts, and children died
Of sins that were Gomorrah's pride,
That Sodomites once perpetrated;
Jerusalem once fell prostrated
When God had waited many a day;
Nineveh paid without delay
The sums it owed, and soon was free,
But this was short-lived liberty.
Soon Nineveh had greater sorrow,
God sent no Jonah on the morrow.
All things are great and then are nil,
They take their course as heaven will;
The man who's careful when he borrows
Has but few cares and fewer sorrows;
Trust not the men, they are not true,[2]
Who'd sign your bond and lend to you;
If you can't pay you will be bled,
They'll take the cover off your bed.
When Egypt had from famine sorrow,
So much of foodstuff did men borrow,
They were reduced to serfs, and yet
They were compelled to pay the debt.
When donkeys want to dance, don't fail
To give them room, hold not their tail.

Who'd wish for things he's never tried
And waits not till the Lord provide
Will suffer grief on every side.

26. OF USELESS WISHING

A fool he'd be whoever would
Want things that do more harm than good,
E'en though his wish could be fulfilled
He'd still belong to folly's guild.
King Midas had a craving bold
That all he touched be turned to gold,

This done, all things, to Midas' dread,
Were turned to gold, e'en wine and bread.
'Tis good his hair he did conceal
Lest donkey's ears he should reveal
Which sprouted there among the reeds.[1]
Woe's him whose wishes turn to deeds;
Full many wish protracted life [2]
Yet cause the soul despair and strife,
With boisterous living, food and wine,
And so they die before their time;
And even if they should grow old
They're pale, misshapen, sick, and cold,
Hollow their cheeks, their skin like crepe,
As though their mother'd been an ape.
Youth plays a happy, varied game
But old age always is the same,
In limb, voice, brain it quakes and shrivels,
It's bald and from its mouth it drivels;
Wives like not men so old and sear
Whom e'en the children scold or fear,
They're crabbed, cross in every wise
And always want to criticize.
Who live too long have great distress,
Accursed misfortunes them oppress,
In grief that constant sorrow breeds
They end their days in mourning weeds.
Nestor, Peleus, Laertes bold
Complained of this when they were old,
Too long, they said, the Lord watched o'er them
Since e'en their sons had died before them.
Had Priam perished young and strong

And lived but moderately long
He'd not seen bitter grief befall
His children, wife, his realm and all.
If Mithridates, Marius,
Great Pompey, also famed Croesus
Had died at some far earlier hour
They would have died in wealth and power.
Wish beauty for yourself and kin
And you'll be wishing naught but sin;
If Helen had not been so fair
She would have stayed in Greece fore'er,
And if Lucrece had ugly been
She'd not have suffered from Tarquin;
If Dinah had been humped and cropped
By Shechem she had not been stopped.[3]
But very seldom can one see
Beauty allied with chastity,
Yet dandies ever like to play
Their tricks and act in fiendish way.
But they are foiled and as a rule
They fare like any arrant fool;
They want a house, a wife, a child
And are by lust for wealth beguiled
And other baubles that the Lord
Has not approved but has ignored.
Our Lord such wishes ne'er approves
And what He grants He oft removes.
Some also strive for power and might
And seek to reach the greatest height
But do not call to mind at all
That height entails a greater fall,

That he who on the ground must crawl
Need never feel a humbling fall.
God gives us everything He will,
He knows what's right and what is ill,
What helps us, what's of real avail,
What brings us trouble, what travail,
And if He did not love us more
Than we ourselves, and from His store
Did grant us what our hearts hold dear,
We'd rue it e'en within a year,
For we are blinded by our greed
To wish for things we never need.
The man who sensibly would live
Let him pray God the Lord to give
Him sound mind, body, soul alway
And keep the fear of death away [4]
And wrath and appetite and greed.
Who's blessed with these, that man indeed
Has led a life of nobler bent
Than Hercules had ever spent
Or Sardanapalus once led
In luxury and featherbed;
He's found full everything he wants
And need not worship gods of chance.
A fool oft courts his injury,
His wish oft brings his misery.

Who never learns the proper things,
Upon his cap the dunce bell rings,
He's led by idiot's leading strings.

27. OF USELESS STUDYING[1]

Students should likewise not be skipped,
With fool's caps they are well equipped,
When these are pulled about the ear
The tassel flaps and laps the rear,
For when of books they should be thinking
They go carousing, roistering, drinking.

A youth puts learning on the shelf,
He'd rather study for himself
What's useless, vain—an empty bubble;
And teachers too endure this trouble,
Sensible learning they'll not heed,
Their talk is empty, vain indeed.
Could this be night or is it day? [2]
Did mankind fashion monkeys, pray?
Was't Plato, Socrates who ran?
Such is our modern teaching plan.
Are they not bred to folly true
Who night and day with great ado
Thus plague themselves and other men?
No other teaching do they ken.
Of such men, writes Origines,[3]
That froglike creatures quite like these
And gadflies who, unbidden, flew in,
Brought over Egypt rack and ruin.
In Leipzig students act this way,
In Erfurt, Mainz, Vienna, ay,
Heidelberg, Basel, any place,
Returning home in sheer disgrace.
The money's spent in idleness,
They're glad to tend a printing press
And, learning how to handle wine,
They're lowly waiters many a time.[4]
Thus money spent to train and school
Has often gone to rear a fool.

If God should heed what mortals say
We'd fare but badly every day,
More tears than smiles would come our way.

28. OF SPEAKING AGAINST GOD

A fool would build a fire bright
To help the sun give warmth and light
Or would expect the torches' beam
To aid the sunlight's potent gleam.
Worse, who'd impugn God's majesty,

Henry of Foolsland he would be,
All other fools he does exceed,
A fool of documented breed.
God's grace and foresight, which endure,
Are so replete with wisdom pure
That human prudence cannot raise
And magnify their endless praise.
Fool, why chide God with idle care?
Man's wisdom can't with God's compare.
Let God prevail howe'er He will,
Rewarding good, avenging ill,
Let Him make storms or skies of blue,
He'll not make weather just for you
No matter how aggrieved you'd be.
To wish brings only misery,
By fretting you commit a sin,
Far more by silence you can win.
We pray that God's will may be done
In heaven, on earth for everyone,
But fools would censure God and preach
That He should do as they would teach.
Better are things by God arranged
Than by your folly half deranged.
The Jewish people teach us true
What murmuring against God will do.[1]
Who was His councilor (is it stated?)
When He both heaven and earth created? [2]
Who gave to Him, and when and whence?
He shall receive his recompense.

Who trusts his piety alone
And others' sins will ne'er condone
Will come to fall o'er many a stone.

29. WHO JUDGES OTHERS

A fool is he whose faith doth rest
On fancy, thinking he's the best,
And never knows that deep in hell
His soul will soon hereafter dwell.
All fools beneath illusions labor,
They think hell's only for their neighbor;

When they see others pale and die
They always know the reason why
And say: "This man was marked by folly,
He wantoned, he was never jolly,
He did that, this one was remiss,
God punished him with death for this."
Thus when they're dead are men reviled
On whom God's favor may have smiled,
Reviled by men of greater sin
Against God, neighbors, next of kin,
They fear no punishment that's nigh,
Though knowing well that they must die,
Where, when and how no one can know
Till through the mouth the soul will go.
But that his soul to hell will fare
No one believes until it's there,
He'll sense the plight he would desire
When he's engulfed by hellish fire.
We think our lives are good indeed,
But only God our hearts can read,
And many a man seems bad on earth
While God appreciates his worth.
Some men are honored while they dwell
On earth but later live in hell,
A fool is he who dares to say
He's free of sins for now and ay,
But every fool doth lack in this:
He's loath to be just what he is.

If many a benefice you'd share
Your ass will fall more oft than fare;
An ass can die from heavy ware.

30. OF TOO MANY
BENEFICES[1]

Fool he with benefice so great
That he can scarcely bear the weight
Yet always takes another pack
And almost breaks the ass's back.
A decent prebend keeps one sleek,

But take a second, then I'd seek
To warn: Watch over your *one* eye,
Lest out the window it should fly.
Who for a second prebend sighs
Will lose the sight of both his eyes.
Yet day and night he'll have no rest
Until with prebends more he's blest,
Then soon the heavy sack will tear
And off to bone yard he must fare.
But now one oft gets dispensation,
Which causes some men false elation,
Who think that they are safe, although
Number eleven be their throw.
Some many a benefice have won,
Who cannot tend a little one,
Although but one would quite suffice.
He builds up prebends, trades or buys,
That he can scarce enumerate them
And scarce knows how to choose or weight them.
He'd fain reside in every one,
He's sociable and full of fun.
Collecting is an arduous lot,
'Tis true, there's death in yonder pot.[2]
For prebends one must now wait long,
Simon, Gehasi[3] run along.
Man's final prebend, mark it well,
Will come to him in burning hell,
'Tis there he'll have a wealthy presence,
Worth more than sixfold earthly absence.[4]

Who sings Cras, Cras [1] like any crow
Will stay a fool till death, and so
His dunce's cap will wax and grow.

31. OF SEEKING DELAY

A fool to whom the Lord does say:
"Improve yourself this very day,
Abandoning your wrong and sin,
A better life you should begin,"
And who remarks: "Let me delay,
And mend my ways some other day,"

And sings "Cras, Cras," as does the crow,
But ne'er his span of life doth know.
Many a fool has come to sorrow
By crying: "I'll do that tomorrow."
Where sins are found, and folly's blight,
There crowds rush in with great delight.
But goodly service, righteous deed,
Are all performed with sluggish speed,
Inviting ever long delay.
"Confession? Yes, but why today?
Tomorrow let God's will be done."
In this you hear the prodigal son.
That morrow never will be felt,
Like snow 'twill quickly come to melt.
But when at length the soul has gone,
Then will at last that morrow dawn.
So terrible misfortune's toll,
The body pays no heed to soul.
And thus in wilderness there died
Those Jews whom God did not decide
To take into the happy land
That He had promised with His hand.
If you would not repent today
Tomorrow will be worse than ay.
To whom this day God's summons call
May later hear no voice at all.
By thousands men are now forlorn
Who planned improvement on the morn.

He guards grasshoppers 'neath the sun,
Pours water into wells for fun,
Who guards his wife as 'twere a nun.

32. OF GUARDING WIVES

They harvest folly, sheer despair,
Who always watch their wives with care,
For she who's good will do the right,
And she who's bad will sin for spite
And manage well to perpetrate
Her evil plans against her mate.

For e'en a padlock placed before
The entrance, be it gate or door,
And many guards about the house
Can't keep her honest toward her spouse.
Danaë, held in tower, grieved,
And none the less a child conceived.[1]
Penelope was loose and free,
And many suitors did she see.
Yet twenty years her husband strayed,
Still chaste and pure she always stayed.
Let only that one claim that he
Of his wife's base deceit is free
Who loves her so as to believe
That she would not her spouse deceive.
A pretty wife on folly's course
Is like unto an earless horse.
The man who plows with such a nag,
His furrows oft diverge and sag.
A wife who would be modest found
Should cast her eyes upon the ground
And not coquet whene'er she can
And not make eyes at every man,
Nor heed whate'er one says and does.
Panders will often wear sheep's clothes.
If Helen had not sent a note [2]
In answering what Paris wrote,
And Dido through her sister Ann,
They'd not have wed a lecherous man.[3]

If through his fingers one can see
And lets his wife promiscuous be,
As cat she views the mice with glee.[1]

33. OF ADULTERY

Adultery's called a trifling thing,
Like casting pebbles from a sling,
Adultery now pays no heed
To laws that Julius once decreed,[2]
For sin no punishment is spoke
Because so many married folk

Now lead the same licentious life)
And trade for theirs another wife
And hush up mutual disgrace
While holding fingers up to face
And peeping through them evermore;
Attentively they feign a snore.
Men now ignore a woman's stain
And mete no punishment or pain.
Men's stomachs are now strong and stout,
For all dishonor can they flout
And be like Cato infamous,[3]
His wife he lent to Hortensius.
Few men now find adultery)
So great a cause for misery)
As those Atrides rightly faced
When they beheld their wives disgraced,
Or else as Collatinus loosed
Revolt when his wife was seduced.[4]
Adultery is now so meet
That Clodius soils every street.[5]
If all those people should be beaten
Who e'er adulterers' fruit have eaten,
As Sallust for his crime once suffered,[6]
Many by welts would now be covered.
If all adulterers should sustain
Abimelech's distressing pain [7]
Or die like sons of Benjamin [8]
Or suffer such distressing sin
As David did from Bersabë,
Many would shun adultery.
Whoe'er at wife's adultery winks

And of reproval never thinks,
Who acts with fixed deliberation,
Toward wisdom has no inclination,
He gives her cause for many a fall
While neighbors gossip one and all
And say he aids her, yes abets,
And shares the filthy pelf she gets,
While she says: "Jack, I love you true,
No man's as dear to me as you."
The cats pursue the mice in haste
When once they've had a little taste.
Women who try out other men
Become so bold and shameless then
That deep they sink into the mire
And only think of their desire.
Let each so treat his wife that he
Will give her cause for chastity
And treat her kindly, spare her stings
And fear not every bell that rings
And quarrel not by night and day
But listen what the bells may say.
And then it seems to me 'twere right
If many a guest you'd not invite,
This is preëminently true
In case your wife is fair to view;
On no one can one quite depend,
Of falsity there is no end.
Helen had still loved Menelaus
If he had not invited Paris,
If Agamemnon had not left
His friend Aegisthus, crafty, deft,

To rule o'er house and home and wife,
He never would have lost his life;
Kandaules foolish came to harm,
He showed a friend his goodwife's charm.
Who cannot keep his joy apart)
Will find it sold at any mart,)
And so I think it wisely done ⌐
If married folk a guest would shun,)
The more if they can't trust in him,
For life is full of stratagem.
Suspicious people soon believe
That others cheat, betray, deceive,
As Jacob of the garment said,
Immersed in gory blood and red;
Asverus thought Haman did mean
Esther to violate, the queen,[9]
And Abraham his wife denied
Before to Gerar's walls he hied.[10]
A miser's better as a guest
Than others' eggs in one's own nest.
Who often far afield will go
A sparrow soon will be, I know.[11]
Who'd boast a lap of burning coal,
Whose trusting bosom snakes enfold,
Who in his pocket rears a mouse,
Such guests are bad in any house.

Some think their wit is very fine,
Yet they are geese right down the line,
All reason, breeding they decline.

34. FOOLS NOW AS BEFORE

A fool who hears what wise men say
But never profits day by day,
Who wants to hear what would behoove
But never wisely would improve,
He wants to own whate'er he spies
And shows all men he's far from wise,

For every fool this flaw doth show:
What's new, for that he'd crave and glow,
But soon of novelty they tire
And other novelty desire.
Fools often travel very far
Yet never learn just where they are,
For every goose when once let loose
Returns and still remains a goose.
'Tis not enough to feel at home
In Pavia, Holy Land, and Rome,
One must have brought back something fine,
Skill, common sense, wisdom divine,
Then such a journey would be good,
But had you full of crowns your hood,
And had you precious stones to burn
No merit I'd therein discern
If many countries you have toured
Yet not to wisdom are inured;
Travel no special honor brings
Unless it teaches special things.
Had Moses in Egyptian clime,[1]
Had Daniel not learned all the time
When in Chaldea he did dwell,
Men had not known them half so well.
Confession some attend with stain
Who'd come forth white and light again,
But still polluted home they fare
And round their neck a millstone bear.

Whoever spurs his ass's hide
Out o'er the donkey's head will slide.
Swift wrath befits a dunce's pride.

35. OF READY ANGER

That fool rides asses every season
Who rages much without a reason
And snarls about him like a dog,
With evil words he's e'er agog,
He knows no letter saving "r"
And brags men fear him near and far,

That he may rage from dawn to dark,
And each good fellow will remark:
"How many dunces fume and roar,
Misfortune gives us fools galore,
But every fool that doth appear
Thinks he's the only Donkey's Ear."
Wrath baffles wise men too because
A wroth man knows not what he does.
Archytas, when a lowly slave
Had wronged him, said unto the knave:
"This gift I would not give you now
If wrath had furrowed not my brow." [1]
And Plato too suppressed his rage,[2]
And Socrates, for they were sage.
Impatience born of irritation
May lead to sin and dire damnation,
Man's patience calms the obdurate
And calming speech breaks hardened hate,
With temper virtue does away,
A man in anger cannot pray;
Lest wrath boil over take good heed,
Bad temper is the idiot's meed.
Better a she-bear's angry mood
When she has lost her youthful brood,
Than brook a fool's indignity
Who has a mind the fool to be;
The sage's conduct's never crass,
The rash man ought to ride an ass.

Who would on self-willed pinions fly
Will aim at birds' nests very high,
Hence oft upon the ground will lie.

36. OF COMPLACENCY

By prickly thorns will he be frayed
Who thinks he needs no other's aid
And deems his cleverness sensation,
A match for every situation.
He'll go amiss on broad highway
And through a wilderness will stray

And find no road that leads him home.
Woe's him who falls when all alone!
Toward heresy such men are bent
Who would not hear of betterment,
With faith in naught but their poor sense
To win both fame and eminence.
A fool may tumble painfully
Who climbs for nests upon a tree
Or seeks a road where none is found;
Who's ladderless stays on the ground.
Contempt will lead to many a slip
And insolence can wreck a ship.
No man is helpful, none respected,
Whoe'er to teachings wise objected;
No one would hear what Noah said [1]
Until both men and beasts were dead,
A base rebellion Korah planned [2]
And perished with his evil band.
Beasts singular will eat a deal.[3]
The man who acts for personal weal
Would rudely rip the cloak and tear it
That has no seams for those who wear it.[4]
Whoe'er from folly's ship keeps clear
Must put some wax into his ear,
The kind that shrewd Ulysses used
When past the Sirens' haunts he cruised,
Escaping them by prudent plans,
Thus thwarting all their arrogance.

Who perches high on fortune's wheel
In harmful tumble soon may reel,
And drenched he'll be from head to heel.

37. OF CHANCE

A fool is he who climbs on high
And shows his shame to every eye,
He hopes to greater heights to go
But fortune's wheel he doesn't know.
All things that venture giddy flight
Will tumble down from greatest height;

Such heights no man will ever gain,
As on the morn he hoped to claim;
Good luck at all times can't abound,
Since Clotho spins the wheel around,
No man can guard his earthly store
'Gainst Death when knocking at the door;
The man of power bears distress,
Many have died through mightiness.
The force that's but sustained by force
Doth have a brief and short-lived course,
Lose love and popularity,
And you have care, anxiety.
If you'd have many men to fear you,
You'll fear full many who may near you:
As sentinel fear's never good,
It never guards you as it should.
The man of power should learn to love
His God and praise Him high above,
The man with justice in his hand
Has power that can long withstand.
In wielding power he was wise
Who is lamented when he dies.[1]
Woe be the king beneath the sod
Of whom men say: He's dead, praise God!
If you'd roll boulders up a hill
They'll tumble back and cause you ill,
And who relies upon his luck
By quick misfortune oft is struck.

Who's ill and lies in direst need
Yet doctor's counsels will not heed
Will bear the damage that's his meed.

38. OF PATIENTS WHO
DO NOT OBEY

A fool is he who does not heed
The doctor's word when he's in need
And at the diet only jibes
That any medico prescribes,
To wine instead of water clings

Or does a deal of harmful things
And takes whatever he may crave
Until he's laid into his grave.
Wouldst victory over ills be winning? [1]
Resist them all in every inning,
For medicine's effect is slow
When illness once has laid you low.
Whoever quickly would get sound
Must show the medico his wound
And suffer pain when it's unclosed
Or lanced or pierced or diagnosed,
Or when it's bound, or washed, or taped,
E'en if his skin is thereby scraped,
So that a life be rescued thus,
A soul be kept from leaving us.
A good physician does not fly
Because a man is apt to die,
A patient should have patience pure
To hope that he will find a cure;
The patient telling doctors lies,
Who when confessing, falsehoods plies,
Or tells his lawyer not the truth
When seeking counsel, he forsooth
Himself and no one else has cheated
And has himself the damage meted.
Fool he who any doctor seeks
And fails to follow what he speaks
And listens but to witches' chatter
And meets his death through magic patter,
Their magic, foolish medicaments,
And lands in hell for lack of sense;

Such superstition now is rife,
It holds forth hope of health and life.
If one compiled such silly tricks
We'd have a book for heretics.
The sick were eager to be cured,
Not caring whence the help's procured,
Some men would summon up the devil
To flee a sickbed's threatening evil,
The devil though makes matters worse
And brings them but eternal curse.
He's damned to folly who when ill
Would seek his health 'gainst heaven's will,
Desiring not with wisdom's store
To be a wise man evermore.
Not wise is he, he's but a fool,
And goes to folly's fatuous school,
A quite inveterate invalid,
Of blindness, madness never rid,
For oft from sin will illness spring
And sinning maladies will bring,
And so if illness you deny,
Keep God the Lord before your eye,
Consult your priest, confess your sin
Before you take the medicine,
And pay good heed that soul be sound
Ere that your doctor comes around.
Yet many foolish men now hold:
Who's bodied, he is also souled.
But living thus you'll be bereft,
Nor life nor soul will then be left;
Eternal illness we'll be seeing

If temporal illness we are fleeing.
Full many rot in cold, dank grave,
Would they had prayed to God to save
And show them mercy, love, good will,
Before they sought a doctor's skill!
Without His grace they would succeed
But died with soul in deepest need.
If Maccabeus had relied
On God and not on Roman pride,
As he decided once before,
He surely would have lived yet more.[2]
Long Hezekiah had been dead,[3]
Had he not turned to God instead
And prayed the Lord that He decree
A meed of His longevity,
And if Manasseh had not turned,
By God Almighty he'd been spurned.
Our Lord to the palsied man did speak [4]
Who had for many years been weak:
"Go, sin no more, be foolish ne'er,
Lest even worse than this you fare."
Some vow, to sickbed's misery fettered,
That now their conduct will be bettered.
The sick restored are often seen
To turn out worse than they had been,
And think that God has been deceived
Till they're by greater ills bereaved.

Who gives his plans publicity
And spans his net for all to see,
Avoid him, dangerous is he.

39. OF OPEN PLANS

A fool seeks sparrows as a prize
And spreads the net before their eyes,
For sparrows easily may flee
The net that everyone can see;
Who threatens people every day
Will sometime really strike his prey,

Who gives his plans a public airing,
Shun him, in danger he is faring.
Had change not come o'er Nicanor
And he'd persisted as before,[1]
Judas would not have read his heart
And never watched his wiles and art.
His conduct of true wisdom savors
Who minds his business, not his neighbor's
In things affecting soul-salvation.
The prying folk of every station
They ply deceit and faithless trick
Like cats that scratch and also lick.
That person is in folly dyed
Who confidential plans can't hide;
A crowd of fools, a lover's zest,
A city built upon a crest,
And straw that slips into a shoe,
They cannot be concealed from view.
A poor man lives in privacy,
Rich men are watched quite eagerly,
By all their faithless retinue
All their affairs are aired anew.
From persons living by our side
'Tis hard to keep what we would hide.
No enemy's more dangerous
Than those who share the house with us.
The man we don't suspect and fear
May steal our lives and treasures dear.

Who sees a fool that takes a fall
But pays no heed to that at all,
He strokes a fool's beard full or small.[1]

40. TAKING OFFENSE
AT FOOLS[2]

Fools daily one may see who fall,
Yet ridicule them one and all
And, scorning them, make pretense wise
But earn a fool's cap—what a prize!
One fool another fool will goad,

Both traveling the selfsame road,
But rocks that cause one fool to stumble
Will also make the other tumble.
Full many a fool Hippomenes [3]
Saw headless, yet like unto these
He courted danger, risked his head,
And but for luck he had been dead.
One blind man calls the other blind,
Yet both are of the stumbling kind.
One crab will scold the other 'cause
He's walking backward on his claws,
Yet none goes forward—in reverse
They follow th' others, which is worse.
If you would be a stepchild rather,
And not a son, then spurn your father.
If Phaëthon had been more shy
And Icarus when he would fly,
Had they but heard what father said,
In tender years they'd not be dead.
The way that Jereboam went [4]
Has never made a man content,
Yet others follow, knowing pain
And grief are marching in the train.
Who sees a fool that takes a tumble
Should be on guard lest he too stumble.
He's not a fool in any season
Who criticizes fools with reason.
The fox eschewed the cave, though urged,
From which no one had e'er emerged.

A bell sans hammer gives no ring,[1]
No foxtail sets it echoing,
Wherefore ignore all gossiping.

41. PAYING NO HEED
TO TALK

If now a man would get along
He must endure much grief and wrong,
See many things before his door
And hear what well he may abhor.
Therefore those men enjoy renown

Who spurn the world and on it frown
And walk through valley, over hills,
To shun the world's rebuff and ills,[2]
Avoiding guilt where'er they go,
And yet they suffer many a blow:
The world does not deserve one whit
That such good men inhabit it.
Who'd righteous be in every matter
Should pay no heed to idle chatter,
Avow your undertaking pure
And lend no ear to idiot's lure.
Had prophets and wise men of old
Paid heed to gossips loud and bold
And overlooked fair wisdom's light
They would have been in piteous plight.
No man on earth of any school
Can always satisfy a fool.
Who'd please the men of every hue
Would be a servant good and true
And would arise ere break of day
And rarely on his mattress stay.
He must have vast supplies of flour
Who'd fill each mouth at every hour,
For no man could control or rule
The talk of every arrant fool.
The world must do what can be done
And she's done much for many a one.
A fool sings "Cuckoo!" oft and long,
As every bird will sing his song.

From fools 'tis good to keep away
Who pelt with rocks and stones for ay,
Not heeding ill or wisdom's way.

42. OF SCORNERS[1]

Learn, fools, what well you may afford,
The fount of wisdom: Fear the Lord!
All knowledge of the holy lies
In paths of understanding wise,
For wisdom glorifies the race,
Enriches men in every place.

A benefactor, he who's sage,
But fools prefer the selfish stage.
So wise are fools, they will not hear,
They mock all wise men far and near;
Who'd teach a scorner to be wise
Will harvest scorn, a paltry prize.
Who punishes a wicked fool
Will harvest sorrow as a rule.
Chastise a wise man, soon you'll earn
His thanks, for he's intent to learn.
The righteous man we must chastise
Will think the punishment is wise.
The unjust often will revile,
Yet suffer scorn himself the while.
The jaybird very scornful is,
Yet many things he needs must miss.
Toss out a scorner through the door,
His scorn lies with him on the floor,
And all abuse and mockery
With him before the door you'll see.
If David had not spared his ire
Nabal had met a fortune dire; [2]
Sanballat rued his scorn and guilt [3]
When the Holy City's walls were built.
By vicious bears were children raided, [4]
By bald men prophets were upbraided,
Shimeï still has many sons [5]
Who hurl as missiles rocks and stones.

Why I love temporal things alone
And scorn the Everlasting One?
The reason: I'm a monkey's son.

43. CONTEMPT OF
ETERNAL JOY

Fool he who ne'er is much concerned
If life eternal he has earned
And utters prayers that he may
Live like a fool till Judgment Day,
Gives every roistering lout his hand

But ends where'er God may command.
O fool, no pleasures here on earth
Can evermore give joy and mirth,
They're harsh and bitter through and through,
Were't otherwise I'd think that you
Had cause to love this evanescence,
Though foolish frailty be its essence.
A fool that person is from birth
Who'd live long years upon this earth:
It's nothing but a vale of tears,
In joys brief, long in grief and fears;
This stay for mortals ne'er is meant
To be quite long or permanent,
Since all will make a journey grand
Into a strange and unknown land.
Full many've gone, we'll come apace,
For we must see God face to face,
Be it for joy or sorrow deep.
Hence tell me, O you foolish sheep,
Has ever greater fool been born
Than who'd stay here and heaven scorn?
In God the Lord you'll not believe
And from eternal life take leave,
A drop of honey here, that's all
You'd have and there a sea of gall,
On earth a moment's jubilation,
There endless joy, perhaps damnation.
Who would such sinful utterance dare
Will find frustration here and there.

Who takes to church dog, hawk, or jay,
Disturbing others who would pray,
The fool's role he with zeal doth play.

44. NOISE IN CHURCH

One must not ask who they may be
Whose dogs in church bark furiously
While people pray at mass or sing,
Who bring a hawk that flaps its wing
And rings its bell with tinkling gay,
That one can neither sing nor pray.

The hood is lowered o'er the hawk,
There's pattering and many a squawk,
Affairs are aired and tongues are loose,
There's clattering with wooden shoes,
That brings disturbance, great ado;
He peers to Lady Kriemhild's pew
To mark if she will turn and gape
And make the cuckoo-bird an ape.
If men would leave their dogs at home
To watch for thieves that prowl and roam,
While men would worship there in church,
If birds were left upon the perch,
And wooden shoes were worn for street
To pick up dirt or mud or peat,
And other people's ears be spared—
But when have fools for others cared?
Dame Nature will the fool betray,
Base folly always has its day.
Christ gave us all a good example,
Coin-changers drove He from the temple,[1]
And men with pigeon-vending urge
He chased in anger with a scourge.
If now He'd oust the men of sin
But few would still remain within;
At first the priest away He'd send
And with the sexton would He end.
God's house deserves much sanctity
Since God's own dwelling place it be.

Who knowingly goes into fire,
Or enters wells in full attire,
Deserves his fate should he expire.[1]

45. OF COURTING MISFORTUNE

Some fools will worship every day
And, as they think, sincerely pray
And call to God with loud appeal:
"O help me, God, my folly heal!"
But still their dunce's cap they don

And every day they put it on
And think that God is saying no,
Yet what they want they never know.
Who leaps into a well through whim
And fearing death that threatens him
Shouts: "Throw a rope, O see my plight!",
Hears neighbors say: "It serves him right,
No one 'Jump in' commanded him,
He could have stayed upon the rim."
Empedocles was such a fool,
He entered Etna's flaming pool;
Whoso had saved him from that hell
Would not have acted wise or well,
For steeped in folly quite insane
He would have made the leap again.
Likewise some think that God's sweet voice
Should call and bid them e'er rejoice
And give them lovely gifts and grace,
But ah, God never sees their face.
Full many waste their every day,
And God is deaf to what they say,
So heaven never shows them favor
E'en when their prayers of wisdom savor.
Who prays and knows not what he prays
The wind he blows and shadows lays;
And many pray for things so bad,
'Twould irk them if those things they had.
Who lives in constant fear and cares
Bears ills no matter how he fares.

Folly has lavish retinue,
The whole world joins it, even you,
If you have power and money too.

46. OF THE POWER OF FOOLS

'Tis need that many fools there be,
For some are blind and cannot see,
But only wit is their ambition,
Though all do know their base condition
Of folly yet would never dare

To ask: Fool, what're you doing there?
And when in wisdom fools cavort
It's wisdom of a foolish sort,
And when no one will praise their ways
Themselves they shower then with praise,
Although the truly wise man thinks
That, broadly speaking, self-praise stinks.
The man who's overconfident,[1]
A man is he of foolish bent,
But he who walks in wisdom's light
Is praised by us with all our might.
That land is blest that has a lord [2]
Whose wisdom is a treasure hoard,
Whose princes always eat aright
But seek no greed or base delight.
O woe's the prince whose land you see [3]
Accursed to puerility,
Whose princes eat at early morn
But all sweet wisdom hold in scorn.
A needy child with wisdom's grace [4]
Is better in its rightful place
Than yon old king who's but a fool
And pays no heed to future rule.
Woe unto those who love what's right [5]
When fools ascend onto the height,
But after fools are once defeated
For righteous persons they're unseated.
An honor 'tis for any land [6]
When good men hold the reins in hand,
But when an idiot has the rule
He ruins many an arrant fool.

Unjust is he whose judgment says:
Trust friendship, mere appearances,[7]
For but a piece of bread or less
A man will oftentimes transgress.
The wise on judging well are bent,
Respect not men for judgment sent.[8]
Judge, councilman should have no bias,
Susanna's judges still defy us,
Who practice wantonness and force,
For righteousness has run its course,
Both swords are rusty, badly worn,[9]
And from the scabbards can't be torn,
Nor will they cut whene'er there's need,
Blind justice is and dead indeed,
And gold alone is deified.
Jugurtha when from Rome he hied [10]
Did utter: "O you venal state,
How soon it would be 'Check' and 'Mate'
Did but some buyer bid for you!"
Like Rome are many cities too,
Where bribery goes on apace
And many another black disgrace.
All money, favors help us naught,
So Moses learned, by Jethro taught.[11]
Greed, money, friendship, favor, power
Break laws and charters every hour.
The princes formerly were sage,
Had learned councilors old of age,
And things went well in every land,
And sin had retribution grand,
And peace prevailed o'er all the earth.

Now folly's pitched its tent of mirth,
Preparing onslaught bold and blind,
To force the princes, force their kind
To leave all wisdom, knowledge true
And seek advantage for the few,
Advising them in childish way
Until they meet an evil day
Which worse will grow with every hour.
Great folly goes with copious power.
Our Lord would let the princeling rule
A long time, were he not a fool,
Becoming bitter and unjust
Through councilors whom none can trust.
No prince should trust that vicious tribe
That takes of money, gift, or bribe:
The man who takes a bribe's not free,
Accepting gifts breeds treachery,
As Ehud killed fat King Eglon [12]
And as Delilah lured Samson,[13]
Gold vases from Andronicus
Did cause the death of Onias [14]
And Ben-hadad did break the league,[15]
Enticed by gifts and base intrigue,
And Tryphon, when he would deceive,[16]
That Jonathan might well believe,
Presented gifts and largess to him,
So that with stealth he might undo him.

Some men persist on folly's road
And draw a cart with heavy load:
The right cart waits in heaven's abode.

47. ON THE ROAD OF
SALVATION

No fool by God has e'er been taught
The miracles that He has wrought
And daily works, wherefore the fool
On earth will perish as a rule
And suffer lasting death above

Because our Lord he does not love
And will not live as God desires.
Here he has pain, there hellish fires,
Here he must pull the heavy load,
There he will go a harder road.
Therefore, O fool, ask not, I pray,
Where hell does lie, or seek the way.
One reaches it with effort slight,
The road is open day and night,
It's broad and smooth and duly worn,
Leads many to a dunce's bourn.
But ah, the road to high salvation—
Pure wisdom's only destination—
Is very narrow, hard, and steep
And few the men that to it keep
Or have the pluck that will endure.
This is the answer clear and sure
To fools who seem too curious
And ask why fools so numerous
Will travel hell-bound night and day,
While few the wise who fare that way.
The world is wanton, blind, untrue,
Fools live aplenty, wise men few.
Many are called but very few
Are chosen. In what class are you?
Six hundred thousand men in all,[1]
Not counting wives and children small,
Were led by God across the sand,
Two only reached the Promised Land.[2]

48. A JOURNEYMAN'S SHIP

A ship for journeymen sails by
With artisans from far and nigh,
With many trades diversified,
And each with work tools by his side.
No trade is honored o'er the land,

They're overcrowded, overmanned,
Every apprentice would be master,
For all the trades a great disaster.
Many to masterhood have turned,
But ah, their trade they've never learned.
One crowds the other to the wall
And thus prepares for his own fall.
Trying to make his product cheap
He fails and out the gate must creep.
If you'll not sell for less than he
You're undersold by two or three.
Their work is good, so they assure,
But really 'tis but very poor:
Many will turn out petty trash
To sell it cheap for little cash.
That man can never earn a tittle
Who pays a deal but sells for little.
One man by trading wrecks himself
And leaves the other man with pelf.
A bargain often may entice,
But sometimes it's not worth the price.
A bargain oft lacks quality,
Is made in haste, as one can see,
And is designed for fleeting eyes.
A craftsman over losses sighs,
For profits ne'er are very high.
"What you refuse to do I'll try."
'Tis slipshod work, poor quality,
But I lay store by quantity.
And I myself, the truth to say,
With such have tarried many a day

Before I could describe such wight,
As yet they've not been judged aright,
I'd need more time if that I'd do,
Good work cannot be hurried through.
An artist to Apelles rushed [1]
His painting negligently brushed,
And said he'd painted this in haste,
With this reply he then was faced:
"Your work, O painter, doth reveal
Great carelessness and little zeal,
With speed you could, if you'd the mind,
Paint many works of such poor kind!"
No praise will hasty work e'er find,
Competitors will soon hold sway.
Shoes, twenty pairs, in one brief day,
A dozen swords, all keen and prime,
But everything is sold "on time."
Such practices will net no savings,
Poor carpenters make many shavings,
The masons dote on gaps and breaks,
A tailor hasty stitches takes
So that the seams can never hold.
The printers squander coin untold,
A weekly wage a day, I'm told.
So rash their reckless, roistering way,
Although their work's laborious ay.
They print and putter, cut a die,
Set type, correct, arrange and pi,
Apply the ink—a printer's game—
Make pigments over burning flame,
Grind colors then, cut spaces new.

Many do work the whole day through,
And yet their work's of poorest brand
If come they do from Monkey Land.
They've learned their trade disgracefully;
Some sail the ship with utmost glee,
They find companions good though plain
Who work and see but little gain
And spend that little in a wink
When wine at festivals they drink.
No care the future bears or sorrow,
The while they beg for alms and borrow.
One man will lend on odds and ends
But make no more than what he spends.
No sale can now be made—'tis odd!—
Before one swears an oath by God,
And after many an oath and plea
One grants a discount cheerfully.
'Tis clear that all the world has grown
To like low bids as in Cologne: [2]
"Half off on that!" bids every wag,
"Good luck!" 'twill injure no one's bag.
And so they sail, full many a guild,
Some vessels are but partly filled.

What you do, that your child will do,
In evil children copy you,
Break jars, your child will break them, too.[1]

49. BAD EXAMPLE OF
PARENTS

Who tells his wife and children much
Of evil things, amours and such,
Let him expect that they will gape
And play the mimic, play the ape.
Good manners, virtue hold no sway,

Wives, children learn our evil way,
Wives follow husbands' lead apace,
From parents children learn disgrace,
And when the abbot likes the dice
The monks will follow in a trice.
The world is full of vicious sin,
And virtue's gone, and discipline.
The fathers bear the heavy blame,
The wife will ape her husband's shame,
The son will do as does the father,
The daughter do as does the mother.
Should it now be so strange to us,
That fools on earth are numerous?
The crab walks as his father went,
Wolves bear no lambkins innocent.
Brutus and Cato long have died,[2]
And Catilines have multiplied.
If wise we are, good, virtuous,
Our children will resemble us.
Diogenes a lad once spied,[3]
Inebriate, to him he cried:
"As did your father, so you do,
A drunken man gave birth to you."
In children's presence take great heed,
They'll copy you in word and deed,
For habits grow, and that's the cause
Why children show so many flaws.
Let each man be a righteous spouse
And keep vexation from the house.

The stupid oft by lust are felled
And by their wings are firmly held:
For many, this their end hath spelled.

50. OF SENSUAL PLEASURE [1]

A temporal pleasure's like unto [2]
A brazen, sensual woman who
Infests the street and plies her trade,
Inviting every amorous blade
To come and practice fornication
At bargain rates—a great temptation—

She begs all men in shameless fashion
To join and quench her evil passion.
Fools seek her out, indifferent, low,
As oxen would to slaughter go,[3]
Or like a harmless, frisky wether
That does not know about the tether
Until it feels the deadly dart
That's shot to penetrate its heart.
Remember, fool, your soul's at stake
And soon in deepest hell you'll bake
If such lewd women you frequent.
Shun lust, then blessings will be sent,
Seek not for lust, licentiousness
Like heathen king Sardanapalus,
Who thought that men should live on earth
In lust and joy and sensuous mirth,
Because they're over when one dies.
Such nonsense silly fools advise,
To trust in pleasures ever fleeing.
Yet this old king was quite far-seeing.
The man of lust and pleasures vain [4]
Buys moderate joy with ample pain;
If temporal lust be sweet, my friend,
It's wormwood, mark its bitter end,[5]
The whole world's base licentiousness
Turns finally to bitterness,
Though Epicurus placed his trust
In worldly joys and wanton lust.

Who cannot keep a secret well
And other men his plans must tell,
He's under great misfortune's spell.[1]

51. KEEPING SECRETS

Fool he who tells his secret plan
To wife or any other man,
Thus mighty Samson, less than wise,
Lost strength and locks and both his eyes.
The prophet Amphiaraüs [2]
He suffered his destruction thus,

For women, as in Writ we're told,
A secret cannot guard or hold;
Who cannot keep a secret hidden,
Who by deceitfulness is ridden
And like a fool will blurt his plan,
He's shunned by every prudent man.
One may be proud of escapades
At night, and lovers' serenades,
But later when we go a-spying
We'll find him on a dunghill lying,
And from his tales it can be seen
Just where in folly he has been.
If you desire that I say naught,
'Twould not be fair that you say aught,
If you cannot a secret hold
Which to my trusting ear you've told,
Why would you ask that I refrain
If you yourself cannot abstain?
If Ahab had not wished to tell
His secrets all to Jezebel,[3]
And hushed the words that he had said,
Naboth had surely not been dead.
Who bears a secret in his heart
To none this secret should impart,
No other man can then reveal
What carefully we would conceal.
The prophet spoke: "My secrecy
I'll guard and keep alone for me." [4]

Who weds and for naught else is fain
Than growth of property and gain
Will suffer quarrels, woe, and pain.

52. MARRYING FOR THE SAKE OF GOODS

Who flays a donkey for its fat
He has no brains beneath his hat,
Who weds an old wife just for gain
Makes one grand splurge, then ne'er again,
And he has very little joy,

No children, either girl or boy,
And happy, carefree days he lacks
Save when he sees the money sacks.
The money bag is often stressed
That's made of him a fool at best,
And by this truth I'm often struck
That such a marriage brings ill luck.
Who muses but of property,
Neglecting good name, piety,
Unhappily that man has wed,
Joy, friendship, comradeship are dead.
Far better seek a wilderness [1]
Than live with such a sorceress:
An angry, scolding, nagging shrew
Whose evil ways will ruin you.
I never trust such men myself
Who sell their youthful years for pelf.
Because one likes the smell of fat
He'd flay the donkey just for that.
But after many days are past
He finds but dung and filth at last.
Full many Ahab's child pursue [2]
And come to sin and later rue.
Now Asmodaeus seems to wield [3]
Much influence in Hymen's field.
Rare is the Boaz now forsooth [4]
Who fain would court and marry Ruth.
One finds but woe, calamity,
And *criminor te, scratchnor a te.*[5]

Ill will and hatred everywhere,
One finds great envy here and there,
Neitharts still live, are never rare.

53. OF ENVY AND HATRED

Fools thrive on jealous enmity,
This chapter shows, as we shall see.
It seems to spring alone from this:
You envy me what I possess
Or crave to garner what is mine
Or bear me ill will all the time.

Yes, Envy is a deadly wound,
Who's stung by her will ne'er be sound.
Bad qualities she has inbred,
She plants fixed thoughts within your head,
By night nor day will Envy rest
To put her evil plans to test.
For Envy will not laugh nor sleep,
Her heart in sadness will she steep,
Her lips are pallid, pinched, and lean,
She's like a sullen cur and mean.
Her eyes are red, she'll never try
To look a man straight in the eye.
With Saul and David 'twas the case,
With Joseph, too, and with his race.
Dame Envy only laughs when she
Has sunk a foe's ship out at sea,
When Envy gnaws with eager bite,
She eats herself alone for spite.
Etna consumed itself alone,
Aglauros turned into a stone.[1]
How poisonous spite and hate can be
In brothers' hatred we can see:
As Cain, Esau, and Thyestes,
Jacob's sons, and Eteocles:
In such deep hatred each did live,
As though he were no relative.
A kinsman oft will hate some other
Far less than he may hate his brother.

If bagpipes you enjoy and prize [1]
And harps and lutes you would despise,
You ride a fool's sled, are unwise.

54. OF IMPATIENCE OF PUNISHMENT

A sign of folly clear and sure
Is that a fool will ne'er endure
To hark and lend a patient ear
When men of wisdom he can hear.
A wise man lists to wise men's lore,

Enriching thus his wisdom's store,
Bagpipes are dunces' instrument,
For harps they have no natural bent,
And naught gives fools a greater joy
Than wand and pipe, their favorite toy.
How shall we mete out punishment
Since fools are many, have no end?
Remember, fool, at every tide
That death is lurking at your side,
And that in ashes once you'll bide.
Among all creatures small or great
Endowed with sense in nature's state
You are the least—a bastard base,
Mere scum and dregs—an old carcase.
Why do you vaunt your mortal power,
Your wealth, youth, station every hour,
When everything beneath the sun
Is foolish, vain, and soon undone?
Far better wise men's condemnation
Than dunces' sheepish cachinnation.[2]
For as a burning thorn will crackle,
So will a fool's dull-witted cackle.
Blesséd the man who always shows
A sense of fear where'er he goes.
A wise man's heart will think of sorrow,
A fool will pipe but reck no morrow.
Say what you will, entreat and plead,
His "Come, eleven!" he'll not cede,
Nor will he pain or lesson heed.

The medico who'd treat and cure
But of his skill is never sure,
That man's an idiot simon-pure.

55. OF FOOLISH MEDICINE

A fool is he, of little skill,
Who tests the urine of the ill
And says: "Wait, sir, and be so kind,
The answer in my books I'll find."
And while he thumbs the folios
The patient to the bone yard goes.

Some men physicians are yclept,
But in that art they're not adept.
They only know what herb books say,[1]
Or healing women old and gray.
They have an art of great appeal,
All ills and ailments it would heal,
No class or age it fain would ban,
Cures young, old, children, wife, and man,
Or humors moist, dry, cold, and hot.
This herb such strength and power's got,
E'en like the salve in Alabaster,[2]
Wherefrom the surgeons make their plaster
And heal all wounds (so goes the rumor),
Stabs, ruptures, cuts, and e'en a tumor.
The doctor-fool keeps all in humor.
Who'd use a salve for sick and weary,
Cure dripping eyes, bloodshot and bleary,
And purge without a urine glass,
He's such a quack as Zuhsta was.[3]
He's like a stupid advocate
Who's poor of counsel, light of pate.
Like some confessor-priest is he,
Who cannot ever learn to see
How he can cure a rank disease
Or mortal sins he may appease.
He walks about in senseless ease.
Some men by foolishness misled,
Can see it not until they're dead.

To earth no power has e'er been sent,
But in good time its way it went
When once its usefulness was spent.

56. OF THE END OF POWER

One finds such fools at every hour
Who would rely upon their power,
As if 'twere infinite, although
It actually melts like snow.
The emperor Julius was no wight,
Rich, mighty he, with prudence dight,

Before he took the lofty throne
And as the emperor was known,
But once the scepter's weight he bore,
He tribulations had galore.
Nor did he heed what prophets said,
So, stabbed by foes, he soon was dead.
Darius ruled a mighty race [1]
And could have stayed home sans disgrace,
He could have kept his wealth and name,
If he had not gone forth for fame,
To conquer this land, yonder king.
The upshot: He lost everything.
Xerxes to Greece shipped hopefully
Troops many as the sands of sea.
So numerous sails were there unfurled,
He might have frightened all the world,
But what, I ask, did Xerxes gain?
Athens he flayed with might and main
As some dread lion kills a hen
And yet fled like a rabbit then.
The great king Nebuchadnezzar,
When he had far more luck than ever
And overcame Arfaxat too,[2]
He thought his lands were far too few,
And yearning after heavenly power
Was turned to ugly beast that hour.
More tales are found of similar bent
In Old and Newer Testament,
Yet I have shown enough of these.
But few men die as they would please,
Those only die of natural ills

Whom no assassin finds and kills,
So take good heed, you men of might,
Though holding fortune's wheel so tight,
Be wise and heed your dying day,
Lest that wheel spin the other way.
Fear God the Lord and serve Him well,
His wrath may send you down to hell,
It catches fire quite easily,
Then powerless again you'll be,
You'll perish, robbed of power and land.
Ixion's wheel would never stand,
It turned, by gentle breezes blown.
Blesséd who trusts in God alone.
That boulder rolled and always will
Roll down again from yon high hill
That Sisyphus did push with fear.
Power and luck last but a year.
Oh, heed the proverb, hear it say:
Ill luck and hair grow every day.[3]
Unrighteous power is but an ill,
Remember Ahab, Jezebel.[4]
A lord may have no foe at all
But by a slave's hand may he fall,
Or friends may force him to the wall
And cheat him oft of rank and might.
Zimri conspired with scoundrel spite [5]
And finally his lord did slay,
Then reigned, but not too many a day.
Alexander ruled the world as king,
A servant killed him with a drink.
Darius many dangers fled,

His servant Bessus stabbed him dead.
Thus power ends for no man's good
And Cyrus drank his own life's blood.
No power on earth is e'er so great
That some day it will not abate.
No friend can boast such mighty friend
That happy days to him he'll lend
Or guarantee a single hour
Wherein he'll have good luck and power.
What now the world deems best of all
Will some day turn to bitter gall.
Presumptuous men who proudly stand
May slip and fall upon the sand
And fate will mock them with a brand.
Great folly 'tis to have great might,
It often lives one day or night.
When all the states on earth I scan,
Th' Assyrian, Persian, Median,
And Macedon, the states of Greece,
Or Carthage, Rome, they found their peace,
They all now slumber under sod.
Our Roman Empire trusts in God,
He's granted it a time and fate,
May He still fashion it so great
That all the world its cause may serve
To such extent as it deserve.

Who, lacking merit, seeks a prize
And on a fragile reed relies,
His plans go backward lobster-wise.

57. PREDESTINATION OF GOD

Some fools display a wealth of wit
Who hide behind the books and Writ,
They think they're striped and famous sages [1]
When they have thumbed a volume's pages.
They eat the Psalter, 'twould appear,

As far e'en as *Beatus vir*,[2]
They think if God has blessed them all
That then from grace they'll never fall.
Since down to hell these men may fare,
On earth they would be debonair
And live with others blithe, in mirth,
And never reck their future dearth.
Fool, cease from all your fantasy,
Or else in fool's stew you will be.
That God rewards where naught is earned,
Believe it, fool, be unconcerned
And wait until a roast fowl slips
To earth and nestles 'twixt your lips.[3]
Were life so simple, then indeed
Most every wight would have his meed
No matter if he works or nay,
But that is not earth's usual way.
With rich rewards should heaven bless
A man who lives in idleness
And grant a knave who wants to nod
His kingdom and the meed of God?
I say no man on earth can live
Whom God unearnéd boons would give,
Or whom our Lord God owes a sou,
God owes no man, nor me nor you.
A free lord gives to whom he will,
He may give little, may give nil
As he may please, who can gainsay?
He knows why he says yea or nay.
A potter fashions out of earth
A pot, to some of little worth,

Can't find salvation in books
(expect)

A jar, a jug of any style
For any liquid good or vile.
No pot will say to th' potter's face:
"I should have been a lordly vase!"
God knows (and He alone can know)
Why everything on earth is so
And wherefore Jacob He preferred
But for Esau no love averred
And why King Nebuchadnezzar,[4]
Who long in sin had taken pleasure,
Was punished and away was cast
But was restored as king at last.
Though Pharaoh was soundly scourged,
A wicked man he yet emerged.
A medicine makes one man well
But drives another nearer hell.
One man, if he will understand
God's wrath and feel His mighty hand
Will rue his sin with many a sigh,
While some upon free will rely,
And seeking heaven's righteousness
Abuse His loving kindliness.
God will not let a sinner lie
Unless He knows the reason why.
If everything were once equated
Alone the rose would be created,
But God desired the thistles too,
Justice for all, for me and you.
He'd be a slave of jealous whim [5]
Who'd think the Lord unjust to him
Because He gave him meagerly

And with another one was free.
If you're a slave of indolence,
Then God bestows no recompense,
But many righteous men on earth
Will suffer bitter want and dearth
And God will treat them, every one,
As though a grievous wrong they'd done,
But idiots you will often find
Who have good luck of every kind
And in their sins are frank and free,
As though they lived in sanctity.
God's ways are all mysterious,
Their cause is known to none of us,
The deeper into this we pry,
The less we know the reason why.
And even men who dream and hope
To know the reason merely grope.
The why of such things men are spared
Before to tother world they've fared,
Wherefore let God's predestination
And all His prudent dispensation
Stand undefiled, be dutiful,
For God is good and merciful.
Let God know everything He knows,
Do right, see how your guerdon grows,
Be steadfast, then I'll guarantee
That down in hell you'll never be.

Who'd quench a neighbor's blazing fire
While flames around his barn mount higher,
He plays upon the dunce's lyre.

58. OF FORGETTING
ONESELF

Who takes all pains that e'er he can
To aid and help some other man
Or win him gain in any shape,
That man's indeed a silly ape
If he has stupidly neglected

Himself and goes quite unprotected;)
He takes the fool's book off the shelf
Who thinks of others, not himself.
Well-ordered love for other men
Means: With yourself you must begin.
Terence was right when once he stated:
"I'm nearest to myself related." [1]
At your own self 'tis wise to glance
Before you see how others dance.
He'll perish long before he should
Who only cuts his neighbor's wood;
Who comes to clean his neighbor's dress
While his is marred with dirtiness;
If fire in neighbor's home you'd stop
While flames shoot through the crumbling top
Of your own house with violence,
For your own good you have no sense.
Who'd push or pull his neighbor's dray,
His own not, he's a fool, I say.
Who carries packs with vim and will,
Except his own, will come to ill;
Who easily can be persuaded
To deeds for which a man's upbraided,
He'll not escape the luring charm
Of fools that take him by the arm
And teach him wisdom via harm.
He'll suffer hardest while he dies
Whom others all can recognize,
While he when landing on the shelf
Knows he's not recognized himself.

Who wants good service every day
But never "Thank you" wants to say
Deserves a club in every way.

59. OF INGRATITUDE

He craves a lot, this foolish wight,
But favors never will requite,
He causes toil and troubled care
But ah, his gratitude is rare.
If profit from a deed you'd find
You must be fair, make up your mind

With joy to give as well as take,
For justice, honor are at stake.
A wearied horse is little use
When once subjected to abuse,
A willing horse for naught is good
If given not the proper food.
A fool he who'd expect a lot
But give no pay for what he got;
The man who always scolds and frets
For righteous recompense he gets,
Some day he should not be dejected
If with a whiplash he's corrected.
If you desire a worth-while treasure
You must pay back in ample measure;
Ingratitude wins paltry gain,
A spring of water will it drain.
Wouldst from old cisterns water draw?
Pour water in, then pour some more!
Door hinges oftentimes have grated
Unless they're duly lubricated.
He never earns a greater prize
Who smaller presents would despise.
To him all gifts should be denied
Whoe'er in small ones takes no pride,
He's senseless, coarse, and stultified.
All sages hate the man as crude
Who's marred with base ingratitude.

My time in fool's broth I must pass
Since I esteem the looking glass;
I'm brother to a silly ass.

60. OF SELF-COMPLACENCY

A fool's broth he does stir and feed
Who thinks he is of witty breed
And so admires his lovely face
That e'er into the glass he'd gaze,
Yet grossly ignorant that he
A fool in yonder glass doth see,

And if an oath he were to swear
He'd say he's wise and debonair,
With ne'er a failing, flaw or dearth,
With not a peer upon the earth,
And swear his conduct's ever fine,
And that unblemished it doth shine.
The mirror never leaves his hands,
Whene'er he sits or lies or stands,
Like Emperor Otho who, they say,[1]
Did take his glass into the fray,
He shaved twice daily smooth as silk
And washed his face in ass's milk.
In this same way the ladies pass
Their time before the looking glass,
The while they prink and don their gear
Much time will pass, almost a year.[2]
Who lays such store by beauty's work
Is like the ape at Heidelberg.[3]
Pygmalion did his statue like [4]
So well, he lost his mind, the tike,
And had Narcissus not espied
His image he would not have died.[5]
Who in the mirror sees his face
Will often see a vile grimace.
The men that show such stupid bent
Will reck nor pain nor punishment,
They've reached so stuporous a stage
That they will balk at being sage.

For dancing this can well be said:
One does not always push ahead,
Betimes one wheels and turns instead.

61. OF DANCING

I'd take all those for fools almost
Who skill and joy in dancing boast,
Cavorting, prancing as they must,
With weary feet in dirt and dust,
But later then I called to mind
That dance and sin are one in kind,

That very easily 'tis scented:
The dance by Satan was invented
When he devised the golden calf
And taught some men at God to laugh,
And Satan dancing still doth use
To hatch out evil, to abuse.
It stirs up pride, immodesty,
And prompts men ever lewd to be.
The pagan Venus gives her hand
And purity is rudely banned.
Could viciousness to joy give birth?
There's naught more evil here on earth
Than giddy dancing gayly done
At kermess, first mass,[1] where the fun
Is shared by priests and laity,
Where cowls can flap in zephyrs free.
They swing their partners in the breeze
Till girls' bare legs high up one sees,
Their other sins I will not treat.
They'd rather swing their girls than eat;
When Jack and Maggy swirl and sway
They never wait a single day,
They strike a bargain willy nilly
And trade a she-goat for a billy.
If some class that as recreation
I call it base abomination;
Some crave for dances many a tide
Whom dances never satisfied.

The man who'd play the amorous wight
And sing a serenade at night
Invites the frost to sting and bite.

62. OF SERENADING
AT NIGHT

The dance of fools would now be o'er,
Though there'd be something still in store,
For we've not mentioned those gallants
Who walk the streets and would entrance
The girls, to whom they're very sweet,

And wend their way from street to street,
While playing lutes for all to hear
At doors from which a girl may peer,
And do not from the street go dashing
Until a night-pot's dregs come splashing,
Or till a rock has struck their pate.
The pleasure's never very great,
Since wintry blasts may nip his nose
Who late at night a-courting goes
With lute, song, piping, boisterous thumping,
In lumber yards o'er timber jumping,
Priests, students, laity hell-bent,
They hum a fool's accompaniment.
One screams, shouts, bleats with might and main
As though he feared he's being slain,
One fool will tell the motley crew
Where they've arranged their rendezvous,
And there the music is begun.
"In secrecy" the thing is done,
So everyone may well agree,
E'en fishers noise it publicly.[1]
One leaves his wife alone in bed
Who'd rather play with him instead,
If he goes duncing none the less
And all ends well, I miss my guess.
No word of those who take delight
In going out like fools bedight;
But call such fool a gaby dense,
At such a pass he'll take offense.

I feared no fools were left for me,
The beggars then I went to see,
Their wisdom was of low degree.

63. OF BEGGARS[1]

Bold begging charms full many a fool,
For begging has become the rule
And ranks among our best professions:
Church orders teem with rich possessions
And yet lament their pauper state.
Poor cadgers, ah, the pity's great!

Rank pauperdom, that is your class,
Though heaps of wealth you should amass,
And Prior shouts: "Bring more, bring plus!"
His is a sack that's bottomless!
Quite similar are the relic-vendors,
The pious dealers and pretenders.
No kermess but they thither fare
And there they advertise their ware:
"In this bag you will find the hay
That once in bygone ages lay
Beneath the crib at Bethlehem." [2]
"An ass bone here of Balaam."
"Of Michael's wing I have a feather."
"St. George's steed once wore this tether!"
"See here St. Clara's laced-up shoes."
To beg some men will always choose,
Though they could work if but they would,
They're young and strong, their health is good,
Save that their back they'll not incline,
These sluggards have a corpse's spine.
Their children in their youth they train
To profit well by beggar's gain,
To learn the cries—a mumper's token—,
Or else they'd have their bones all broken
Or so be maimed with welt and bruise
That they would scream from sheer abuse.
Of such two dozen seek their gain
At Strassburg in St. Thomas Lane,
Others in foundlings' homes are cast,
But beggars very rarely fast.
In Basel where the scoundrels lurk

They carry on much rowdy work,
They have their thieves' slang everywhere,
It helps them out where'er they fare.[3]
Full every beggar boasts a Moll,
She lies, cheats, plies her folderol,
Scouts where her Johnny may find swag,
He twigs the wine that gives a jag,
In all gin-mills his luck he tries
And "roll the bones," that's how he buys,
Until he's plucked them here and yon.
Discovered now, he rambles on
Across the countryside to fare,
Steals webfoot here and cackler there,
Whose necks he slices off or breaks
While hobo gang his escort makes.
To humankind 'tis a disgrace
That all men after money chase.
All sorts of heralds once could claim [4]
They spoke rebuke of public shame
And earned themselves an honor so;
Now every fool pretends to crow [5]
And wants to bear a herald's stave:
Thus begging, money he would save,
Indeed, he'd like his clothes in tatters.
Beggardom every country spatters.
One needs to have a silver cup
And seven measures daily sup.
He uses crutches when he's out,
But not when no one is about;
He throws a fit before a crowd
So everyone will shout aloud;

He borrows children by the score
So he'll have mouths to feed galore,
Equips an ass with baskets nine,
As though he'd seek St. James's shrine.[6]
He limps, he's hunched and very sick,
He ties his leg to crutch or stick
Or hides a bone 'neath garments thick.
Should anyone inspect his wound
He'd find it very shrewdly bound.
Beggars I grant a deal of space,
They're plentiful in every race
And evermore their numbers grow,
For begging's pleasant, that they know,
Except for those who have no choice,
The rest in cadgers' weeds rejoice.
By begging they can get ahead,
Some even get to eat white bread,
And they don't drink the cheaper wine,
But Reinfal,[7] Alsace, that's their line,
And begging brings them many joys,
These toying, courting beggar boys,
For after they have spent their share
They're always beggars now as e'er,
They may go begging anywhere.
As beggars many men live high,
Who have more coin than you or I.[8]

Some men would ride morn, noon, and late
If they could only dodge their mate,
But women's grip is obdurate.

64. OF BAD WOMEN

When I began I did not shun [1]
A solemn protestation,
Good women never I'd forsake,
Nor injury in my book they'll take;
Against me men would soon complain
If evil ones I'd not disdain,

For those who trust in wisdom's name
Will not be prone to vice and shame.
A good wife calms a husband wroth,
Ahasuerus swore an oath,
By Esther then he was disarmed,
Abigail David quickly charmed.
But evil wives give counsel bad,
As Ahaziah's mother had.[2]
Herodias her daughter bade
To amputate the Baptist's head,
By women Solomon was moved
To worship idols he reproved.
A woman has a magpie's tongue
And likes to exercise her lung;
Pierus had a brood of young,[3]
Their tongues were smeared with venom dire,
They burned ablaze and stung like fire.
One mourns, one prattles, one tells lies,
Another lives to criticize,
And e'en in bed this good wife frets,
No rest her suffering husband gets,
Must hear a sermon grave and deep
While many a barefoot monk's asleep.
Some tug against a nagging wife
Yet they must yield through all their life.
In shrewdness women lead the van,
Not matched are they by any man.
His words she never will obey,
She heeds not what he'd teach or say,
For man misfortune's often sprung
From woman's loose and babbling tongue.

Amphion found his joy denied
When all his lovely children died.[4]
If women's talk is our contention
Calphurnia [5] should come to mention.
Bad women show their evilness,
And Joseph's wife is proof of this.
No wrath can evermore mount higher
Than such a woman's boiling ire,
She's like a lioness in mood
Who's been deprived of suckling brood,
Or like a bear of cubs distressed,
Medea, Progne [6] prove this best.
In all the books of history [7]
More bitter nothing e'er can be
Than wives whose hearts are like a net
That catches fools and holds them yet.
Three things the earth do agitate,[8]
The fourth it will not tolerate:
A servant who has come to rule,
A gluttonous, voracious fool,
An odious, evil, poisonous wife,
Once she is married, prone to strife,
The fourth all friendship spoils indeed,
A maid who should her dame succeed.
Three things insatiable I fear,
The fourth cries ever: "Bring more here!"
A wife, a hell, and any ground
That swallows water all around,
The fire will never say: " 'Tis good!
I have enough, bring no more wood."
Three things I cannot comprehend,

The fourth—there I've no news to send:
When through the air an eagle flies,
On rocks a snake that crawls and lies,
A ship that sails the water wild,
A man who still is like a child.
Of similar kind a wife would be
Who, planning on adultery,
Will lick her chops and wash them clean
And say, "Not evil have I been."
A leaky roof ere winter's through
Is like a woman who's a shrew:
He has his hell and torture now
Who with such woman pulls a plow.
Vashtis [9] did many daughters breed,
Their husbands they will never heed.
Nor of those women will I think
Who give their men a poisonous drink,
Like Portia [10] and Agrippina, [11]
Belides [12] and Clytemnestra,
Who stabbed their husbands in their bed,
As Pheraeus was stricken dead. [13]
Quite different is Lucretia
Or Cato's famous Portia.
But wanton wives are far from rare, ⟩
For Thaïs [14] dwelleth everywhere.

The world is full of superstition,
Men prophesy by stars' position
And every fool deems this his mission.

65. OF ATTENTION TO
THE STARS[1]

Fool he who'd promise more than he
Can keep with full propriety,
More e'en than he'd desire to do.
Physicians well may promise you
But many fools will promise more

Than all the world could hold in store.
For future things one feels a bent,
What stars and what the firmament
And what the planets' course proclaims
And God's wise providential aims.
They wish to know and would discuss
Th' Almighty's plans for all of us,
As though the stars prescribed to you
What you should do and should not do,
As though our Lord were not much higher,)
Not guided by His own desire, /
And letting even Saturn-born
Be good and pure as is the morn,
While Sun and Jupiter have had
Some children that are very bad.
A Christian true should never heed
Base heathen arts of any creed:
One can't by scanning planets say
If this be our propitious day
For business, war, or marrying,
For friendship or for anything.
Whate'er we've done, where'er we've trod,
Our conduct should rely on God.
He lacks a faith in God's creation
Who trusts in any constellation,
Believing certain things are good
And so propitious that we should
Start things of moment only then,
And if they're not accomplished when
The stars are lucky, then delay,
Since that's an unpropitious day.

And he who sports no brand-new thing
At New Year's—goes not forth to sing,
And hangs no greens about the room,
He thinks he sees approaching doom
As once Egyptians seemed to fear.[2]
And then, when comes the bright New Year,
The one who gifts does not receive
Will fear a year when he must grieve
And other superstitious fancy,
Palm-reading, e'en ornithomancy,
Or symbols, signs, and books of dreams,
Or search for things by Luna's beams,
Or black arts done with pomp and show.
There's not a thing men wouldn't know.
Who says: "I've all that I desire!"
Lacks many things, the brazen liar.
Not only do men prophesy,
From starry course they also try
To read the smallest things there are—
A fly's brain lit by twinkling star,
Whate'er'll be said and what be done,
If you'll have luck, if you'll have none,
Your health, your very destination,
They'll read it from a constellation.
With folly all the world's insane,
It trusts the fool, the most inane.
In calendars and prophecy—
In these the printers profit see,
They'll print whatever one may bring,
Yes, e'en the most disgraceful thing.
Such things go scot-free, are believed,

The whole world wants to be deceived.
If such art were observed and taught
And not with dangerous evil fraught,
So that for man's soul 'twould be well,
As Moses did and Daniel,
Of wickedness it would not savor,
'Twould have our confidence and favor.
The cattle's death they do divine,
The blight of corn, the failing wine,
When rain will come, and when 'twill snow,
When sun we'll have, when wind or no.
The peasants like it—good their reason:
It helps them plan a prosperous season,
For they may hoard their corn or wine
Till prices upward may incline.
When Abraham read books like these,
And sought Chaldean prophecies,
That consolation then was gone
That God had sent in Canaan.[3]
Yet naught it is but blasphemy
To treat such matters frivolously,
To force th' Almighty we'd aspire
And bend His will to our desire.
God's love and favor now have fled,
We seek the devil's art instead.
When God forsook the old king Saul [4]
The devil heeded well his call.

Who measures heaven, earth, and sea,
Thus seeking lore or gaiety,
Let him beware a fool to be.

66. OF EXPERIENCE OF ALL LANDS[1]

I do not deem him very wise
Who energetically tries
To probe all cities, every land,
And takes the circle well in hand
That thereby he may well decide

How broad the earth, how long and wide,
How deep and large the seas expand,
What holds th' extremest sphere of land,
And how at ends of earth the sea
Clings tight to its extremity,
If round the earth a man can fare,[2]
What men live here, what men live there,
If underneath our feet below
Men walk the nether earth or no,
And how they hold their ground down there,
That they fall not into the air,
And how with rule and compass you
May cut the whole great world in two.
Archimedes, too, who knew a lot,
Drew circle in the sand, and dot,
That many things he might compute,
But all the while he played the mute,
He feared he'd blow the sand away
And all the circles might not stay.
Before he'd speak, he'd suffer pain
And let himself be foully slain.
His skill was in geometry,
His death, though, he could not foresee.
With ardor Dicearchus tried [3]
To measure every mountainside,
Mount Pelion, he then confessed,
Loomed up, the highest mountain crest.
He never measured with his hand
The Alps in mountainous Switzerland,
Nor measured he how deep is hell,
To where he went and still must dwell.

And Ptolemy described the girth,
The length and breadth of all the earth,
He drew the length from Orient
And ended it in Occident,
Degrees one hundred eighty he
Set down, toward midnight sixty-three,
The breadth from equinoctial ran.[4]
Toward midday 't has a narrower span,
While twenty-five degrees are shown
Of land, as far as now is known.
Then Pliny figured that in paces,
Strabo used miles to measure places.
Since then more countries far away
We've found past Thule,[5] past Norway,
As Iceland and Pilappenland,[6]
Which ancient writers never scanned.
They've found in Portugal since then
And in Hispania naked men,
And sparkling gold and islands too
Whereof no mortal ever knew.[7]
Marinus failed most grievously,
To figure earth by means of sea.
The master Pliny [8] once did say
That vain it is in every way
To measure out the world's expanse
And then to cast a further glance
Beyond the earth, beyond the sea;
In this all men err grievously,
Into these problems each would delve,
Yet can he understand himself?
In knowledge many will persist

Of matters e'en that don't exist.
Once Hercules set in the sea
Two brazen pillars plain to see,
The tip of Africa is one,
By the other Europe is begun.
To ends of earth he paid much heed,
But his own fate he would not read:
For all his deeds of bravery
He died by woman's treachery.
Bacchus fared forth with retinue,
Crossed every land and ocean blue,
The only aim that he was willing
To own was teaching drinking, swilling,
And where no wine or grapes were near
He led men on to mead and beer.
Silenus [9] sought no urging strong,
He joined our ship and went along
With women lewd and other rabble
Who sing and play and laugh and babble.
A drunken scamp was he in fine
Since he was very fond of wine;
If he had ever toiled at aught,
Carousing, drinking he'd have taught.
Men still go roistering everywhere,
Silenus through our land doth fare,
Some drink all day and never stop,
Whose fathers never touched a drop.
But what did Bacchus ever gain?
He had to leave his merry train
And fare to hell the while he's cursed
To tipple not for joy but thirst.

The heathens always sang his fame,
A god they called him, praised his name,
And e'en to this, our present day,
The goddess Berchta [10] yet holds sway;
So Bacchus e'en today is praised,
Though great the evil he has raised.
Bad customs always persevere
And viciousness has mastery here.
The devil e'er will strive to see
That mankind shows him fealty.
But time it is that we reverted
To other topics we've deserted;
Why should we humans seek to be
More than we are in verity?
We never know what gain it brings
To study many lofty things,
No one his hour of dying knows,
Which like a shadow comes and goes. [11]
Although his arts are great, no doubt,
He's but a mad and foolish lout
Who rates this lightly in his mind:
That toward himself he's always blind
And puzzling problems would dissect
Quite alien, then himself neglect.
Self-knowledge never was his aim,
He strives for honor and for fame
And thinks of no eternal life,
How spacious 'tis, with beauty rife,
Where live the souls of sterling worth.
Blind fools can only see this earth
And find their joys and pleasures vain

Which bring more injury than gain.
Some have explored a foreign land
But not themselves can understand.
If like Ulysses men got wise,
As when he fared 'neath foreign skies
And saw new lands, men, towns, and sea,
Acquiring new sagacity;
If they were like Pythagoras—
Of Memphis he a native was—[12]
And Plato Egypt once did see
And also went to Italy
With hope of learning ever more
And making rich his wisdom's store;
Appolonius [13] went to every place
Where'er he found a wise man's trace,
He followed it without surcease,
His skill and knowledge would increase,
And everywhere he learned new lore
Of things he'd never heard before.
He who would take such trips as these,
That e'er his wisdom might increase,
He could be pardoned one sole vice,
Though even that would not suffice.
For those ay longing to depart
Cannot serve God with all their heart.

How did the silly Marsyas fare?
He lost his hide and lost his hair,
And yet his bagpipe still was there.

looking at the
anatomy of the
fool →

67. NOT WISHING TO
BE A FOOL

Fools all possess this quality:
They are unable quite to see
That people mock them and deride,
Whence Marsyas lost hair and hide.
But folly is so very blind,

A fool is all the more inclined
To think he's witty when men mock
And make of him a laughing stock:
His faith is solid as a rock
That all men in his wit believe—
Until the pipe falls from his sleeve.
The rich man gathers hosts of friends
Who walk the sinful way he wends
And swindle him for sinful ends.
They persevere until he's poor
And he exclaims: "My friends grow fewer,
O Godamercy, how they wane,
No friend consoles me, stills my pain!
If sooner I had realized
I'd still be rich and not despised!"
He must a stupid fool appear
Who squanders in a single year
The sums for all his lifetime meant,
In one brief, reckless splurge they're spent.
He hopes to end his earthly stay
And join his pelf in heaven some day,
But then when nothing he can see
But scorn, contempt, and misery
And when he's tattered all and bare,
He's stabbed by penitent despair.
Bless him who faithful friends can find
Through goods that he must leave behind,
Who'll comfort him and with him stay
When he's undone by sheer dismay.
Full many a man the idiot plays
And takes on idiotic ways,

And even though he's boiled and flayed
From ignorance he'll not be swayed,
He'll shut his ears quite unafraid.
The fool he is, the fool he plays
But no one likes his foolish ways.
Although his folly's manifest
No one applauds his wit or jest,
And men will comment then at once:
"The dunce would like to play the dunce,
In everything he suffers dearth,
He's but a fool, has little worth."
A curious thing it is on earth
That many a man would fain be shrewd,
Yet folly's mantle he's indued
And likes to think he should be praised,
But men say: "He's in folly raised."
But many idiots know I too
Who've once been hatched by some cuckoo;
They speak of wisdom every minute,
Pretending they are experts in it;
As witty as they'd fain be rated
So stupid are they estimated.
If fools were brayed upon a stone,[1]
As often with the pepper's done,
And they were crushed a year or more
They'd still be fools as evermore.
The fools lament to one another:
Wonolf is now Btriegolf's brother.[2]
Some men would let themselves be flayed
And tied with ropes from foot to head
If only that would net them gold

And bring them affluence untold,
And some in bed would gladly be
And have the rich man's malady,[3]
Or take a scolding like a knave,
If only riches were their slave.
With little no one is content,
He who has much, on more is bent,
From riches arrogance will spring
But humbleness they seldom bring:
Must dung not stink like anything?
And many a man who childless lives,
Has brothers not nor relatives,
Yet slaves and labors day and night,
By riches ne'er contented quite,
He never asks himself: "Ah me,
For whom toil I in drudgery?"
God grants some men a happy lot,
Their souls have everything but not
The wisdom sage and forethought fine
To use their wealth in goodly time.
They save, economize, and spare
To please some lavish, gluttonous heir.
With water Tantalus is cursed,
Yet cannot satisfy his thirst,
Though he sees apples everywhere
Yet has no joy of fruit so fair,
For with himself he does not share.

Who passes time with fool or child,
Unless he's at their jesting smiled
An arrant fool will he be styled.

68. NOT TAKING A JOKE

A fool is he who does not feel
That with a fool he has to deal,
Fool he who answers bark with bark
And fights with drunkards in the park,
Who fain would play with child or fools
And won't abide by folly's rules.

Who wants to hunt must rouse up game,
The bowler sets the pins in frame,[1]
Admit you lie if naught you lack,
Howl if you rove with wolfish pack:
"Give words for words" is fool's device,
"Give good for ill" commands high price.
But who requites the good with evil
Will ne'er be rid of any devil.
Who laughs when others weep and grieve
Will meet the same fate some fine eve.
Wise men with wise associate,
A fool will have a fool as mate.
The reason no one loves a fool:
Self-love is always folly's rule.
A fool feels more of jealous dread
When other people forge ahead
Than joy he knows that all adore him
And kneel in reverence before him.
By this remark I've merely meant:
The proud would rule and regiment.
Haman's delight was not intense [2]
That all men did him reverence,
He grieved far more that Mordecai
Looked down on him, would not obey.
No need to look for fools have you,
They show themselves in all they do.
If you'd be wise, as all men should,
You'll shun all idiots for good.

Go, toss into the air the ball
And do not guard against its fall
If you would anger one and all.

69. DOING EVIL AND **NOT**
BEING ON GUARD

You are a silly if you do
What others should not do to you;
Before you would abuse another,
Reflect if you would like it, brother.
As once into the woods you shout,

So will your voice come echoing out;
Who'd push a man into a sack
He must himself expect a whack.
The man whom others' faults disgust
Is like to hear his own discussed.
As Adonibezek had done [1]
To others, such reward he won.
Berillus in the ox was roasted,[2]
Once meant for others, he had boasted,
And such the fate of Busiris,
Of Diomede and Phalaris.[3]
For others many dig a pit,
But they themselves fall into it.
Haman made gallows for a foe,
To these same gallows he did go.[4]
Trust everyone but use your eyes,
For too much trust is oft unwise,
Find out what lies behind your man:
False trust has cost full many a span.[5]
Eat not with one of envious eye [6]
Nor sit at table with him by,
For he may plan how you'll be caught
In wiles you never would have thought.
Though he say: "Friend, O drink and eat!"
His heart for you will never beat,
And he may think: "I give it lief,
As lief as if you were a thief."
Some men will smile a friendly smile
But eat your heart out all the while.

Who'll never glean in summer's heat,
In winter he'll have naught to eat
And like the bear lick hands and feet.[1]

70. NOT PROVIDING
    IN TIME

Some men are worthless and inane,
They're fiickle like a weather vane
And consequently leave undone
The many things they have begun.
Naught can they do when times are right,

Things will escape them over night.
For usually they're so remiss,
They never know what they may miss,
Or what they'll need in future pinch,
Unless the goal lies but an inch
Away; their planning never goes
Much further than from mouth to nose.
The man who gleans in summer's heat,
So that in winter he may eat,[2]
He's wise in more than one respect.
But who in summer would neglect
His work and slumber 'neath the sun,
Must have in storage ton on ton,
Or through the winter's cold must see
The presence of adversity,
And suck his fingers hard and long
Until his hunger pangs are gone.
Who when it's summer makes no hay,
With grief in winter will he pay.
He'll drag a rope that's tied together,
And beg cheap hay in stormy weather.
He who no winter plow has led,[3]
May beg in summer time for bread,
He'll suffer misery and grieve,
Ask much but little will receive.
Learn, fool, the ant to imitate,[4]
Provide before it is too late,
That you may never suffer want,
When other men rejoice and vaunt.

He'll get much raillery uncouth,
Who fights like children tooth for tooth,
And thinks that he can blind the truth.

71. QUARRELING AND
GOING TO COURT[1]

Now of that fool I would report
Who always wants to go to court,
And amicably end no suit
Before he's had a hot dispute.
When cases would protracted be,

And men from justice hide or flee,
They must be summoned, warned, apprized,
Banned, outlawed, even ostracized,
They hope that then they'll twist the law
And come out free through any flaw,
As though the law a wax nose were,
Not realizing they're the hare,
That goes into the law clerk's soup.
The judge, attorney—all the group
Of jurists feed from clients' dish
And win a handsome mess of fish;
Delay, protraction is their aim,
'Tis thus they trap and catch their game:
Small cases e'en like big ones look,
A trickle's made into a brook,
A foreign speaker must be brought,
Imported here from far-off port,
That he may well pervert the case
And cheat the judges to their face.
Full many hearings there must be,
So that there'll be an ample fee,
And greater sums red tape will take
Than all the sums we have at stake.
The money won in lawsuits will
Ofttimes not pay your parsley bill.[2]
They think that truth can never see
When suits are lengthened endlessly.
The man who'd rather sue than eat
Should have some nettles on his seat.

Vile, scolding words do irritate,
Good manners thereby will abate
If sow-bell's rung from morn to late.[1]

72. OF COARSE FOOLS

A new St. Ruffian now holds sway,
Men celebrate him much today
And honor him in every place
With words and ways that spell disgrace,
And make a jest of ribaldry,
Though belted not with decency.[2]

Sir Decency is doubtless dead,
Fool holds the sow's ear, wags her head,
And makes the sow-bell loudly ring
So that the sow her ditty sing.[3]
The sow leads on and cannot fail,
She holds the fools' ship by her tail,
That laden down no wreck it be,
For that would bring great misery.
The wine no fool today would heed
That's quite inferior wine, indeed.
Full many a litter breeds the sow,
And wisdom lives in exile now;
The swine on decent people frown,
The sow alone now wears the crown.
Whoever rings her bell, that man
Is now the one who leads the van,
While he who does such foolish work
As that famed priest of Kalenberg,[4]
Or as Monk Islan long of beard,[5]
He thinks that he's himself endeared.
Some men in folly are so free
That if Orestes [6] them could see—
He had no brains beneath his hat—
He'd say: "Sane men can't act like that."
"Come clean to village" lost its sense,
For peasants drink and give offense.
Sir Alderblock is roundly fêted,
With Roughenough and Seldom Sated.
Most every fool doth love the sow
And wants to have his grease box now,
Which he keeps filled with donkey's fat.[7]

But rarely is it bare of that,
Though everyone would take a piece,
To keep his bagpipes well in grease.
Now grossness everywhere has come
And seems to live in every home,
And sense and prudence both are dead.
What now is written, what is said,
Is covered o'er with donkey's fat.
Carousers know and cherish that.
The sow the *matins* does recite,
The donkey sings the *prime* all right,
St. Ruffian sings the *tierce* with might,
Hatmakers' boys recite the *sext*,
Coarse felters [8] do compose the text.
Rude rabble doth recite the *none*,
And gluttoners the words intone,
The *vespers* from a sow's voice ring,
Filth, gross untidiness then sing.
And lastly the *compline* is done,
When *all is full* at length is sung.
The donkey's fat is potent grease,
With sow's fat it is mixed with ease.
One reveler smears it on another,
If he would have him be his brother.
Reserve and modesty 'twill smother.
Nor God nor honor then are spared,
Lewd things are scrutinized and aired,
The one who's quite the foulest swine
Is given a brimming glass of wine.
Applause is his with vim and zest,
He's asked to tell another jest.

They say: "A great success you've scored!
You keep us thus from being bored!"
As fool to fool they all declare:
"Be sociable, gay, debonair!
Feti gran schier e belli schier! [9]
Let's all be cheerful while we're here,
Good fellows should rejoice, not pout,
Let's laugh and sing, carouse and shout!
We've but a little while on earth,
Let's spend it wassailing, in mirth.
The man who dies will never rise
And never walk 'neath sunny skies.
Has any mortal ever learned
Of mortal men from hell returned, [10]
That they might tell us how it's been?
To have a good time's not a sin!
The priests can say whate'er they may,
Let them forbid this, that for aye!
If this were sinful, as they claim,
Then why, why do they do the same?
If priests did not discuss the devil,
And shepherds saw in wolves no evil,
No one would profit very much."
'Tis fools alone who utter such
Remarks, and with their brutal crew
Insult the world and God and you,
But finally their gain is rue.

For priesthood some declare desire,
They don a priest's or monk's attire,
But later their regret is dire.

73. OF BECOMING A PRIEST

Another type I'd have you mark
That on the fool's ship should embark
Has recently been much increased,
For every peasant wants a priest
Among his clan, to dodge and shirk
And play the lord, but never work;

It's not done out of veneration
Or for the sake of soul's salvation,
They want a high-placed relative
On whom the other kin may live.
"Training," they say, "we need not give
Him much, he'll learn it easily,
No need for scholarship I see
So long as benefices be."
Priesthood to them is something slight,
As though it were a trifling mite;
Ofttimes young priests are now so crude,
They seem just like a monkey's brood,
Shepherds who flocks should tend and keep
But could be trusted with no sheep.
In church affairs they're as astute
As Miller's ass upon the lute.[1]
But if to orders they're admitted
For this the bishops should be twitted,
Soul shepherds they should never be
Unless they're friends of decency.
Unwise the shepherd who'd abuse
His flock and all his sheep confuse,
But now these young and foolish beasts
Have one ambition—being priests,
This is the hope that they unfold,
But everything is not of gold
That on the saddle brightly gleams,
It's merely dung that costly seems.
A youth that enters priesthood's state
May later execrate his fate
Because he took the step in haste,

By begging later to be faced.
If he had had a living good
Before he donned the gown and hood,
It never would have gone so far.
Full many priestlings summoned are
And have to bless the fish and meat
At lordly feasts where others eat.
A patent's rented out and hired,
So that a title be acquired:
To cheat their bishop they believe,
But only their own selves deceive.
No poorer creature lives on earth
Than priests who suffer want and dearth.
They must pay fees to one and all,
To bishop, vicar, and fiscal,
Collator and to many a friend,
Housekeeper, children without end,
These lash him with a cruel whip
And land him on the dunce's ship.
Thus joy is killed and pleasures pass,
O God, so many priests say mass,[2]
'Twere better far did they refrain
And graced the altar ne'er again.
Your sacrifices will not win
The Lord when done with sin in sin.
To Moses God the Lord did say [3]
That every beast should stay away
And should not touch the holy mound,
Else black misfortunes would abound.
Uzzah,[4] who saw the ark and dared
To touch it, was by death not spared;

Korah, Abiram, and Dathan [5]
The censer touched and perished then.
The sacred meat seems good to eat,
With monkish coal some warm their feet,
Who'll later roast and stew in hell.
I'm preaching to the sensible.
Full many a youth ordained we see
Who has not reached maturity,
And ere he knows what it will do
Of good or bad, he's in the stew.
Habituation oft will do it,
But sadly some men have to rue it
And curse their friends with loud complaining
Who bear the blame for this ordaining.
Most enter monasteries blind,
Not old enough to know their mind,
They enter not by heaven's will
And only hope to eat their fill;
They pay no heed to priestly vow,
They never make a reverent bow,
Especially in orders where
Observing rules is very rare.
Such cloister-cats are insolent
Because they are not tied and pent.
Far better close the orders all
Than monks that into sinning fall.

Some men on hunting spend their all
But find the profit very small
Though they may shout the hunter's call.

74. OF USELESS HUNTING

Aye, hunting can be quite inane,
One spends much time with little gain;
Although it's meant for sport and pleasure
It's sumptuous beyond all measure.
The many kinds of dogs you need
Are quite expensive in their feed,

The dogs and hunting birds you've got
Have little use but cost a lot.
No hare or partridge brought to ground
Will cost you less than one full pound.
It's irksome work and little fun
To follow game, to ride and run
On hill, in vale, in woods to bide,
To set a trap, in ambush hide.
Some rouse more game than they can take,
Their nets but poorly they did make;
Some hunters "catch" the selfsame hare
That they have bought at mart or fair.
Some hardy hunters even score
When hunting lion, bear, or boar,
Or chase the chamois to his haunt,
But in the end they'll suffer want.
Now peasants hunt amid the snow—
The rich man's privilege long ago:
He hunts but nothing can espy,
The peasant sold it on the sly.
Nimrod took up the hunting horn [1]
When he by heaven was forlorn,
And Esau hunted; [2] was he not
A sinner who his God forgot?
Few hunters now like Hubertus
Or even like Eustachius, [3]
Who threw away the hunter's rod,
Else they could not have served their God.

In shooting let your aim be true,
For if you missed the target, you
Would land among the fool-ship's crew.

75. OF BAD MARKSMEN

If marksmen gave me their permission
I'd have a shooting competition
For fools, a range along the shore,
Where fools could targets miss galore,
And bowmen's prizes we'd be setting,
The champion the best prize getting.

If you shoot for elimination
You must use wise discrimination,
Aim straight and not too low or high
If you would strike the target's eye,
And shun an all-too hasty try.
Some men will shoot too high or low,
They break the string or bolt or bow;
In bending bows some make a slip
Or on the bolt they lose their grip.
Too soon the arrow's oft released
Because the bowstring's overgreased.
For one the mark stays not the same
And so he cannot take his aim;
One's tried it o'er and o'er again
But all his efforts seem in vain;
To lose the porker he is fated,[1]
At last he'll be eliminated.
Hast ever witnessed matches which
Proceed without a single hitch?
"This happened." "That was not the case"—
With such excuse one saves his face.
"Had this not been, had that been done,
The prize I surely would have won."
Of marksmen I a plenty know
Who hear of contests with the bow
To which they come from every clime,
To take a part at given time—
The champions under any skies,
Of whom no one can win the prize
Unless he never misses once.
Now many an archer's such a dunce:

He knows he'll lose, yet in a dither
He undertakes the long trip thither,
And tries the victory to attain.
I'd take his costs for all his gain,
Say nothing of the entrance fee,
The sow his empty sleeve will be.[2]
At wisdom many men would aim
But miss the mark as well as fame,
The reason is they cannot sight,
Misjudging depth, misjudging height;
One does not wish to cock his eye,
One fails because he will not try,
One takes a shot like Jonathan,[3]
His arrow lands behind the man.
If you'd hit wisdom's pith and marrow
I'd recommend you such an arrow
As Hercules possessed of yore,
Wherewith a victory to score [4]
And strike his victim's very core.
Who'd shoot at wisdom all his rounds
Should take good heed to stay in bounds,
For if he fails the mark, mayhap
He's fitted for the dunce's cap.
Who over reckless shots must grieve
Will bear the sow within his sleeve;
A hunting, jousting, shooting wight
Has great expense but profit slight.

Knight Peter of the Olden Years,[1]
I have to pinch your silly ears,
Both you and I are arrant fools,
Though knightly spurs are your proud tools.

76. OF GREAT BOASTING

Of louts and fools I also sing
Who boast of many a lofty thing
And want to be what they are not,
The whole world's vision they would **blot**

Because it never honors them.
From noblemen they claim to stem
The while their father banged and pounded [2]
And in the cooper's trade was grounded,
Or in his fortune he progressed
By buying out the dispossessed,
Or else a Jewish spear he held
Wherewith full many a man he felled;
Now he would claim his blood is blue
As if no man his father knew.
His name was Master Jack of Mayence, [3]
The while his son is Squire Vincenz.
Some boast of lofty elevation
And vaunt in constant emulation,
But 'neath the skin base fools they be
Like Peter Knight of Porrentruy [4]
Who made the claim he was a knight
That joined at Murten in the fight,
Whereas he was so fain to flee
And hide in marshy, muddy lea,
His pants so spattered were with dirt
That there was need to wash his shirt;
Yet shield and helm he bore away
To prove he was of knightly clay.
A hawk is like a heron dressed, [5]
And on the helmet eggs in nest,
And on the nest a moulting cock,
He's brooding out the little flock.
I know that all the foolish host
Of this would like to vaunt and boast:
That they have always led the van;

Whenever some retreat began
They looked behind with sorrowing
To see if foes were following.
Some men of fighting brag a lot,
How one they stabbed, another shot,
In truth they were so far away,
No shot could e'er have reached their prey.
His coat-of-arms a peasant draws
With decorative lion's paws,
A helmet crowned on golden shield,
And he's a knight of Bennefield.[6]
Some men are noble through their mother,
In Ruprecht Meadows lived their father;[7]
So many wear their mother's arms,
But as to father they have qualms,
Some own a seal and patent good,
They prove they are of noble blood.
They're first, they claim quite rightfully,
To be dubbed in that family,
And I nor blame nor disagree.[8]
'Tis virtue makes nobility,
For breeding, honor, virtue can
Alone proclaim the nobleman,
But if unvirtuous you be—
No breeding, honor, modesty—
Of nobleness for me you're bare,
E'en though a prince your father were;
Nobility with virtue goes,
Nobility from virtue flows,[9]
And many claim a high degree
Who know not Sextus nor Decree,

No Digest, Institute, Clementin.[10]
They only own a parchment skin
On which their right is fully writ,
It documents their ample wit
And shows that bagpipes they can play.[11]
Here Dr. Grab-It holds the sway,[12]
A learned and a witty wight
Who by the ears grips all men tight
And does more than most doctors might,
Who've been at famed schools many times,
At home and eke in foreign climes
Which average fools can never see
Who dote upon a high degree.
As "doctor" they would be addressed
Because in crimson gown they're dressed
And had as dam a monkey pure.
I know one well, he's Jack Manure;
To all who listen he will say
He's been in Sweden and Norway
And in Granada and Cairo,
And where the pepper plants do grow.
In truth he ne'er so far did rove,
But when his mother at her stove
Was frying cakes or sausage there
He'd hear and smell it anywhere,
For bragging lies so frequent fall
I simply couldn't count them all,
Since this is every dunce's lot:
He wants to be what he is not.

To gambling many are inclined,
No other sport is on their mind,
But future losses will they find.

77. OF GAMBLERS

Some foolish idiots I could name,
They love the cards, the dice, the game,
Preferring never to exist
Before from gambling they'd desist,
And day and night they game and rattle
With cards and dice, and drink and prattle,

And all night long they warm their seat
And never sleep and never eat,
But they must always drink a lot,
For gaming turns your liver hot
And makes you parched and full of thirst,
And then the morning is the worst:
One's face is like a pear in hue,
One goes behind the door to spew,
The color of their fellow knave
Is like a corpse's laid in grave,
Or else his face shines in the sun
Just like a smith's when day is done.
His head has suffered from abuse,
He yawns all day without excuse,
As though his aim were catching flies.
No man were fain to earn a prize
For sitting through a sermon deep
An hour, yet falling not to sleep,
But, head concealed in mantle's slit,
He'd show the priest 'twere time to quit;
When gaming though, how very odd!
He'll sit and sit and never nod,
And many women are so blind
That they forget their sex and kind
And know not that propriety
Forbids such mixed society.
They sit together 'mongst the men
And never feel dishonored when
They shake the dice and bet and game,
For all good women great the shame.
The distaff they should tend and wet

And gamble not with men and bet.
If each one stays among his kind
No need for any shame he'll find.
When Alexander's father told
His son to race for prize of gold,
Because to running he was bred,
The stripling to his father said:
" 'Twere meet and proper that I do
Whate'er my father wants me to,
And surely I'll be glad to run
Against some other ruler's son,
You'd never need to urge the case
If I against a peer could race."
But nowadays it's come to pass
That priests and knights of noble class
Sit down with barber's helper Jack
Whose soul their excellence must lack.
'Tis never good a priest to see
At gaming with the laity,
For they should always bear in mind
The hate long felt against their kind,
Else Neithart [1] may their pathways cross
And take revenge with gain or loss,
And they should bear in mind at least
That gambling is forbid the priest.
The man who gambles with himself
Will rarely sacrifice his pelf
And need not fear a bad reverse
Nor imprecations nor a curse.
But let me make it very clear
What's meet for gamesters far and near

And hearken to what Vergil sings,[2]
Who speaks like this of all these things:
"Avoid the gambler all the while
Lest lustful avarice beguile,
For gaming is a senseless vice
Which kills your reason in a trice.
Ye valiant, heed your virtuous name,
Lest that be harmed by dice and game.
A gambler coin must have and daring,
When luck is bad be not despairing,
No wrath or curse his gains advance.
Who plays with cash must take his chance,
For many come with coins not few
And leave the house without a sou.
Who plays alone for ample winnings
Will not have many lucky innings,
For peace he'll have who gambles not,
And he who plays must feed the pot.
Who wants to sit in every bout
And try his luck with every lout,
He must be blessed with shekels many
Or else go home without a penny.
You've furies three, desiring more?
Then take me, thereupon have four." [3]
With sin most gambling is beguiled,
On gamblers God has never smiled,
The gambler is the devil's child.

Most fools are under pressure ay:
Those who are fools in many a way,
The donkey rides them every day.

78. OF OPPRESSED FOOLS

The dunces' guild is numerous
And I was nigh forgotten thus,
I'd missed the boat upon the pier
But that the ass breathed in my ear.
I'm he whom all things do oppress,
I'd hide my face for shamefulness,

If but the donkey'd leave me free
And not upon my back would be.
If but my patience will suffice
I'll shake the donkey in a trice,
But I've a great sodality,
They're pressed by what oppresses me.
Take him whom no one dares advise,
Who's furious when wrath's unwise,
Who buys misfortune, mourns for naught,
Seeks strife when peace were better sought,
Who likes his children petulant,
Who treats his neighbor not as friend,
Who lets his shoe pinch worse than sin,
Whose wife must seek him at the inn,
The fool-book's none too good for him.
Who uses more than he can earn,
Who borrows much, which melts in turn,
Who shows his wife to eager eyes,[1]
A fool is he, an ass unwise.
Who thinks on all his sin on earth
And pain to which our sins give birth,
Yet laughs and jests at every pass,
He should not ride upon the ass,
The ass should ride upon this dunce
And press him down to earth at once.
A fool is he who sees the good
But e'er to evil turns his mood.
Untold the fools from far and wide
Whom such an ass takes for a ride.

When clerks and knights have once waylaid
A sturdy peasant plain and staid,
Their victim will be squeezed and frayed.[1]

79. KNIGHTS AND CLERKS

The clerks and knights one ridicules
For having joined the class of fools,
Both eat from out the selfsame pot,
One's blows are overt, th' other's not,
One risks his health 'neath any skies,
His soul in dusky inkwells lies.

The knight will build a blazing fire,
The clerk a peasant doth desire
Who's fat and drips as well he could
To make his cabbage lush and good.
If each of them did as he should
Each would be fully worth his board,
One with the pen, one with the sword.
Both knight and clerk we well could use
If they did not their rights abuse
And if at law they did not scoff
And live from stirrup unto mouth.
But since for personal interest
Each one of these shows zeal and zest,
They'll pardon me if that I slip
Them midst the dunces in our ship.
I did not ask that they go there,
Themselves they proffered me the fare
And offered me of their accord
To bring more customers aboard.
Clerks many, hypocrites I see,
They practice wanton chivalry,
Like riders' squires they snatch and pillage
For food in countryside and village.
It is indeed a great disgrace,
Unsafe are highways every place
For travelers seeking gain or grace.
And yet I know why this is so:
Safe-conduct makes the shekels flow.[2]

O, I have wandered far and wide,
No empty flask hung by my side:
This message fools may well betide.

80. FOOLISH NEWS

Though messengers I might ignore
And all their folly should not score,
Of it will they remind me e'er,
For fools must have a messenger
Who bears a letter 'twixt his lips
So that no rain upon it drips.

He walks the roof with cautious care
And hopes the tiles will stand the wear [1]
And always he will try to do
E'en more than masters want him to,
But whither he's been told to go
Because of wine he doesn't know
And tarries long in alley, street
Because there many folks he'll meet.
Some nearby lodgings him entice,
Examining each letter thrice
To see what may be written in it,
He spreads its message in a minute.
At night a bench doth hold his bag
While he drinks wine and gets a jag,
Without an answer coming home.
Such fools I mean—such fools alone.
They chase our ship in full career
And find it too 'twixt Aix and here. [2]
They should presume ('twill be no task!)
To bear in mind their little flask,
Their liver, privates both are dry
From running fast, from many a lie.
Snow offers men a cooling fine
When it is found in summer time, [3]
So too a messenger who's true,
Who's done his duty well for you.
I praise the messenger one hires
Who carries out what one desires.

Here come the butlers, servants, cook
Who all to things domestic look,
They tend the ship in every nook.

81. OF COOKS AND
WAITERS

A messenger preceded us
To find out where our vessel was,
We gave him salty soup quite ample
So he his little flask might sample.
He ran so very speedily

That he did drink incessantly;
We offered him a letter long,
His will to wait though was not strong.
Now we come walking down the street—
Cooks, maids, and butlers, servants neat,
Who work in kitchens, wait and serve
And treat all men as they deserve.
We've no regrets at any turn ¹
For we expend what others earn.
Above all when our master's gone
And sees not what is going on
We visit inns and there carouse,
And then bring guests into the house
And give and take full many a swig
From cans and jugs and bottles big,
And when at night our masters snore
And locks and bars are on the door,
We drink the wines with comrades boon
And tap the largest barrel soon
Which will not show that it's been bled.
We take each other then to bed,
But each a pair of socks we wear
That we're not heard upon the stair.
And if they hear some creaking sounds
They'll say it's cats that make their rounds.
And when a little time has passed
And master thinks that he still has
A keg of wine he hasn't drunk
The spigot answers: Glunk, glunk, glunk,
A token this that now the keg's
Near empty to the very dregs.

And we can skillfully prepare
A wealth of dishes served with care,
Thereby the palate always wooing
With cooking, boiling, frying, stewing,
With roasting, baking, pepper pot.
Of sugar, condiments a lot
We do prepare an oxymell [2]
So that our master vomits well
Or takes a purging laxative
With enema and syrup stiff.
This recks us not, for we can treat
Ourselves: we'll have more food to eat,
And we ourselves devour a lot,
We snatch the best from out the pot,
For though we died of hunger we
Would be accused of gluttony.
The butler says: "Fry me a link
Of sausage, cook! You'll get a drink."
The butler, he the wine's defier,
The cook, he is the devil's frier,
He's used to all the stifling heat
Which later on in hell he'll meet.
Starved cooks and butlers ne'er one sees,
They serve up food in quantities,
Our ship is popular with these.
When Joseph into Egypt came
The prince of cooks fell into blame, [3]
Nebusar-Adan won Jerusalem. [4]

My mind had almost made a slip
Since I procured no extra ship
When on to peasants' vice I skip.

82. OF PEASANTS' SQUAN-
DERING

The peasant folk had simple ways
In not extremely distant days,
To them was justice never dead.
When Justice from the cities fled
She went to live in huts of straw

And peasants bare of wine she saw,
While now on drinking wine they're set.
They plunge themselves in heavy debt,
And though their corn and wine sell well
They borrow more than I can tell,
And payments are alway belated.
They must be excommunicated,[1]
Of goodly twill they now complain,
They want no jackets cheap and plain,
From Leyden, Mechlin they export
Clothes cut away and slit and short,
With colors weird and quite absurd,
Upon the sleeve a cuckoo bird.
Now city folk from peasants learn
Great wickednesses in their turn,
From peasants springs all knavery—
Each day a new discovery.
Simplicity has left the earth:
Of wealth the peasants have no dearth,
They hoard their corn and wine by stealth
And other things inducing wealth,
Thus driving prices ever higher,
Until the thunder comes with fire,
For barn and corn a funeral pyre.
And now for such a reason too
We've hatched full many a cuckoo
Who burgher, peasant used to be,
Now he'd profess nobility.
A noble would be baronet,
A count a prince's title get,
At royal crowns the princes aim,

And many knights (a grievous shame!)
Use not their swords for righteousness.
A peasant wears a silken dress
And round his neck gold chains he bears.
A burgher's wife now often wears
Clothes better than a countess would,
For where wealth is there's hardihood.
One goose another's raiment sees,
For that untiringly she'll tease.
"I must have this if I'm to live!"
Thus nobles lack prerogative,
A tradesman's wife one often finds
Who wears more gauds of various kinds,
Skirts, rings, cloaks, broid'ries scant and rare,
Than in her home is anywhere.
It's ruined many a good man's life,
He must go begging with his wife,
From jugs in winter time drinks he
To keep his wife in finery,
And if today she has her fill
She sells it soon to junkman Will.
Who every whim of wives would please
When he feels hot will really freeze.
All lands into disgrace have got
And none's contented with his lot,
And none remembers now his sires,
The world is full of fool's desires,
Nor need I overstate a bit:
The trident in the bag must fit.[2]

From naught these fools derive a pleasure
Unless it smack of gold and treasure,
In fool's fold now I take their measure.

83. CONTEMPT OF POVERTY

Of money-fools there's never dearth,
One could not count them all on earth,
To honor money they prefer,
To poverty they all demur.
Men cannot live on earth alone
With virtue, if that's all they own,

For wisdom now is spurned and scored,
Respectability ignored,
It will not prosper now a whit,
Nobody wants to mention it,
And who for riches has an itch
Will hatch a plan for getting rich
And heeds no sin at any season
Nor murder, usury, nor treason,
Which now is common here on earth,
All evil's done for money's worth.
What's just for money's sake is sold,
Some men'd be hanged because of gold,
The gold it is that buys them free,
For money sinners go scot-free.
I'd say it plainly what I'd say:
The little thieves are hanged alway,
Gadflies from spider webs can flee
But gnats are caught and can't get free.
Ahab was never satisfied [1]
With all his kingdom far and wide,
He wanted Naboth's land beside,
So poor, god-fearing Naboth died.
Into the sack the poor must haste,
Give money, then you have good taste.
Stark need, which now has little worth,
Once bore a name upon the earth,
To Golden Age it once was dear,
No money-lovers were there here,
Nor any private property,
Common was all to you and me;
Contented were we and we used

Whate'er th' untilléd soil produced
And what Dame Nature chose to grow.
But once the plow they came to know
With greed they oft were fain to whine
And say: "If thine were only mine!"
And virtue here might well have stood
If men craved only what they should.
A gift of God is poverty
Although men treat it mockingly,
The reason is that men refuse
To think: The poor have naught to lose,
And scarce to him can come a lack
Who always had an empty sack,
And any man can swim the best
Whoever's naked, who's undressed.
The poor sing through the woods with cheer,[2]
For losses they need never fear.
The poor man has his liberty
To beg his way, for he is free,
Though hard looks he may often see,
And though he's driven from the door
He'll be no poorer than before,
For better counsel poorness offers
Than any opulency proffers,
That's proved by Quintus Curius [3]
And also by Fabricius
Who wanted neither goods nor gain,
For honor, virtue, these his aim,
For poorness once gave fundament
And rise to prudent regiment,
Most towns by poverty were grounded,

All arts by poverty were founded,
Of evil poverty is bare,
All honor takes its rise from there.
To all the peoples far and near
A long time poverty was dear,
The Greeks subdued through poverty
Lands, cities, peoples o'er the sea;
Both poor and just was Aristides
And stern and plain Epaminondas,
Poor Homer was, but widely read
And Socrates was wisely bred,
Phocion stood high in lenity.
The Bible says of poverty:
There's naught on earth whate'er its fame
But once from poverty it came.
The Roman Empire—high its name—
From poverty at first it came,
For who will note what's much expounded
That Rome by shepherds once was founded
And long by peasants poor was ruled
And then by riches was befooled,
He'll realize that poverty
Did Rome more good than property.
Had Croesus but been poor and wise
He would have kept what he did prize.
When Solon, asked that he confess
If he possessed true happiness,
Since he had power, wealth, and worth,
He answered: One should not on earth
Call mortal happy ere he dies,
Since none knows what before him lies.

Who claims that he's secure today,
He does not know the future way.
The Lord spake: "Woe to you and fear,[4]
Ye rich, your joy is only here,
Your joy in futile goods ye see,
Blest are the poor with spirit free."
Who's wealthy through a lying tongue,[5]
A worthless man by fear unstrung,
He feeds himself upon his woe
Till choked by Death and then laid low.
Treat poor with base iniquity [6]
And profit by their poverty
And you will find a richer boor
Who'll swindle you and make you poor.
Upon such goods turn not your eye
That soon will take to wings and fly,
For wings 'twill grow, like eagles fare [7]
From hence and fly into the air.
If riches were a blessing sure
Would Christ have been so bare and poor?
Who says: "For me the only curse
Is this: I've nothing in my purse,"
He's ignorant of wisdom's way,
He lacks far more than he can say.
Precisely this he never knows:
He's needier than he'd suppose.

Some men with plows are very spry
Yet end in trouble by and by,
The cuckoo finds their eggs on high.

84. OF PERSISTING IN
THE GOOD

Some use a sturdy hand to plow [1]
And first with zealousness they bow
To wisdom, for good works show will
Yet never reach the highest hill
That toward the realm of heaven's inclined;

Alas, they often look behind
And yearn for that Egyptian land [2]
Where all their dreamed-of flesh pots stand,
Reverting e'er to sins so great,
Like dogs to food that once they ate,[3]
That several times they do devour.
Their intent's bad at every hour.
A wound will heal but slowly when
It has been opened up again.
The sick man, deaf to all advice,
So that his ills grow in a trice,
Will oft discover that he may
Remain a sick man many a day.
Not starting's better, I insist,
Than start and presently desist.
God speaks: "I wish that you were not
Lukewarm but either cold or hot,[4]
But since you'd rather be but luke
I'm much displeased and must rebuke."
Although a man much good has done,
The right reward is oft not shown
If he gives up before the end.
From greatest evil God did fend
And once redeem the wife of Lot,[5]
But later, when she heeded not
The word of God and looked behind,
A salten pillar one could find.
A fool returns to cap and bell,
A dog will like his vomit well.

Can wealth, strength, youth, nobility
Have peace and quiet, Death, from thee?
What's born to live, to feel life's boon,
If mortal, that must perish soon.

85. NOT PROVIDING FOR DEATH

We're cheated, friends, I know it well,
Whoe'er upon this earth do dwell,
Because in time we don't provide
For death, which never spares our hide;

We've known it long and know it yet,
For each of us an hour is set,
To when, how, where, 'tis true, we're blind,
Yet death will leave no man behind.
To die and flow away we're bound
As water flows into the ground.
Hence we are fools with donkey ears,
We never see in all the years
That God allows us life and breath
That we should e'er provide for death.
The truth of this we needs must see:
From Death we must, can, should not flee.
The wine-pledge solemn did we drink [1]
And from the bargain cannot shrink,
Our first and final hours are mated,
And when the first man God created
He knew then how the last would die.
But folly cheats us shrewd and sly,
That we neglect the truth each day:
That Death won't let us tarry ay,
Our pretty horse he'll take away,
Our greening wreaths and garlands fair.
His name is truly Jack Sans Care;
Whom Death would grasp, let him beware,
If he be young or fair or strong
He'll take to leaping high and long,
And this I call the leap of death,
He'll sweat, freeze, writhe, and hold his breath
And like a worm will twist and wiggle
And finally will writhe and jiggle.
O Death, thy power is quite untold,

Thou snatchest off the young and old,
O Death, thy name is execration
To mighty nobles high of station,
To those precisely who delight
In nothing else but temporal might.
Death breaks with hard, impartial foot [2]
The hall of kings, the shepherd's hut,
He heeds nor pomp nor wealth nor power,
Takes peasant, Pope in one brief hour.
A fool who flees from day to day
The things he cannot halt or stay,
He thinks that if his dunce bells ring
Death ne'er will do him anything.
On such condition everyone
Comes here: That he will soon be done
And be the property of Death
When soul flees body void of breath.
Impartially Death takes away
The things o'er which our life holds sway.
"You die, but you, my friend, will bide,"
Yet no one stays a long, long tide,
Who e'en a thousand years did stay
Death ultimately took away.
From father down to son's a score
Of years—a coat's age—nothing more.
In tender years the son oft dies,
He knows it who a calfskin buys.
Of death there's never diminution,
Who dies not well finds retribution.
Those men are all to folly born
Who o'er the dead will weep and mourn

And would begrudge to them the rest
With which we hope we'll all be blest.
Too soon that place one cannot see⟩
Where one will dwell eternally. ⟨
To many a man it is a boon
If God in heaven calls him soon,
For many death has been a gain,
Since thus they're rid of grief and pain.⟩
Some men for death have had the mood
And some would die with gratitude
If Death before their time they'd see.
Death even sets some prisoners free,
A life-long prison term is o'er
When he's been through the prison door.
Luck gives some men a paltry share⟩
But Death deals equal lots and fair. ⟨
Death's like a judge who hears no plea
Of any man for clemency,
For Death will everything requite,
He spares no man the smallest mite,[3]
He shows no man obedience,
For at his summons all hie hence
And dance as he may lead the way,
Pope, kaiser, bishop, king, and lay.
But many do not seem to know
That soon a-dancing they must go,
That they must dance in rows (or totter)
The Westerwelder or the trotter.[4]
Who'd gird himself and well prepare
Would not be taken unaware.
Full many a blockhead Death did call

Who pondered long his funeral,
So much had he upon it spent
That even now there's wonderment.
A mausoleum for her dear
Spouse Artemesia did rear,
She fashioned it with such expense,
With luxury, munificence,
That 'mongst the seven wonders known
To earth it can be counted one.
In Egypt graves are very famed,
The pyramids are aptly named,
In such a grave did Chemnis store [5]
His goods and all his wealth galore;
Three hundred sixty thousand men
Piled up this tomb, if right I ken,
For herbs alone he spent so much
(On other costs I will not touch),
No prince today so rich has grown
That he could pay that all alone.
Amasis built a pyramid [6]
And Queen Rhodope also did.[7]
'Twas naught but folly, great, untold,
For men to squander so much gold
On graves wherein naught else is thrown
But sacks of ash and rotting bone,
And waste much money bare of sense
To build for worms a residence,
Not thinking where the soul may be
Which lives for all eternity.
Souls need no costly cenotaph,
A marble stone they never have,

No shield hangs here, no helmet, banner,
No coat-of-arms in lordly manner
And no inscription writ on stone,
The best shield is a skull-and-bone
For worms and snakes and toads to gnaw,
A shield that kaiser, peasant bore.
Who boasts a paunch now fine and sleek
May feed his retinue next week,
There'll be a fighting, tussling free,
Your friends will crave your property,
And this they're hopeful to attain,
The devils soon the soul will gain
And triumph over it with pother,
From one bath take it to another,
From biting cold to biting heat.
Witless we live and indiscreet
That for the soul we never care,
But bodies heed we everywhere.
Earth's consecrated but to God,
Who well has died lives well in sod,
The sky doth vault o'er many dead
Who 'neath no burial stone are laid.
How could you rest in better place
Than where the stars light up your face!
God finds the bones at His own leisure,
In graves a soul will ne'er have pleasure.
Who dieth well, his grave's the best,
The sinner's death is never blest.

Who fears from God no punishment
Because no thunder yet He's sent,
His thunder God on him will vent.

86. OF CONTEMPT OF GOD[1]

A fool who feels for God despite
And strives against Him day and night
And thinks that He is like mankind
And speaks not when He's mocked, maligned,[2]
For many a man possesses trust—
When thunder does not straightway thrust

A fire on him and strike him dead,
Because to evil ways he's bred,
Or when he dies not suddenly—
That fearful now he need not be,
Since God has quite forgotten him,
Postponing punishment for him,
Perhaps He'll e'en reward him, too.
Such sinful thoughts mark the cuckoo,
Who's always to the bad adhered.
When God spares man what he has feared,
He dares to grasp and pull God's beard,
As though his Lord he would deride,
And in such folly He'd abide.
O listen, fool, and learn today,
Do not rely on such delay,
It is a cruel punishment
That by th' Almighty must be sent,
For even though He spares you so,
The punishment postponed will grow.
God lets some men sin long before
He may chastise them all the more
And square accounts and pay them back
(We say that it doth clean the sack).
Some die sin-free, without disgrace,
God shows them mercy, goodly grace,
He takes them young from this earth's face
So that their sins may not increase,
And rob their soul of heavenly peace.
God's promised those who do repent
His love—acquitment He has sent,
But ne'er to sinners does He say:

"So long in this life you may stay
Until you do repent, improve,
Or till repentance you will move."
The mercy God may show today
Tomorrow he may take away.
Hezekiah [3] won from God reprieve,
And, came his time, he did not leave
The earth, but lived for fifteen years.
Belshazzar [4] sooner died, in fears,
That hand did kill his joy and mettle,
That wrote its Mane, Phares, Thetel.[5]
His weight, it seems, was all too light,
And so he lost his splendor bright.
He had not marked his father's woe,[6]
Who had been punished years ago,
And who had rued his evil deed,
Wherefore God, harkening, did heed,
So that as beast he never died,
But penitent, with God allied.
For mortal God has writ before
His time, his sins, so much, no more.
Hence hasten not base sins to do,
Who sins too much will soon be through.
Full many died this very year
Who could have changed their conduct here.
If they'd but turned the glass one day
The sand would not have run away
And on this earth a while they'd stay.

Who with his oaths 'gainst God is free
Lives shameful, dies in misery;
Woe's him and his persistency.

87. OF BLASPHEMING GOD

The greatest fools, I know them all
And yet I know not what to call
Such fools who never tire of sin
And brag they are of devil's kin,
For they must show in every wise
That God doth hate them and despise,

And they deny Him, bare of sense.
One charges God with impotence,
For God's own tortures God would blame—
His millet, entrails, kidney, brain.[1]
Who cannot swear new oaths with might—
Oaths barred by decency and right—
Is but a chicken-hearted wight.
One must have crossbow, have a spear
And fight four foes without a fear
And tilt the bottle debonair
And o'er the wine cups curse and swear,
Or over cards for lowly stakes.
'Twill not surprise if heaven makes
An end to earth, turns all to ash,
And causes heaven's vaults to crash.
Thus men malign their God, blaspheme,
All honor's left the earthly scene,
No legal punishment doth follow,
For that we suffer pain and sorrow.
It happens now so publicly
That all can mark it, hear and see.
In judgment God Himself would sit,
For long He cannot bear with it,
For He commanded mortals well
To stone blaspheming Israel.[2]
Sennacherib did curse the Lord
And with disgrace and scorn was gored.[3]
Lycaon [4] and Mycentius [5]
Endured, and famed Antiochus.[6]

Say: "God's too prone to punishment
And plagues us often with intent,"
And plague to you will soon be sent.

88. OF TORTURE AND PUN-
ISHMENT BY GOD

A fool who notes in wonderment
That God sends men His punishment
And lets one pain pursue another,
Despite full many a Christian brother
And many holy priests on earth,

Who all their time in want and dearth
Devote to fasting, ardent prayer.
But hear me: 'tis no wonder e'er
That you will not find one estate
In which the evil is not great,
Where yet there's no degeneration.
Wise men discuss this situation: [1]
"If you destroy what I do raise,
We'll both regret it all our days
And all our work will be for naught."
For thus the Lord in wrath has taught: [2]
"If my command you will not hear,
I'll send you plague and death and fear,
Drought, hunger, pestilence, and war,
Heat, frost, cold, hail, and thunder's roar,
And make it worse from day to day
And from your prayers I'll turn away.
Though Moses, Samuel beseech me,
Their prayers and pleadings will not reach me,
I loathe the soul on sinful path,
I, God, will punish it in wrath."
Regard the Jews and all their kin,
What they have lost through grievous sin,
How often God expelled their band,
Through sins, from out the Holy Land.
The Christians, too, have lost it now,
They've merited God's ireful vow.
I fear that we may lose still more,
And worse we'll fare than e'er before.

Whoe'er for bagpipes trades his mule,
Will not enjoy his trade, the fool,
He'll walk when riding's been his rule.

89. OF FOOLISH TRADING

A fool has greater trouble e'er,
Because his soul to hell will fare
Than any hermits ever face
In wilderness and lonely place,
When he serves God with fast and prayer.
One sees what trouble pride can bear,

It prinks, paints, laces up, and ties,
And suffers stress in every wise.
Greed drives men over seas to go,
Through storms and rain and heavy snow,
To Norway and Pilappenland.[1]
From lovers rest and peace are banned.
And gamblers have no joy and leisure;
The mounted thief has greater measure
Of care when he goes venturing.
Of wild carousers I'll not sing,
For heartburn is their constant bane
And pressure, often secret pain.
The climber's time is not the best,
He fears the rivals in the nest.
Its own limbs greed doth boil and bake,
No man's content for heaven's sake
Or patiently doth search his soul—
'Twas Noah's, Job's, and Daniel's goal.
Too many men in evil fare,
Those choosing good are very rare,
The good by wise men's much adored,
The bad will come of its accord.
Who gives up heaven for trumpery,
A fool is he whoe'er he be.
He never will enjoy his trades
Who gives what's deathless, takes what fades.
To say it in a word, he has
Secured a bagpipe for an ass.

Your father, mother honor ay,
That God grant you long earthly stay
And no disgrace upon you lay.

90. HONOR FATHER
AND MOTHER

A fool who gives to his young brood
What he may need for personal good,
Relying on this hope forever:
His children will desert him never
And keep him in his need, instead.

But every day they wish him dead.
He seems a burden, seems a pest
To all his brood, a hateful guest,
And yet it almost serves him right,
For he's a dull and witless wight.
He harks to kind words smoothly shod
And should be beaten with a rod.
But that man lives not long on earth
Who does not prize his parents' worth.
His lamp will fade and grow quite dim [1]
Whose parents are not dear to him.
Since Absalom opposed his sire [2]
He found his end in hellish fire,
And so a curse was laid on Ham,
When he disclosed his father's shame. [3]
Balthesar suffered sorrow too [4]
Because his father he did hew.
Sennacherib died by his sons, [5]
No realm thereby the villains won.
Tobit asked that his son revere [6]
His mother, that he hold her dear.
With such intent King Solomon [7]
Rose for his mother from his throne
And Coriolanus for his own.
God gave the Rechabites their meed, [8]
To their own father they gave heed.
The man who'd live, the Lord doth say, [9]
His parents he should honor ay,
He'll have a long and prosperous day.

In church full many fools hold sway
Who prate, help, counsel every day
That ship and cart get under way.

91. OF PRATTLING IN CHURCH

Some men in church or in the pew
Will prate advice the whole year through
How ship and skiff he best prepares
Who off to Narragonia fares.
The war in Italy's discussed

And lies are told (to my disgust)
And many a novel yarn is spun,
Thus then the matins are begun
And last until we vespers read,
And many come to church for greed,
For they do business there in church,
Else they would leave it in the lurch.
'Tis better nevermore to come
And all the time to stay at home
And close the prattling bench in haste
And have the goose mart elsewhere placed
Than tending personal affair
In church—it has no business there.
The business some have not completed
They bring to church where then it's treated,
How they may start the ship and cart
And latest news to friends impart,
And taking pains in every way
That their ship suffer no delay.
He'd rather leave the church for good
Than grease the wagon as he should.
Of those men hardly dare I speak
Who into church do merely peek,
They scarcely show themselves before
They've made their exit through the door.
What good and reverential prayers
Are prayed by men of such affairs!
They're paid rich prebends while they gape
Upon the bearded organ ape.[1]

Who lauds himself in vanity
And always on the crest would be,
The devil traps that man with glee.

92. PRESUMPTUOUSNESS
OF PRIDE

He kindles fires on roofs of straw
To whom world fame is highest law,
Who acts for notoriety,
For in the end he too will see
That he has been misled by pride

And but on rainbows has relied.
Who builds upon a pier of pine,
His plans will fail and never shine.
If e'er for worldly fame you've striven
Expect no more above in heaven.
Some dunces vaunting may be seen
That they've in Romance countries been
And learned in yonder school and this,
Bologna, Pavia, Paris,
Or at Siena sapience,
Or in the school at Orléans,
And there the organ ape they met
And Maître Pierre de Conniget,[1]
As though in our own German life
No reason, honor, sense were rife,
That art and science we might learn.
No need to foreign schools to turn.
Who'd study here in native land
Will now find many books at hand,
You can't excuse yourself, you see,
Without misleading shamefully.
Once men thought learning could but ay
Be sought at Athens far away,
And then in Italy 'twas found,
But now here too on German ground.
Our only failing's love for wine,
To it we Germans do incline,
And good hard work is rarely done.[2]
Bless him who has a prudent son!
I never liked a learned man
Who pride and profit will not ban

And boasts that he is shrewd and bluff.
The wise man's scholarly enough.
Who learns for haughtiness and pelf
Wins passing glory for himself,
Just like a wench who prinks with glee
And mirrors for the world to see,
When devil's nets she doth prepare,
That many souls to hell must fare,
For that's the owlet, that's the stick ³
Wherewith the devil plays his trick.
He's led full many a man astray
Who thought that he was witty ay.
Balaam gave Balak counsel odd ⁴
And Israel brought wrath to God,
They were defeated in the fray
Which through the women came their way.
Had Judith not dressed up and spruced,
Holofernes had not been seduced.⁵
Once Jezebel did paint her face
When King Jehu she would disgrace.⁶
The wise man says: "Turn thee away
From woman, she will tempt thee ay." ⁷
A foolish wench is insolent,
She gives herself with vile intent
And seems to think 'twill never hurt
With fools to ogle, jest, and flirt.
His thoughts are bad who sees a wench,
It sets him on the idiot's bench,
He follows up his goal absurd
Until he's caught the cunning bird.
If clothes had been on Bersabë ⁸

She'd not have known adultery.
Dinah went out lewd men to see [9]
And so gave up virginity.
A humble wife's with honor decked,
And she deserves the world's respect,
The woman who to pride would tend,
Her haughtiness it knows no end,
She always strives to lead the van,
No man with her would live, nor can.
The greatest wisdom God e'er gave
To him who does what men would crave,
But if their goal seems bad to us:
To do the thing that's decorous.
But who by women would do right,
He must be more than serving knight.
For oft through weakness they achieve,
Where cunning skills cannot deceive.
The pride of those who know God's hate
Will rise and rise and ne'er abate,
Yet finally, you'll find, it fell
To Lucifer's domain in hell.
Hark, pride, the hour's not far away,
When you yourself will speak and say:
"What joy brings me my haughtiness, [10]
I sit in grief and deep distress,
What good are wealth and prosperous station,
World's honor, fame, and reputation?
They are but shadows faint and wan,
In one brief moment are they gone."
Bless him who spurns and scorns such things,
And onto deathless matters clings.

A fool on earth can't find enough,
But in the end he finds rebuff.
Above all, pride should be maligned,
By nature is it so designed
That e'en the highest angel could
Not stay in heaven; and Adam should
Leave Paradise in sheer disgrace.
For pride there's ne'er on earth a place.
For in the end all pride must dwell
With Lucifer in pools of hell.
Let pride seek him who fathered pride,
It would to hell and there abide.
Hagar, through haughtiness beguiled,
Was banished with her little child,[11]
Pharaoh was destroyed through pride,[12]
And Korah with his people died.[13]
Indignant, angered God appeared,
When haughtiness the tower reared.[14]
Proud David numbered all the folk,
But pestilence his self-love broke.[15]
Herod was clad in vanity,
As though he had divinity.
To godly honor was he urged
But by the angel he was scourged.
Who lives in pride's humiliated,
Meekness by God is highly rated.

The usurers are vile and rash,
The man of poverty they thrash,
They'd care not if the world should crash.

93. USURY AND PROFIT-EERING

We'd punish him for all his tricks,
From him we must remove the ticks
And pluck his pinions with elation
Who buys up goods on speculation,
The wine and corn in all the land,

No sin, dishonor stays his hand,
So that a poor man cannot flee
Starvation with his family.
Thus prices mount, it must be clear,
They're higher now than those last year,
If wine now costs a scant ten pound,
Next month 'twill certainly be found
You'll pay full thirty when you buy.
The same is true of wheat, spelt, rye.
The great abuse need not be stressed
Of money, kind, and interest,
Of loans, pawn business oft unsound:
In one day some will earn a pound
More profit than a year should hold,
They lend in silver, ask for gold,
You borrow ten, eleven's due,
They're more usurious than the Jew.
Their business now the Jews may lose,
For it is done by Christian Jews.
With Jewish spears they run about,[1]
I could name many such a lout,
Unsavory are their transactions
Yet are not stopped by legal actions.
With joy they greet the hailstorm's might
And see the hoarfrost with delight,
But often too, deprived of hope,
You'll find men hanging from a rope.
Harm common weal and help your own,
And you're a fool, but not alone.

putting your own good above the common good

Some cast an eye on others' ware
And hope to bury them as heir,
But they die, their testators ne'er.

94. OF HOPE OF GETTING LEGACIES

A fool is he who hopes to be
Another's heir and legatee
Or take his place in council wise,
His goods and post at his demise.
Another's death he will await

But does not know the plans of fate.
He'd bury others, rascal knave,
Who may plant pear trees on his grave.
Who other men to graves would send
And doesn't know where he will end,
He shoes the ass upon whose back
To Foolsland he will beat a track.
Young, strong, and jolly men may die,
And calves' hides one can often buy,[1]
Though smaller than a cow's they be.
Let each one praise his poverty
And not desire that it may grow.
Fate deals us mortals many a blow.
Bulgarus was the legatee,[2]
His sons died unexpectedly.
Priam saw all his children killed
Although his realm to them he'd willed.
'Gainst David Absalom did plot,[3]
But at the oak he found his lot.
Some come to riches overnight
Of which they'd never thought a mite.
Some men have such vile legatees,
They would prefer a dog to these.
Not everybody's wish comes true,
As Abraham's [4] and Simeon's, too.[5]
Be free of care, when God but will
Your fortune's goal He can fulfill.
Our home's [6] the one best legacy,
Where we desire some day to be.
Yet that home few can hope to see.

On holidays men go to church,
And leave their labors in the lurch,
Yet some for work and business search.

95. OF BEING MISLED
ON HOLIDAYS

A citizen of Apeland he [1]
Who saves the work and tasks there be
To do upon a holiday.
The ape-cart is his private shay.
One wants his horses shod that day,

Another buttons has to sew
Which should have been done long ago
The while he gamed with friends and wined.
Another has his shoe points lined,[2]
That rags and lint are in them pressed.
Another tries on pants and vest,
No other day would suit him ay,
It must be some high holiday.[3]
The cooks a fire do soon prepare
Before the church is opened e'er,
And then they feast and gormandize,
Before most men from bed arise,
The taverns, too, are full of folk,
Who every kind of wine would soak,
Especially on holidays
When other work aside one lays,
They get their carts and drive away.
Men turn to fools on holiday.
Some think the holiday's assigned
For little tasks that God won't mind:
A game of checkers can't be wrong,
Or playing cards the whole day long;
On servants sundry tasks are laid,
No master cares if child or maid
Would worship, list to sermons wise
Or for the early mass arise,
And over mead we find them toiling
Which through th' entire week was boiling,
No trade, it seems, will feel disgrace
By doing work on holidays,
So eager they to earn a penny,

As though no days were left, not any,
Some stand and chatter in the street
While others game, carouse, and eat.
For wine some lavish what they'd seek
To earn by working all the week.
A bungler he, a niggard, lout [4]
Who stays not till the party's out
All day and night till cats awake
And sunbeams through the windows break.
Jews jeer at us with words that flay,
That we neglect the holiday
Which they observe with heart and lip,
So that into the dunce's ship
I would not place them, but they err
In other ways like some mad cur.
A poor man on a holiday
Sought sticks; they stoned him then straightway. [5]
The Maccabees once would not go
On Holy Day to ward the foe, [6]
And many of these were stricken dead.
One does not bake the heavenly bread [7]
On holy days, as God has said.
But oft we work in foolish way
And save the work for holiday,
The work we shirk some other day.
O fool, respect the day of rest,
With workdays man will e'er be blest,
E'en after you decay in grave;
The road to vice by greed is paved.

A fool is he who mourns all day
For things that he cannot allay,
Or rues that he has done some good
To one who has not understood.

96. GIVING AND REGRET-
TING

A fool is he who gives a gift,
But soon his inclinations shift,
He makes a dour and angry face
That gladdens no one, shows no grace;

He loses gift and gratitude
Who would regret his generous mood.
So persons who do something fine
Through heaven's grace or will divine,
And yet regret their noble way
If God rewards them not straightway.
Who would give gifts in spirit mellow
Must laugh and be a jolly fellow
And not say: "I regret my deed,"
If gratitude and love he'd need.
God contemplates his gift with sadness
Who does not give in joy and gladness.
What's yours, retain it if you will,
To force a man to give is ill,
The gift a man bestows with grace,
'Tis such that's welcome any place.
Thanks usually can be found,
Though they be slow in coming round,
For very often things are righted:
With "two for one" we're all delighted.
Though one sees gratitude disdained,
One finds some men in honor trained,
Wise men of gratitude and sense
Who for the rest give recompense.
But he who boasts of liberal mind
Deserves no prize of any kind
And should expect no gratitude.
A boastful giver's oft too crude,
For people always look askance
At one who boasts munificence,
Nor will he profit from it hence.

There's laziness in all the classes
And most among the servant classes;
Pay any wage, it will not please,
Still they will spare their energies.

97. OF INDOLENCE AND SLOTH

No better fool where'er you go
Than one whose pace is always slow,
So lazy he that he will burn
His shinbone e'er he'll stir and turn.

As smoke is bad for human eyes,
As vinegar the teeth defies,[1]
So too the slothful man for one
Who'd have him on an errand run.
A lazy man is useless too,
Except to be a bugaboo.[2]
Long must he sleep in any case
Behind the stove, his proper place.
He's happy who with pickax works,
The idle man's the one who irks,
An idle man can try the Lord,
Good work God always will reward.
The devil notes all idleness
And sows his seeds in wickedness.
One cause of sinfulness is sloth,
The Israelites it rendered wroth.[3]
When David too was idle he
Did kill and do adultery.[4]
The fact that Carthage was undone
Cost Rome her overthrow anon;
Since Carthaginians were defeated
Worse injury to Rome was meted
Than in the wars that went before
One hundred sixteen years or more.
The lazy man who'd stay at home
Says: "Outdoors savage lions roam." [5]
The mad dog keeps to his home station,
Sloth ever finds justification,
'Tis sloth that swings now back now fore
Like any hinge upon a door.

Idle hands get in
trouble →

Here witness many fools of fame,
They're fools and they possess the name,
For them the other fools feel shame.

98. OF OUTLANDISH FOOLS

There are so many worthless folk
Whom ugly fool-hide serves as cloak,
Inured to folly without fail
And tied onto the devil's tail.
They can't be cured howe'er we try,

I'll keep my peace and pass them by
And let them hold their foolish stance
And not depict their ignorance,
Turks, pagans, Saracens—in brief
All those who have no true belief,
The heretics to boot (a plague!),
Who have their fool's abode in Prague; [1]
At other countries too they aim
And e'en Moravia they claim.
They don the fool's cap uglily
Like those who not the Trinity
And one true God would e'er revere,
Who ridicule our faith and jeer.
They're never simple fools and meet,
They have the cap beneath their feet,
So public is their folly that
They lack the cloth to make a cap.
Those too commit apostasy
And in the devil's grip we see:
Mad women,[2] evil wenches too,
Procurers, panders not a few
And other men of sinful kind
Who all in foolishness are blind.
Of those I also would have sung
Who've killed themselves, on gallows strung,
Or who abort or drown their young:
They earn no legal comfort here,
No teaching, not a taunting jeer.
But they are carefree fools and jolly,
They've earned a cap through all their folly.

I beg you all, sires small and great,
Regard the common weal and fate,
The fool's cap leave for my poor pate.

99. OF THE DECLINE
OF THE FAITH[1]

When I regard neglect and shame
Which everywhere appears the same
Of prince and lord, of city, land,
No wonder then the tears do stand
In these mine eyes and flow so free

That one should see disgracefully
The faith of Christians ebb, recede.
Forgive me though I have indeed
Included e'en the princes here.
Luckless it is that we must hear
That Christians' faith has met distress,
For daily it diminishes.
At first the cruel heretic
Did tear and wound it to the quick
And then Mohammed shamefully
Abused its noble sanctity
With heresy and base intent.
Our faith was strong in th' Orient,
It ruled in all of Asia,
In Moorish lands and Africa.
But now for us these lands are gone,
'Twould even grieve the hardest stone.
We've lost and see ourselves now banned
From Asia Minor, Grecian land
And all of Greater Turkey too,
Which to our Faith is quite untrue.
'Twas where the seven churches were,
And John we know wrote letters there.
Such good and faithful countries fell,
One'd vow it quite impossible.
In Europe we've been forced to see
The loss but very recently
Of kingdoms, even empires two [2]
And mighty lands and cities true,
Constantinople, Trapezunt,[3]
Lands known to each and every one,

Achaea and Etolia,
Boeotia and Thessalia,
Thracia and Macedonia,
Attica, yes, and Mysia,
Triballi [4] too and Scordisci, [5]
Bastarnae, [6] also Taurici, [7]
Euboea, now called Nigrapont, [8]
Pera, [9] Kaffa, [10] also Idrunt, [11]
Not mentioning what we have lost
Yet otherwise at heavy cost:
In Morea, Dalmatia,
Styria, Carinthia, Croatia,
In Wendish march, in Hungary.
So strong the Turks have grown to be
They hold the ocean not alone,
The Danube too is now their own.
They make their inroads when they will,
Bishoprics, churches suffer ill,
Now they attack Apulia,
Tomorrow e'en Sicilia, [12]
And next to it is Italy,
Wherefore a victim Rome may be
And Lombardy and Romance land,
We have the archfoe close at hand,
We perish sleeping one and all,
The wolf has come into the stall
And steals the Holy Church's sheep
The while the shepherd lies asleep.
Four sisters of our Church you find,
They're of the patriarchic kind:
Constantinople, Alexandria,

Jerusalem, Antiochia,
But they've been forfeited and sacked
And soon the head will be attacked.¹³
Our sins I blame and not the others',
We have no patience now with brothers
Nor pity we their misery.
Each state would grow and greater be;
We're like the oxen famed in tale
Who watched the rest without avail
Until the wolf consumed them all,
The last one sweated, then did fall.
We find each man to his wall turning ¹⁴
To ascertain if it is burning,
Not thinking e'er to quench with vim
The fire before it reaches him.
He suffers grief and penitence,
Discord and disobedience,
They do our Christian faith no good,
In vain we shed our Christian blood,
None realize how close it be,
They fancy they'll come off scot-free,
Until misfortune hounds their gate,
And then they stir and crane their pate.
For Europe's gates are open wide,
The foe encircles every side,
With sleep or rest he's not content,
On Christian blood alone he's bent.
O Rome, when kings you had to fear
You were a vassal many a year,
To freedom later you did pass
When ruled by men of common class,

But when you turned to haughtiness,
To riches, aye to mightiness,
And burgher facing burgher stood,
Not heeding any common good,
Your power mostly passed away,
O'er you an emperor held sway,
And in imperial glory's sheen
For fifteen hundred years you've been,[15]
Lost ground and made but little gain,
E'en as the moon begins to wane
And smaller grows and dimmer too,
And now but little's left of you.
Would God you'd be augmented soon,
In that way too be like the moon.
Of Roman Empire everyone
Desires a slice to call his own.
The Saracens with many a band
First took the Holy Promised Land
And then the Turks gained many a mile,
To tell it all would take a while.
Some cities now resort to war
And heed the emperor no more,
Each prince would take a slice of goose
And pry himself a feather loose.
No wonder it's a platitude
That now our realm is bare and nude.
Each one is warned that he must not
Demand e'en what he should have got [16]
And that with caution he avoid
To take from men what they've enjoyed.
By God, you princes, please behold

What injury there'll be untold
If once the empire should decay,
Not even you will live for ay.
All things have more efficiency
When they exist in unity
Than when there's discord in the world,
For concord's banner once unfurled
Will give us strength to thrive and grow,
But where discordance seeds may sow
The greatest, noblest things are razed.
The Germans once were highly praised
And so illustrious was their fame,
The Reich was theirs and took their name;
But soon we found a German nation
That brought its own realm ruination.
In studs decadent without fail
Each horse bites off its own poor tail.[17]
They're on the march, they have appeared,
Cerastes, basilisk, the feared.
He'll poison but himself the while
Who'd give our realm a poison vial.
But all you lords, you states and kings,
Do not permit such shameful things!
If you'll support the ship of state
It will not sink but bear its freight.
Your king is all benignity,[18]
He'll don for you knight's panoply,
Rebellious lands he will subdue,
But you must help, he needs you too.
The noble Maximilian,
He merits well the Roman crown.

They'll surely come into his hand,
The Holy Earth, the Promised Land,[19]
He'll undertake it any day
If he can trust in you and may.
Cast off your scorn and tauntings all,
God's host it is but very small.
We've lost a great deal, are bereft,
Yet many Christian lands are left,
Good kings, lords, men of common cares,
Some day the world will all be theirs,
They'll win, surround it quick and bold
If but together they will hold.
Faith, peace and love we do require,
I hope to God the end's not dire!
You rule the land and every place,
Awake, renounce all black disgrace,
Be not the sailor in the deep
Who midst his duty fell asleep [20]
The while the storm clouds gathered dark;
Or like a dog that does not bark,
Or like a guard that watches ne'er
And shirking duty shows no care.
Arise and end your dream and see:
The axe is truly in the tree.[21]
O God, give all our rulers sense
To seek Thy honor so immense
And not their own avail and greed,
Then I'll have sorrows none indeed,
Then soon Thou'lt give us victory,
For which be praised eternally!
I warn th' estates in every land,

Whatever be their titles grand,
That they should not be like a crew
Who disagree and battle too
When they are out upon the deep
And wind and storm the sailcloth sweep.
Ere on a course they can agree
Their worthy ship a wreck may be.
If you have ears then list to me:
Our ship is swaying frightfully,
If Christ doth not watch o'er us right
We soon will be in darkest night.
Ye, therefore, who through your high station
From God received the designation
To march forever at the head,
Let evil not of you be said;
Do what befits your lofty station,
Swell not our harm, humiliation,
Let not the sun and moon abate,
The head and limbs deteriorate,
For things seem bad, whate'er I scan,
While living I'll warn many a man.
The frivolous who pay no heed
I'll give a fool's cap, that's their meed.

Who now can stroke the fallow steed [1]
And dotes upon a scurvy deed
Deserves a haughty courtier's meed.

100. OF STROKING THE
FALLOW STALLION

I wish I had a covered ship
Wherein all courtiers I would slip
And those who eat at nobles' board
And hobnob with a mighty lord
So that they may be undisturbed

And by the rabble never curbed.
They're not at ease when others roam,
They're picking feathers, stroking comb,[2]
One coddles, whispers close to ear
And curries favor in a year
And feeds himself by licking plates.
A lord is he who lies and prates,
To whom owl-stroking's now a creed [3]
And flattering the fallow steed.
To flour-blowing he's inclined,[4]
He hangs his coat to suit the wind.
By bearing tales some men go fore
Who'd otherwise see but the door.
If you can mingle wool and hair [5]
Then stay at court, you're needed there,
For you a welcome there will be
Since courtiers need no honesty;
Their every action folly spells,
They'll never leave me cap and bells.
Some groom the stallion so with vim
They get a body blow from him
Or else a kick against a rib,
Which lands their plate into the crib.
The horse would do no injury
If men would treat it prudently.
If men were as they simulate,
Of pious and of honest state,
If each one acted like himself
Fool's caps galore would grace the shelf.

flattery

differences between appearances and reality

He goes a careless, frivolous way
Who credits what the others say,
A prater many can betray.

101. OF BLOWING
INTO EARS

A fool who puts into his head
And credits things that men have said,
He is a dunce that merits jeers,
With sensitive and spacious ears.
All honesty those persons lack

Who would assail behind one's back
And strike without e'er warning him,
With chance of fending very slim.
To lie in ambush men like these
Do now esteem a masterpiece,
It can't be warded off, prevented,
By everyone it is attempted,
With lying tales, with calumny,
With many kinds of perfidy
That can be dressed and colored high
So men may better cheat and lie
And make us credit what we hear
But to defendants lend no ear.
His doom will many a man attend
Who never could himself defend
And prove that he is innocent,
He's trapped and bagged with base intent.
Haman would deal Mordecai death.[1]
Slave Zeba duped Mephiboseth [2]
And Alexander was extolled [3]
Since he believed not what was told
By those who slandered Jonathan.
Oh woe betide the credulous man!
Adam'd been blessed did he believe
No false and tempting word of Eve,
And Eve no word the serpent said.
The credulous to crimes are bred.
Trust not a man in any wise,
The world is false and full of lies;
The raven's black 'neath any skies.

In alchemy it's plain to see,
As 'tis in vinous chemistry,
What falsity on earth there be.[1]

102. OF FALSITY AND DECEPTION

Deceivers many, cheats I see,
They join the dunce's revelry.
False counsel, love, false friends, false gold,
The world is full of lies untold.
Fraternal love is dead and blind,

Each one conspires to cheat his kind,
That he may never lose, but gain,
Though hundreds suffer ruin, pain.
No honesty is anywhere
No matter how the soul may fare,
On shirking, slacking one is bent,
Though thousands die in this event.
Much meddling now there is with wine,
One tries deception all the time.
Saltpeter, sulphur, bones of dead,
Potash, milk, mustard, herbs ill-bred [2]
Through bungs are pushed into the kegs.
The pregnant women drink these dregs,
That they bear children premature,
A wretched sight one can't endure.
From out such drink diseases grow,
Some people to the churchyard go.
Lame horses now are shod and braced
That on the sick-cart should be placed,
In felt their feet are then imbedded,
As though at night for matins headed.
Although they totter weak and lame,
They're traded for immoderate gain.
We suffer from this cheating game.
The weights and measures now are small,
The ell-stick's not an ell at all,
The shops are dark, with lights so tiny,
One cannot see the cloth is shiny.
While one admires with friendly air
The foolkins on the table there, [3]
The seller gives the scale a shove,

That toward the ground it lunge and move
And asks: "How much of this, I pray?",
And with the meat his thumb does weigh.
The road is plowed and sowed with corn,
The coin is old and badly worn,
'Twould break in any hand that had it
If baser metals weren't added.
Coins ne'er are worth their value stated,
False money crops up unabated, ✗
False counsel too; monk, priest, Beguine,[4] ✗
Lay brothers, they are false, unclean,
For wolves in sheep clothes now are seen.
But let there not forgotten be
Our quite deceptive alchemy:
Pure gold and silver doth it yield
But this in ladles was concealed.
Their trickery is sly but ample,
They start by offering a sample
And soon a toad comes into play,[5]
Some men the cuckoo drives away.[6]
Who used to live in happiness
He pours and fills the monkey glass
And then a powdery mass will burn
So that himself he can't discern.
For most it's worked destructively
And few have gained prosperity.
'Twas Aristotle, he did say:
"The form of things persists for ay."
Full many catch this dread disease
But little profit comes to these.
The copper takes the place of gold,

Mouse dirt for pepper corns is sold,
The pelts and furs are dyed so crude
And dressed with little aptitude
So that the fur will shed and tear
And not a quarter year will wear.
The muskrats give an odor vile
So one can smell it half a mile,
Bad herrings smuggled by a bold,
Shrewd merchant oft for fresh are sold.
In every street the hucksters stand,
The peddler reaps a profit grand.
The old with new can be diluted,
Nowhere can cheaters be disputed.
No trade is what it's claimed to be,
Men sell their wares with falsity,
Dispose of them with zealous skill
Although their quality be nil.
Blesséd no doubt is every man
Who'd guard against deceit and can.
The child deceives its relatives,
No heed to kin the father gives;
The host the guest, the guest the host,
Bad faith and guile the many boast.
The Antichrist it doth forbode,
His dealings take a devious road,
His thoughts and acts and words forsooth
Are turned to falsehood, base untruth.

103. OF THE ANTICHRIST [1]

I've sent the vanguard on ahead
Of those to falsehood born and bred,
Yet many are there left who trip
And prance about the dunces' ship,

Themselves and others they would twit
By falsifying Holy Writ.
Our faith is kicked by them and cursed,
The paper ship is then immersed,[2]
Each tears away a bit of border,
'Twill sink the ship in shorter order.
The oars and straps are snatched away
That it be wrecked without delay.
Some think they are so very shrewd
That sense enough they have indued
That now by all their subtle wit
They can interpret Holy Writ:
In this they fail in many a wise,
Their wrongful teaching we chastise.
From other writings they could cull
(Of which the earth is very full)
Much knowledge too and information,
But zealous they of such a station,
They would be first in each respect,
That's how the ship will soon be wrecked.
Such men must be intoxicated,
They know the truth and right when stated,
And yet the ship they would capsize[3]
To show their light to others' eyes.
These prophets false one ought to flay,
God warns against them every day.
Who twist the Holy Writ and preach
What th' Holy Ghost would never teach,
Their scale is wrongful, false, and ill,
They weigh with it whate'er they will,
Make one thing heavy, one thing light,

So faith's indeed in sorry plight.
We stand 'mongst perverts everywhere,
The scorpion begins to stir
Through schemers base of whom did tell
The prophet, famed Ezekiel.[4]
The men who violate the law [5]
For Antichrist's great wealth have awe,
A treasure he has laid away
But short and measured is his day,
Though numerous his friends may be
Who go with him in falsity.
His retinue will be untold,
And when he pays his shining gold
And shows that he's not treasureless
He will not have to use duress,
They'll come and join of their accord,
And money coaxes more aboard.
They'll help him wherewith well he may
Enlist good people every day,
But brief and sad will be their trip,
They will be wrecked with skiff and ship,
Though traveling everywhere for ay,
Distorting truth in every way,
Yet truth will live and ever be,
Expelling all their falsity
Which now from no estate is banned,
I fear the ship will never land.
St. Peter's ship is swaying madly,
It may be wrecked or damaged badly,
The waves are striking 'gainst the side
And storm and trouble may betide.

But little truth is now asserted
And Holy Writ is quite perverted,
It's now defined some other way
From what the tongue of truth would say.
Forgive me, you whom I may hit.
In th' large ship Antichrist does sit,
He's sent a message out to man,
False things he spreads where'er he can,
Creeds, dogmas false in every way
Now seem to grow from day to day.
The printers make the case more dire,
If some books went into the fire
Much wrong and error would be gone.
Some think of profits now alone.
They look for books in every clime,
But ah, corrections take no time.
They muse: How shall we cheat th' elect?
For many print, but few correct.
It's evil, yet they deem it fine
If they can copy line for line.[6]
They stain themselves with base intent,
Some print their way to banishment.[7]
These men the vessel cannot bear,
A fool's cart theirs, so let them fare,
That one may chase the other there.
The time comes, that it comes is clear,
The Antichrist is very near.
And mark this well at my behest:
Upon three things our faith does rest:
On absolution, doctrine, books,
To these foundations no one looks.

The books are published ton on ton,
Because there's too much printing done.
In our times all those books come forth
Which long ago our parents wrought.
So numerous are they here and there,
They count for nothing anywhere
And no one pays to them much heed,
So 'tis with science, so with creed.
In number schools were ne'er so great,
As now are found in every state,
And scarce a city now is known,
That calls no higher school its own.
There many scholars now are trained
Who nowadays are quite disdained,
And knowledge gets a scornful glance,
Most men do look at it askance.
The scholars needs must feel a shame
For studies, gown, their very name.
The peasants now attain the fore,
And scholars hide behind the door.
Men say: "These lazy apes,[8] these beasts,
The devil's cursing us with priests!"
That's ample evidence that science
Lacks honor, love and breeds defiance.
'Tis thus that studies will be wrecked,
For knowledge prospers through respect,
And when no honor's paid to science
Most men will view it with defiance.
Yes, absolution stands no higher,
For it no man has great desire,
It's sought by none, and what is worse,

Some even shun it as a curse.
For absolution naught they'd spend
If home to them we had it sent.
But finally 'twill reach you ay
In Aix or farther e'en away.[9]
By us 'tis hated just as well
As manna was by Israel.[10]
Israel manna did contemn,
They said 'twas valueless to them,
Their soul despised it bitterly
And made of it a mockery.
Thus absolution is at once
Despised and hated by the dunce.
From this a lesson I'd indite:
Our faith today is like a light,
Before 'twould be extinguished quite
It flickers, then it flares up bright.
I'm tempted candidly to say:
We do approach the Judgment Day,
Since mercy's held in cold despite
We're now approaching total night,
Such things have never happened yet,
The vessel sways, it may upset.[11]

If pushed by flattery, by threat,
Your truthfulness can be upset,
The Antichrist will snatch you yet.

104. CONCEALING TRUTH

A fool is he who'd be inclined
To sore annoyance if he'd find
Himself accosted, forced forsooth
To hush and palliate the truth,
Deserting wisdom under stress
To take the path of foolishness

Which he without a doubt doth fare
Whoe'er for threatening words has care,
Since God is always on his side
And doth protect him every tide
Who's wed to stern veracity
So that he ne'er does injury
To his foot; who with truth will stay
Will soon drive all his foes away.
A wise man stands by truth, though he
The ox of Phalaris may see.[1]
Canst stand beside veracity?
Then travel with stupidity.
If Jonah'd had no lying whim
The whale would not have swallowed him.[2]
Elijah set on truth no price,[3]
Hence he arrived in paradise.
John fled the fools' meandering,
Hence Jesus saw the baptizing.
A man who's punished lovingly
In him ill will at first you'll see
But later he may change his mood
And offer naught but gratitude.
He'll speak more praise for words that sting
Than he'll for those of pleasant ring.
No gifts would Daniel take that day
When 'gainst Belshazzar he did say [4]
And spoke the truth with little dread:
"Thy gifts bestow thyself," he said.
The angel 'twas that did prevent
Balaam from taking presents sent,[5]
Likewise from violating truth,

So he was foiled and balked forsooth.
The ass chastises him who's riding.
Two things can never be in hiding,
The third will always be abiding: [6]
A city built on lofty land,
A fool if he sit, walk, or stand
Will show his foolish quality,
But truth is seen eternally
And will not spoil though laid away,
However fools may shriek all day.
All men respect veracity;
Fools thrive on scorn and mockery.
Full often have I been maligned
Because this ship I have designed:
They tell me that I ought to paint it
And that no bark of oak should taint it, [7]
But let some linden sap refine it [8]
And spruce it up right well and shine it.
But I would let them freeze forsooth
Ere saying anything but truth,
For truth lives on eternally,
A beacon light that men can see
E'en when this book in shreds may be.
Truth's stronger far than persons vile
Who me or e'en themselves revile.
If I should heed what they may say
I'd be as great a fool as they
Whome'er my ships will bear away.

The man who would on truth insist
Must meet this, that antagonist
Who'll try and force him to desist.

105. PREVENTION OF
THE GOOD

A fool is he in flesh and blood
Who'd keep another man from good
And seek to fend, ward off, prevent
What brings himself no detriment,
Applauding others who like him

In idiots' broth must sink or swim.
For fools have evermore intrigued
'Gainst those who with the good are leagued.
One fool dislikes another fool
And yet a man from folly's school
Is usually glad that he
Is not the only fool there be,
And so he always tries to find
Some men of his own fatuous kind
And plans how he be not alone.
The bauble is the dunce's own.
When fools see one who would forsooth
Be righteous and abide in truth
They say: "A bigot is this man,
He'd fain be a Carthusian! [1]
Hypocrisy is that man's share
And in our Lord he would despair.
To us too God will once decree
A death that full of grace will be,
Albeit he by night and day
On knees reclines to wake and pray,
He'd fast and build him hermit huts,
To God and world his heart he shuts.
By heaven we were not created
That monks or priests we should be rated,
We'd not abjure the world as foul,
For we would never wear a cowl
Or cap unless it tinkled too.
Behold the fool, the base cuckoo,
Much good on earth he would have done
And even more reward have won

Had he but learned judiciousness
And gone the road of blessedness
And never groveled like a beast
And lived in cell to feed and feast.
So many things he doth renounce,
He has no joy, no single ounce.
If just like this man everyone
Should put Carthusian garments on,
Who would increase the population
And give men wisdom, information?
Of God's desire he makes abuse
Who treats himself like this recluse
And thinks but of himself alone."
Such incantations fools intone.
The earth is their entire vocation,
They never seek the soul's salvation.
Fool, listen, e'en if you were wise
There'd still be fools enough to prize;
Though you should have a monkish air
Fools plenty here on earth would fare.
If all men spoke such sentiment
No one to heaven would be sent.
E'en if your mind should function well
Some men would always go to hell.
If I did have two souls in me [2]
To fools I'd give the one soul free,
But since I have one soul alone
There's need for me to guard the one,
God loves not Belial as His own.

Who lights his lamp here, warm and bright [1]
And lets the oil give cheering light,
That man shall ever have delight.

106. REFRAINING FROM GOOD WORKS

A fool is he who, if he lives,
When God His final judgment gives,
To self-blame and culpation's bound
Because he has suppressed his pound
Which God did give him once of yore,

Wherewith he should acquire more.
From him God takes his pound away,
He suffers pain by night and day.
So they who have their lamp upset
Or not their oil have lighted yet
And go to seek oil everywhere
When far away the soul would fare.
Four creatures small on earth we find,[2]
They're wiser far than human kind:
The ant, that never shirks its work,
And conies that in rocks do lurk,
The locusts, that no kings command,
They sally forth in martial band,
The spider ay on hands does fare,
Yet lives with rulers anywhere.
If you find honey, sharp combs too,[3]
Eat only what is good for you
And never eat too much of sweet,
Lest you may have to vomit it.
Although a sage die suddenly,
Destroyed his soul will never be.
The fool, however, who's unwise [4]
Doth perish while his frame resides
Fore'er in darksome grave, a hole;
He leaves to others goods and soul.
No greater fool was fashioned ay
Than one who recks no future day
And only goes his temporal way.
Some trees do burn in hell below
On which good fruit would never grow.

While o'er the right one finds the crown,
The fool's cap o'er the left is shown.
All fools the selfsame way have gone,
They're castigated, they're forlorn.

107. OF REWARD FOR WISDOM

Some fools seek knowledge high and higher,
To M.A., Ph.D. aspire,
Though people deem them very bright,
These fools can't understand aright

How they'd attain that knowledge rare
Wherewith to heaven they may fare,
And that all wisdom 'neath the sun [1]
To God is folly men should shun.
Some think they have the proper way
But lose the path and go astray
And miss the life that's true and rare.
Blest he who'd never stray and err
When he has found the proper way;
The side road often leads agley
And takes a person off the street
Unless God thinks it is not meet.
Young Hercules was wont to brood
What road by him were best pursued,[2]
The road of joy and vain delight
Or that of wisdom clear and bright,
There came to him amid such thought
Two women whom, though saying naught,
On seeing he did recognize:
The one was full of lust and vice
And well adorned with phrases sweet,
She gave him hope of joyful treat,
But in the end he'd die with pain
And neither joy nor pleasure gain;
The other one seemed pale, hard, sour,
Her mien was joyless every hour,
She said: "No joy I promise you,
No rest, and labors not a few,
On virtue you will virtue heap
And recompense eternal keep."
Then Hercules went where she led,

Joy, idleness, delight he fled.
Would God, as we do always seem
To wish for life to suit our dream,
That we might also crave for us
A life that's ever virtuous,
We'd truly flee from many a way
That over fool's road leads agley,
But since no one of us has scanned
The place where we will later land
And blinkingly we live in night,
We do not heed the road that's right
And often lack the knowledge where
The steps we take will make us fare,
And that's the reason why it's true
We oft repent whate'er we do.
If we succeed with grief and pain
We crave yet more with heart inane.
'Tis best explained by mortals having
An inbred, yes, a natural craving
For what is right and good on earth,
We crave it ever since our birth.
But since, alas, that cannot be
(We err in dark obscurity)
The Lord has given us the light
Of wisdom, making all things bright.
To darkness wisdom puts an end
If but to wisdom we attend.
It shows us too the difference
'Twixt folly's course and prudent sense.
Such precious wisdom these did prize:
Pythagoras, Plato the wise,

And Socrates, who through their creed
Won lasting fame and honor's meed
Yet could not picture bright and clear
The real wisdom dwelling here,
Wherefore of them the Lord did say: [3]
"Their knowledge, skill I'll toss away
And wisdom too, who here are wise,
Let children have it—this their prize."
To children only wisdom's taught,
Which they from heavenly regions brought.
Whoever's learned so wise to be
Is honored for eternity
And sparkles like the firmament.
Those who on righteousness are bent
And teach themselves the proper way
And others too, they shine for ay
Like Lucifer in Orient
And Hesperus in Occident.
Bion,[4] the master, makes us see:
As the suitors of Penelope
Could win her not by escapades
And then began to court her maids,
So those men too who cannot quite
Appreciate true wisdom's light
Come close to it through virtuous grace
(The maids) but never see its face.
All worldly joys have gruesome end,
Let each one watch where he may wend.

You fellows, come and be on hand,
We're headed for Schluraffen land [1]
And yet we're stuck in mud and sand.

108. THE SCHLURAFFEN SHIP

Think not we fools are all alone,
For brothers large and small we own
In every country everywhere,
Our ranks are swelled beyond compare,

We travel far to every land
From Narbon to Schluraffen land,
From there we go to Montflascon [2]
And reach the land of Narragon. [3]
Each port, shore we investigate
And travel far with dreadful fate,
As yet however we've not scanned
The port where we would like to land,
Our traveling will never end
For no one knows to where he'd wend.
We find no rest by day or night,
For none of us sees wisdom's light,
And many a comrade with us errs,
They're satellites and courtiers, [4]
They follow us where'er we go,
The last are they on shipboard though,
And come along in hope of gain.
They're heedless, senseless, quite inane,
With much precariousness we fare,
For no one heeds or glances e'er
At compass, map or hourglass
Or watches how the time doth pass.
The constellations heed we little,
Boötes, Ursa not a tittle,
Arcturus not, nor Hyades,
And so we strike Symplegades. [5]
Our vessel suffers quite a stiff
Bump when it runs against the cliff,
The cliffs destroy the hull and deck
And few can swim to clear the wreck.
We billow through the stormy main

And hardly get to land again
Through Scylla, Syrtis, and Charybdis
And know not where the proper course is.
Of wonders all this is the least:
We spy full many a marvelous beast,
Dolphins and sirens do we meet,
Who sing us many a ditty sweet
And make of us a sleepy band
So ne'er we have a hope to land,
And we discover by and by
The Cyclops with the cyclic eye.
Ulysses stabbed this eye in turn
So Cyclops never might discern
Him, doing him no injury,
Except to bellow furiously
Just like an ox that feels a blow.
Away Ulysses then did go
And let him bellow, weep, and groan
And tossed at him full many a stone.
That Cyclops eye it grew again
As he espied this foolish train,
So widely opened he his eye,
His countenance was hid well-nigh.
His mouth it reached from ear to ear,
He swallowed fools both far and near.
The others who escaped that hour
Antiphates them did devour [6]
With all his Laestrygonians
Who deal with fools of many brands,
For nothing else these people eat
Day in, day out but dunce's meat

And drink their blood instead of wine.
The fools will live there like the swine.
This tale by Homer was invented
That men with wisdom be contented
And not go blithely out to sea.
He lauds Ulysses heartily
Who gave good counsel, wise plans taught,
While war at Troy was being fought,
And how for ten years then with pluck
He plied all seas, enjoying luck.
When Circe with a magic drink
Turned men to beasts that never think,
Ulysses was uncanny shrewd
That he took neither drink nor food
Until the sorceress he deceived
And all his comrades he relieved
With herbs called "Moly," 'tis believed.
Thus many a hardship he'd elude
By wisdom sage, by counsel shrewd,
But since untiring he would fare
Luck could not bless him everywhere,
For one day came an evil blast
That wrecked his sturdy ship at last,
And all his comrades had to drown,
His rudder, ship, and sail went down.
Again his prudence aided him,
Alone and naked he did swim
And yet misfortune came again
When by his son the man was slain [7]
While knocking at his rightful door,
His prudence could not help him more.

Him no one knew on native grounds
Except the faithful baying hounds,
And so he died since no one would
Confess they knew him, as they should.
With this I touch our native plane,
In deepest mire we look for gain,
We'll suffer shipwreck, plain to see,
Mast, sail, and rope will shattered be,
We cannot swim in such a sea,
The waves are high as high can be.
When someone thinks he sits on top
They dash him downward, let him drop.
The wind will drive them up and down,
The ship and all the fools will drown
When once it's sunk with all of them,
For we lack sense and stratagem
To swim ashore and leave the deck,
As did Ulysses midst the wreck.
Though naked, he with more did come
Than he had lost or had at home.
We travel, risking many a slip,
The waves engulf the sturdy ship
And take full many from the crew;
The passengers will mourn and rue,
The owner suffers losses great,
The vessel sways, waves ne'er abate,
And probably a gale will follow
Both ship and passengers to swallow.
Help, counsel wise from us have fled
And finally we'll all be dead.
The wind drives on with violence,

Oh stay at home, ye men of sense
And let our fate a lesson be:
Don't go to sea with levity,
Or else with winds you'll have a fray
As did Ulysses every day.
But though his ship went under fast
Ulysses reached the shore at last.
Hence fools are drowning more and more.
Let each one haste to wisdom's shore
And take the rudder firm in hand,
So that he's conscious where he'll land.
Who's wise will get to shore with ease,
We've fools enough apart from these.
The best is he who'll always know
What he should do and what forego,
Whom no one needs to drill and teach,
Since wisdom he himself does preach.
Good he too who no other spurns
And discipline and wisdom learns,
But who of these is not aware
With all the other fools must fare.
But if perchance he's missed the ship
Upon the next one will he slip.
To cronies easily he'll cling
And with them "Gaudeamus" sing [8]
Or else the dunce's melody.
We've many brothers left at sea
And eke this ship a wreck will be. [9]

A fool is he who does not see,
When dogged by mishap he may be,
That wisely he must be resigned;
Misfortune will not be declined.

109. CONTEMPT OF MIS-FORTUNE

Misfortune makes sighs numerous
And yet it's sought by many of us,
Hence never should a man complain
When boats are wrecked in stormy main.

Misfortunes may be small, I own,
But rarely one arrives alone.
An ancient proverb used to say:
Ill luck and hair grow every day.[1]
'Tis better ne'er to start a thing,
One knows not what its end will bring.
Whoe'er would travel o'er the sea
To luck and weather let him see.
He'll make false headway rapidly
Who travels 'gainst the wind at sea.
With friendly wind the wise man sails,
A fool upsets his ship and fails.
The wise man firmly holds in hand
The rudder, then he reaches land.
A fool has learned no navigation
And often suffers ruination,
A wise man pilots friends and all;
Ere he's aware, a fool will fall.
Had Alexander used no care,
When out to open sea he'd fare,
Which tossed his ship from side to side,
Had he not heeded time and tide
He would have perished mid the brine
And not been poisoned drinking wine.
Pompey won great celebrity
By forcing robbers off the sea.
He drove away the pirates all,
In Egypt, though, he took a fall.
Those prizing wisdom, virtue grand,
Though naked, they will swim to land,
Thus speaks Sebastianus Brant.

Some chide all men for this or that
And hang the bells upon the cat [1]
Yet hesitate to own to that.

110. SLANDER OF THE GOOD

Full many a man will have delight
In all the fools of whom I write
And useful lessons too will learn,
How fatuousness he may spurn,
But some resent the implication,
They think I've prejudiced their station

But dare not say it openly.
They scold the poem more than me
And on the cat the bells they place
Which once their fool-ears used to grace.
A mangy horse for long can't bear
The curry comb upon his hair.
Toss out to many dogs a bone,
The one that's hit will howl alone,
For knowingly I'd fain admit:
All fools will censure me and twit,
And say: This man it can't behoove
To censure fools and e'er reprove,
And show why each is far from good,
For each one says whate'er he would
And moans about a pinching shoe.
My fool's book, does it anger you?
I beg of you to pass it by,
I ask no one to come and buy
Unless you'd enter wisdom's state
And take the cap from off your pate.
I've made an effort mine to doff,
It will not come entirely off.
You chide what ne'er you comprehend?
Then you require this book, my friend!
Each man to what he would desire,
To what he fondly would aspire;
Who'd contradict veracity
And would be wise, a fool is he.[2]

To play the fool would e'er be fun
If one could stop when he'd begun,
But who would try it soon will learn
That he'll be blocked at every turn.

III. APOLOGY OF THE POET

A fool is he, a silly loon,[1]
Who pays a workman far too soon,
He never plies an honest trade
Who ere he's finished would be paid.

The pay for work that's scarce begun
Is seldom earned by anyone.
All work will slowly go ahead
Rewarded with devoured bread.
If they had paid me in advance
To spare the fools my savage glance,
I'd heed them not and tell them how
The payment had been spent by now,
And I would not be satisfied,
For things on earth will ne'er abide,
They're useless folly, idle, vain.
Had I writ this for earthly gain
I fear the meed had been but small,
I'd not have written this at all,
But since I've done it, as I should,
For godly honor, worldly good,
No coin or empty favor could
E'er tempt me, nor the temporal lust,
So help me God, in whom I trust.
And yet I know I'll find much blame
For things I've written o'er my name.
From good men I will not resent it,
I'll take the censure if they've meant it.
Heaven my witness here: If I
Have mentioned aught in which I lie
Or contradict our Lord's intents,
The soul's salvation, honor, sense,
Such censure I will gladly bear,
I'd guard our faith here, anywhere.
Of every man I pray but this:
That he will take it not amiss

And will not scold me angrily
Nor think of me disgracefully.
I wrote it not with such design,
But well I know what fate is mine.
From flowers blessed with fragrance sweet
The bee takes honey, 'tis her meat,
But when the spider comes to feed,
She looks for poison, that's her meed.
This no one's spared: That we're inclined
To act as does our very kind,
Where nothing good doth lie about
No good can e'er be taken out.
Who pays no heed to wisdom's cry
Will slander me and pass me by,
But by his utterance he'll be shown
To be an idiotic clown.
For many a fool I've seen who'd try [2]
To elevate himself on high
Like Lebanon's green spreading tree,
Who thought of folly he was free.
I waited long, I heard him not,
I sought him, yet he answered not.
That place one finds nor far nor wide
Where that same fool did once reside.
If you have ears, then mark and hear!
I'm silent, but the wolf is near.
A fool chides many a man before
He realizes what's in store.
If you could shadow every neighbor
You'd see the cares with which they labor.
Peruse this dunce's book or no,

Why my shoe pinches I do know.
If men should scold me, saying: "Please,
O doctor, cure your own disease,
For you are also foolish, odd—"
I know it, I confess to God,
Of folly I was never free,
I've joined the fool's fraternity.
I pull the cap which I would doff,
Yet my fool's cap will not come off,
But I've applied great industry,
And much have learned, as you may see,
That numerous arrant fools I know,
And hope, if God but wills it so,
That I'll improve in time through wit
If God will grant such benefit.
Let each one guard lest he may fail
And lest fool's curry comb prevail
And lest the wand grow old in hand.
Let every fool this understand,
So speaks Sebastianus Brant,
Who urges men to wisdom's state
No matter what be their estate.
Good workers never come too late.

Of fools such tidings I did tell
So that all men would know them well;
But if you're prudent through and through,
Read Vergil's words, they're meant for you.[1]

112. THE WISE MAN

A good, wise man of prudence rare,
As one can find scarce anywhere
In all the world, is Socrates—
Apollo gave him gifts like these—.
His own judge he, and wisely taught.

Where he lacks wisdom, fails in aught,
He gives himself the acid test,
Heeds not the nobleman's behest
Nor things the common herd would beg.
He's oval-shaped, is like an egg,
That never alien blemish may
Adhere to him in slippery way.
How long in Cancer days are bright,[2]
How long in Capricorn the night,
He plans with wisest industry
That e'er his house in order be,
That every syllable he'd say
May fair be deemed in every way,
That e'er the T-square will be true
And firm what he may measure too
And ward off all adversity
Which off in distance he may see.
Ere welcome sleep doth bless his eyes
He thinks and would himself chastise
For what he's done the livelong day
And what he's failed to do or say
And what betimes he should have done
And what untimely he's begun;
Why this he did without a reason,
Without decorum, out of season,
Or wasted time quite uselessly
Or stuck to something stubbornly
Which better might have been corrected,
Or why the paupers he neglected,
Wherefore his heart was oft not free
Of sorrow, base antipathy,

And why this deed he did not shun
But left the other one undone
And why himself he'd often bleed,
Preferring gain to honor's meed,
Oft doing wrong in word, mien, deed,
And giving honesty no heed,
And letting nature play her part,
But disciplining not his heart.
Thus work and word he ponders ay
From morning e'en to end of day
And musing things in pensive mood,
Rejecting evil, praising good;
The path it is of wisdom's brood.
'Tis such a man that's limned for us
In verse by famed Vergilius.
The man who'd live like that on earth
In God's eyes he would merit worth,
True wisdom he would understand,
'Twould take him home to fatherland,
May God place that in every hand,
I hope, Sebastianus Brant.

Deo gratias.

END OF THE SHIP OF FOOLS

Here ends the Ship of Fools, which for profit, salutary instruction, admonition and pursuit of wisdom, reason and good manners, also for contempt and punishment of folly, blindness, error, and stupidity of all stations and kinds of men, with special zeal, pains, and labor is compiled by Sebastianus Brant, doctor in both laws. Printed at Basel at the Shrovetide which one calls the Fool's Festival, in the year after Christ's birth one thousand four hundred ninety-four.

1494

Nothing without Cause

JO. B. VON OLPE

COMMENTARY

A PROLOGUE TO THE SHIP OF FOOLS (EIN VORRED IN DAS NARREN
SCHYFF)   57

Probably all three cuts are by the Master of the Bergmann shop
(cf. Introduction, p. 20). The words "har noch" (cut 2) mean
"come along." For Dr. Griff, see note 12 to chap. 76, p. 381.

1. For the reasons why *land* vehicles are introduced, see Introduction, p. 11 f. Under the third cut verses 23–27 of Psalm 107
(Vulgate, Psalm 106) are quoted in Latin, viz., "Hi sunt qui
descendunt mare in navibus," etc.

2. Original: *der ist fatuus der gfatter min,* a pun on *fatuus,*
Latin for "foolish," and German *gfatter,* "godfather."

3. Terence *Andria* I. 1. 41: "veritas odium parit."

4. Frankfurt was famous for its fairs (*Messen*).

1. OF USELESS BOOKS (VON UNNUTZEN BUCHERN)   62

The cut is by an inferior artist.

1. The three (sometimes four) lines are the motto to the
chapter which follows; often though not always they describe
the woodcut under it.

2. The original has a pun: *des tütschen ordens,* referring to the
famous German Order of Knights and to those ignorant of
Latin.

3. *Gucklus,* a variant of the classical Latin *cuculus.*

2. OF GOOD COUNCILORS (VON GUTEN RETEN)   64

Woodcut: Inferior artist.

1. The reference is to young, inexperienced councilmen who
have no opinions of their own and become the tools of their
older, often unscrupulous colleagues. Cf. lines 9 and 10 of the
text below. Barclay translates: "Such is as wyse a man/As he
that wolde seeth a quycke Sowe in a Pan."

2. II Sam. 16 and 17. Chusi is Hushai. In many of his biblical
references Brant may have used other sources not known to us.

3. Matt. 7: 2.   4. Prov. 21: 30.

3. OF GREED (VON GYTIKEIT)   66

Woodcut: Inferior artist. The words "gnad her" (mercy, sir)
are a greeting.

4. OF INNOVATIONS (VON NUWEN FUNDEN)   68

Woodcut: The older fool is Uly or Ueli, a notorious tippler, and *stouffen* means "goblet." Since the chapter does not refer to drinking, the cut may be an older cartoon, revived for this chapter and later dated 1494. *Ungeschaffen* means "ugly."

1. St. Lienhart was the patron saint of prisoners.

2. *Schusselkorb* seems to be a medieval hairdresser's appliance for setting and shaping curls.

5. OF OLD FOOLS (VON ALTEN NARREN)   70

Woodcut: Inferior artist. "Haintz Nar" means "Henry Fool."

1. Susanna: cf. *The Apocrypha and Pseudepigrapha of the Old Testament in English*, with introductions and critical and explanatory notes to the several books edited in coöperation with many scholars by R. H. Charles. Vol. I, Apocrypha. Oxford, Clarendon Press, 1913, p. 650 ff.

6. OF THE TEACHING OF CHILDREN (VON LER DER KIND)   72

Woodcut: Master.

1. I Sam. 4.

2. According to Plutarch *Paidagogia* vii. 3, Phoenix was the teacher of Achilles. The following examples are from the same source.

3. *Winterbutz*, a strawman representing winter, who is routed by spring.

7. OF CAUSING DISCORD (VON ZWYTRACHT MACHEN)   76

Woodcut: Master.

1. II Sam. 15.   2. Num. 16.

3. I Macc. 7. Charles, *Apocrypha*, p. 91.

4. II Sam. 1.   5. II Sam. 4.

8. OF NOT FOLLOWING GOOD ADVICE (NIT VOLGEN GUTEM RATT)   78

Woodcut: Master.

1. Tob. 4: 19. Charles, *Apocrypha*, p. 213.

2. Gen. 19: 26.   3. I Kings 12.   4. Dan. 4.

5. Macc. 9. Charles, *Apocrypha*, p. 96. The allusion to Joram is not biblical. See I Esd. 1: 19. Charles, *Apocrypha*, p. 21.

6. II Sam. 17. Brant means not Saul but Absalom and Hushai.

9. OF BAD MANNERS (VON BOSEN SYTTEN)   80

Woodcut: Inferior artist.

1. The story of the man who bit off his father's nose for rearing

him as a gallows bird is as old as Aesop, but no known source before Brant mentions the son's name.

10. OF TRUE FRIENDSHIP (VON WORER FRUNTSCHAFFT)   82
Woodcut: Master.
   1. That is, Damon.   2. I Sam. 31: 5.   3. Matt. 22: 39.
   4. The closest biblical references would be Num. 11: 11 and 14: 11. But perhaps Brant had another source.

11. CONTEMPT OF HOLY WRIT (VERACHTUNG DER GSCHRIFT)   84
Woodcut: Inferior artist. Note the bier, the snakelike club, and the books.
   1. In 1476 a shepherd and piper of Niklashausen on the Tauber, Hans Behem, asserted that he had seen the Holy Virgin. He was finally burned as a sorcerer. See *Haupts Zeitschrift*, VIII, 312 ff.
   2. We follow Zarncke, but *ertoubt* may mean merely "deaf."
   3. We might see in this a startling prophecy of the approaching two hundred years of religious strife which Germany was facing with the advent of the Reformation.

12. OF HEEDLESS FOOLS (VON UNBESINTEN NARREN)   86
Woodcut: Inferior artist.
   1. I Macc. 12: 42 ff. Charles, *Apocrypha*, p. 113.
   2. II Macc. 8: 10. Charles, *Apocrypha*, p. 142.
   3. The Jews are meant.   4. II Sam. 2: 17.

13. OF AMOURS (VON BUOLSCHAFFT)   88
Woodcut: Master.
   1. For other instances of the use of this idea, cf. H. Bluhm in *Modern Language Notes*, LVI, 139.
   2. Cf. Ovid *Metam.* i. 468 ff.
   3. Medea did not burn either child, she slew them both.
   4. Judg. 19: 20.
   5. Read "Bath-Sheba." The form in the text is from the Basel Vulgate of 1490. Cf. II Sam. 11.
   6. That is, Delilah. Judg. 16.   7. I Kings 11.
   8. II Sam. 13.   9. Gen. 39.
   10. Aristotle was ridden by Phyllis, according to medieval legend.
   11. The sorcerer Vergil was suspended in a basket by a concubine, according to medieval legend.

14. OF INSOLENCE TOWARD GOD (VON VERMESSENHEIT GOTZ) 92
    Woodcut: Master.
15. OF FOOLISH PLANS (VON NARRECHTEM ANSLAG) 94
    Woodcut: Master.
    1. Cf. Luke 14: 28–30.   2. Dan. 4: 26–30.
    3. Gen. 10: 8–10 and 11: 9.
    4. It is not clear why Brant associates labyrinths with the Nile.
16. OF GLUTTONY AND FEASTING (VON FULLEN UND PRASSEN) 96
    Woodcut: Master.
    1. Gen. 9: 20.   2. Gen. 19: 33.
    3. Matt. 14. But the drunkenness of Herod is not stated.
    4. Exod. 32.   5. Isa. 5: 11.
    6. Told by Herodotus and Justinus.   7. I Kings 20: 16.
    8. When he killed Clitus.   9. Luke 16: 19 ff.
    10. Prov. 23: 34.   11. Prov. 23: 31–32.
17. OF USELESS RICHES (VON UNNUTZEM RICHTUM) 100
    Woodcut: Inferior artist.
18. OF SERVING TWO MASTERS (VON DIENST ZWEYER HERREN) 102
    Woodcut: Inferior artist.
19. OF IDLE TALK (VON VIL SCHWETZEN) 104
    Woodcut: Inferior artist.
    1. Prov. 18: 13.   2. I Sam. 25.   3. Prov. 29: 11.
    4. Examples from Plutarch *Paidagogia* xiv.
20. OF FINDING TREASURES (VON SCHATZ FYNDEN) 108
    Woodcut: Perhaps Master.
    1. Brant means Achan. Cf. Josh. 7. Achor is the valley in which
    Achan was stoned.
21. OF CHIDING AND ERRING ONESELF (VON STROFFEN UND SELB
    TUN) 110
    Woodcut: Inferior artist.
    1. Cf. Matt. 7: 4 and 5.
    2. Gentilis (eighth century) and Mesue (fourteenth century)
    were physicians who wrote treatises on fever. Brant's sources
    for their mode of death are not known.
    3. Cf. Juvenal *Satires* viii. 140.
    4. Judg. 20. The sin of the Israelites does not follow clearly
    from the biblical text. Perhaps Brant thinks that they sacrificed
    to God too late. See verse 26.

22. THE TEACHING OF WISDOM (DIE LER DER WISHEIT)   112
    Woodcut: Master.
    1. For this chapter, cf. Prov. 8.
23. OF VAUNTING LUCK (VON UBERHEBUNG GLUCKS)   114
    Woodcut: Inferior artist.
24. OF TOO MUCH CARE (VON ZU VIL SORG)   116
    Woodcut: Inferior artist.
25. OF BORROWING TOO MUCH (VON ZUO BORG UFF NEMEN)   118
    Woodcut: Inferior artist.
    1. Promissory notes will bring the wolf to your door, but he will not relieve your distress by eating up the notes. The woodcut refers to this.
    2. Prov. 22: 26 and 27.
26. OF USELESS WISHING (VON UNNUTZEN WUNSCHEN)   120
    Woodcut: Inferior artist.
    1. Cf. Ovid *Metam.* xi. 102 ff. Brant does not reproduce accurately the story of Ovid. The cut follows Brant's text.
    2. Juvenal *Satires* x.   3. Gen. 34.
    4. Juvenal *Satires* x. 360, but modified by Brant.
27. OF USELESS STUDYING (VON UNNUTZEM STUDIEREN)   124
    Woodcut: Master.
    1. In his notes, pp. 346–55, Zarncke has an excursus on the tortures to which students were exposed.
    2. Ridiculous examples of the sophistic method of teaching.
    3. *Homil.* iv to chapter 7 of Exodus.
    4. Strobel believes that it means: the unsuccessful student turns waiter.
28. OF SPEAKING AGAINST GOD (VON WIDER GOTT REDEN)   126
    Woodcut: Inferior artist.
    1. Num. 14.   2. Rom. 11: 34, 35.
29. WHO JUDGES OTHERS (DER ANDER LUT URTEILT)   128
    Woodcut: Inferior artist.
30. OF TOO MANY BENEFICES (VON VILE DER PFRUNDEN)   130
    Woodcut: Inferior artist.
    1. The abuses in filling church offices were a subject for much discussion. See Zarncke, pp. 359–62. But Brant does not consider the evil in its political aspects.
    2. II Kings 4: 40.

3. Simon, the magician; Acts, 8. For Gehasi, see II Kings 5.

4. A "presence" was the profit from a residential benefice, an "absence" (according to Brant, at least) that from one enjoyed *in absentia*. The latter were more lucrative.

31. OF SEEKING DELAY (VON UFFSCHLAG SUCHEN)   132
Woodcut: Master.

1. Latin for "tomorrow." Note the cut.

32. OF GUARDING WIVES (VON FROWEN HUETTEN)   134
Woodcut: Master. "huet fast" means "guard well."

1. Ovid *Metam.* iv. 610 ff.   2. Ovid *Her.* xvi, xvii, also vii.
3. *Frömd*, lecherous, lewd.

33. OF ADULTERY (VON EEBRUCH)   136
Woodcut: Inferior artist.

1. The best explanation of the cat is that she represents the wife, who soon learns to enjoy adultery, as the cat learns to enjoy catching mice. Tickling the husband's nose with a reed means lulling him off his guard through flattery.

2. Brant refers to the *Lex Julia* of Emperor Augustus.

3. Cato the Younger. Cf. Plutarch's life of him, chap. 25.

4. Lucretia.   5. Juvenal *Satires* vi. 345.

6. Gellius xvii. 18.   7. Gen. 20: 18.   8. Judg. 19, 20.

9. Esther 7: 8.   10. Gen. 20: 2.

11. That is, suffer the fate of a sparrow, in whose nest the cuckoo places its eggs to be hatched.

34. FOOLS NOW AS BEFORE (NARR HUR ALS VERN)   140
Woodcut: Master.

1. Exod. 2; Acts 7: 22.

35. OF READY ANGER (VON LUCHTLICH ZYRNEN)   142
Woodcut: Master.

1. Valerius Maximus iv. 1.

2. The examples are from Plutarch *Paidagogia* xiv. 14.

36. OF COMPLACENCY (VON EYGENRICHTIKEIT)   144
Woodcut: Master.

1. II Pet. 2: 5, and I Pet. 3: 19 and 20.   2. Num. 16.

3. Translation of *singularis ferus* in Psalm 80.

4. Refers to the indivisibility of the Church.

37. OF CHANCE (VON GLUCKES FALL)   146
Woodcut: Master.
    1. Cf. Schiller, *Wilhelm Tell:* "Wer Tränen ernten will, muss Liebe säen."

38. OF PATIENTS WHO DO NOT OBEY (VON KRANCKEN DIE NIT VOLGEN)   148
Woodcut: Master. In the first edition this accompanied No. 55 by error.
    1. Ovid *Amores* 91, 92, 115, 116.
    2. I Macc. 4, 9 and 10, and chaps. 8 and 9. Charles, *Apocrypha,* p. 79. But there is no basis for Brant's notion that Judas died because of his alliance with the Romans.
    3. II Kings 20.   4. Matt. 9: 2.

39. OF OPEN PLANS (VON OFFLICHEM ANSCHLAG)   152
Woodcut: Master.
    1. II Macc. 14: 30 ff. Charles, *Apocrypha,* p. 152.

40. TAKING OFFENSE AT FOOLS (AN NARREN SICH STOSSEN)   154
Woodcut: Master.
    1. He strokes his own beard and is a fool.
    2. A pun is involved, for *an narren sich stossen* means also "to bump against fools."
    3. Cf. Ovid *Metam.* x. 561 ff.
    4. I Kings 13: 33, and 14: 10 and 11.

41. PAYING NO HEED TO TALK (NIT ACHTEN UFF ALL RED)   156
Woodcut: Master.
    1. That is, pay no heed to a maligner; he is like a hammerless bell.
    2. Is Brant thinking of his friend a Lapide, who entered the Carthusian monastery in 1487—a step which Brant may often have been inclined to take himself? See Zeydel in *Modern Language Quarterly,* IV, 209 ff.

42. OF SCORNERS (VON SPOTT VOGELEN)   158
Woodcut: Master.
    1. This entire chapter is based upon chap. 9 of Proverbs.
    2. II Sam. 25.   3. Nehem. 4: 1 ff.   4. II Kings 2: 23 f.
    5. II Sam. 16: 5 ff.

43. CONTEMPT OF ETERNAL JOY (VERACHTUNG EWIGER FREYT)   160
Woodcut: Master.

44. NOISE IN CHURCH (GEBRACHT IN DER KIRCHEN)   162
Woodcut: Master.
  1. Matt. 21: 12 f.

45. OF COURTING MISFORTUNE (VON MUTWILLIGEM UNGEFELL) 164
Woodcut: Master. "In geschicht recht" means "It serves him
right."
  1. A variant of these lines is found in some of the Faust books.

46. OF THE POWER OF FOOLS (VON DER GEWALT DER NARREN) 166
Woodcut: Master.
  1. Prov. 28: 26.   2. Eccles. 10: 17.   3. Eccles. 10: 16.
  4. Eccles. 4: 13.   5. Prov. 28: 28.   6. Prov. 28: 12.
  7. Eccles. 28: 21.   8. Prov. 24: 23.
  9. That is, the spiritual as well as the temporal power.
  10. Sallust *Bell. Jug.* 35.   11. Exod. 18.
  12. Judg. 3: 16 ff.   13. Judg. 16: 5 ff.
  14. II Macc. 4: 32 ff. Charles, *Apocrypha*, p. 137.
  15. I Kings 15: 18 ff.   16. I Macc. 12: 43. Charles, *Apocrypha*, 113.

47. ON THE ROAD OF SALVATION (VON DEM WEG DER SELLIKEIT) 170
Woodcut: Master.
  1. Exod. 12: 37.   2. Joshua and Caleb.

48. A JOURNEYMAN'S SHIP (*No title in original*) 172
Woodcut: Master. The coat-of-arms on the sail is that of Basel.
  1. Plutarch *Paidagogia* ix. 20.
  2. Trading was reputed to be particularly sharp in Köln, and
bids there were notoriously low.

49. BAD EXAMPLE OF PARENTS (BOS EXEMPEL DER ELTERN) 176
Woodcut: Inferior artist.
  1. Cf. chapter 6.   2. Juvenal *Satires* xiv. 41.
  3. Plutarch *Paidagogia* iii. 3.

50. OF SENSUAL PLEASURE (VON WOLLUST) 178
Woodcut: Master.
  1. Prov. 7: 10 ff.
  2. The original has *wollust* for "pleasure." In Brant's day this
did not quite mean "lust" as yet, at least according to Zarncke.
  3. Prov. 7: 22, 23.   4. Horace *Epistles* i. 2, 55.
  5. Prov. 5: 4.

51. KEEPING SECRETS (HEYMLICHEIT VERSWIGEN)   180
Woodcut: Inferior artist.
1. Cf. chapters 9 and 39 above.   2. Servius *Ad Aen.* iv. 455.
3. I Kings 21.
4. Isa. 24: 16. The Vulgate has: Secretum mihi, secretum meum mihi.

52. MARRYING FOR THE SAKE OF GOODS (WIBEN DURCH GUTZ WILLEN)   182
Woodcut: Master.
1. Prov. 21: 19.   2. Athaliah. II Kings 11.
3. According to Tobit 3: 8 ff., Asmodeus is the devil of marriage. Charles, *Apocrypha*, p. 209.
4. Cf. the Book of Ruth.
5. "I accuse you, I am scratched (pig Latin) by you."

53. OF ENVY AND HATRED (VON NYD UND HAS)   184
Woodcut: Master. The key to this cut is found in the medieval Neithart Fuchs collection (Kürschner's *Deutsche National-Litteratur*, VII, 163, 189)—see the two cuts there—where Neithart, dispensing wine, releases bees to plague the peasants. Cf. also *ibid.*, p. 165: "Da lag ich in den vasz verschmogen, etc." Neithart is mentioned in line 3 of the motto. A fire on top of a hill in the background probably refers to the raging of hatred and envy as described in line 1 of the triplet. Bees and wasps also mean envy.
1. Aglauros: Ovid *Metam.* ii. 730 ff.

54. OF IMPATIENCE OF PUNISHMENT (VON UNGEDULT DER STRAFF)   186
Woodcut: Master.
1. The instrument of fools; harps and lutes were of higher caliber.
2. Eccles. 7: 6.

55. OF FOOLISH MEDICINE (VON NARRECHTER ARTZNY)   188
Woodcut: Master. In the first edition this was erroneously placed with chap. 38.
1. *Krüterbüchlin* (herb book) was the regular term for a medical book.
2. The reference may be either to a salve box or to a book of receipts. Archer Taylor, *Problems in German Literary History*

of the Fifteenth and Sixteenth Centuries, p. 71, believes the reference is to the unnamed woman who anointed the feet of Jesus in the house of Simon, the leper, at Bethania.

3. Supposedly a notorious quack who practiced in Basel.

56. OF THE END OF POWER (VON END DES GEWALTTES)   190
Woodcut: Same as No. 37.
1. That is, Darius Hystaspes. But the reference should be to Darius Codomannus.
2. Jth. 1.   3. Cf. chap. 109, lines 7–8, p. 356.
4. I Kings 21 and 22.   5. I Kings 16: 9 ff.

57. PREDESTINATION OF GOD (FURWISSENHEYT GOTTES)   194
Woodcut: Master.
1. Striped clothes were a sign of worldliness and distinction, as opposed to the clerical and learned states.
2. That is, they do not get further than the first two words of Psalm 1.
3. A reference to the land of milk and honey later connected with the *Schluraffenland*. Cf. chap. 108 and Introduction, p. 9.
4. Cf. Daniel. Brant cites from *Decretum* ii. 23, 4, 22.
5. Matt. 20: 1–16.

58. OF FORGETTING ONESELF (SYN SELBS VERGESSEN)   198
Woodcut: Master.
1. Terence *Andria* iv. 1, 12.

59. OF INGRATITUDE (VON UNDANCKBERKEYT)   200
Woodcut: Master.

60. OF SELF-COMPLACENCY (VON IM SELBS WOLGEFALLEN)   202
Woodcut: Inferior artist.
1. Juvenal *Satires* ii. 99 ff.   2. Terence *Heaut. Tim.* ii. 2, 11.
3. Upon the old bridge over the Neckar at Heidelberg stood the figure of an ape, with humorous verses mocking vain passers-by.
4. Cf. Ovid, *Metam.* x. 243 ff.
5. Ovid. *Metam.* iii. 407 ff.

61. OF DANCING (VON DANTZEN)   204
Woodcut: Master.
1. The first mass at which a young priest officiates—an occasion for celebration.

62. OF SERENADING AT NIGHT (VON NACHTES HOFYEREN)   2(
   Woodcut: Master.

   1. The reference, missed by Zarncke and the other com
   mentators, is to an old Strassburg custom, forbidden by Cit
   Council in 1466, whereby fishermen held a procession ever
   Whitmonday, bearing fish in vats and making much nois
   ridiculing and insulting passers-by and spreading scandal. C
   Stöber's review of Zarncke's edition in *St. Galler Blätter*, x
   (1855).

63. OF BEGGARS (VON BETTLEREN)   20
   Woodcut: Master.

   1. Beggars gave the authorities in the Middle Ages muc
   trouble. Basel regulated their life and traffic well and estab
   lished a camp for them at the Kohlenberg, where they ha
   special privileges.
   2. Brant puns on the word, making it "Bettelheim" (beggars
   home).
   3. The next twelve lines contain examples of underworld slang
   They cannot all be adequately translated.
   4. The heraldic poets, like Suchenwirt, who glorified noble:
   and their families.
   5. That is, to write heraldic poetry.
   6. St. James of Compostella in Spain.
   7. Rivoglio, an Italian wine.
   8. This chapter, now usually referred to as the argot
   (*Rotwelsch*) chapter, was used by Gengenbach in his *Liber
   vagatorum*.

64. OF BAD WOMEN (VON BOSEN WIBERN)   212
   Woodcut: Same as No. 35.

   1. Prologue, l. 123 ff.   2. That is, Athaliah. II Kings 11.
   3. The father of the Pierides who challenged the Muses and
   were turned into magpies. Ovid *Metam.* v. 295 ff.
   4. Ovid *Metam.* vi. 146. The mother of the children was Niobe.
   5. Calphurnia, so called by some, by others (e. g., Valerius
   Maximus, 8, 3) Gaja Afrania, is a legendary woman whose
   chattering in court is supposed to have prompted the practice
   of debarring women from speaking in court. Perhaps the name
   Calphurnia was suggested by that of Caesar's shrewish wife.

6. Ovid *Metam*. vi. 587.   7. Eccles. 7: 26, 27.

8. Prov. 30: 15 ff. Brant takes up verse 21 first.

9. Esther 1: 11 ff.   10. Juvenal *Satires* vi. 638.

11. *Ibid*. vi. 620.   12. *Ibid*. vi. 655.

13. Ovid *Ibis* 321. The reference is to Alexander of Pherae.

14. The concubine of Alexander the Great.

65. OF ATTENTION TO THE STARS (VON ACHTUNG DES GSTIRNS)   216
Woodcut: Master.

1. This chapter becomes more amusing when we consider that Brant himself, in his shorter poems, often revealed faith in portents. Eberth, *Die Sprichwörter in Seb. Brants Narrenschiff*, however, believes that Brant's superstitiousness was only feigned.

2. *Decretum*. ii. 26.

3. Cf. Gen. 15. But Brant must have had other sources.

4. I Sam. 28.

66. OF EXPERIENCE OF ALL LANDS (VON ERFARUNG ALLER LAND) 220
Woodcut: Inferior artist.

1. This chapter, interesting because of the reference to the first voyage of Columbus, also throws light upon Brant's geographical concepts.

2. *Um die ganz welt*. In the Middle Ages generally it was held that the earth is round.

3. Ca. B. C. 320.   4. That is, the equator.

5. A land in the far north.   6. Is Lapland meant?

7. Assuming that "in Portugal" and "in Hispania" are characteristically loose expressions, we interpret these lines as a reference to the recent discoveries of Columbus, of which Brant knew, having collaborated with the publisher Bergmann in editing the famous Columbus letter.

8. Pliny the Elder *Hist. Natur*. ii. 1.

9. The friend and partner of Bacchus.

10. Brant thinks that the popular "Berchtentag" observed in South Germany on January 6, when masked processions take place, has something to do with Bacchus.

11. Cf. Eccles. 7: 1, and Psalm 144: 4.

12. It is not clear where Brant got this information.

13. Appollonius of Tyana, who lived ca. A. D. 100.

67. NOT WISHING TO BE A FOOL (NIT WELLEN EYN NARR SYN)   226
Woodcut: Inferior artist.

1. Prov. 27: 22.

2. Concepts for "delusion" and "deception" found also in Reinmar von Zweter (thirteenth century) and Boner (fourteenth century). The words *won* (Wahn, delusion) and *btrieg*, *betriegen* (*Betrug*, *betrügen*, deception, deceive) are involved.

3. That is, the gout.

68. NOT TAKING A JOKE (SCHYMPF NIT VERSTON)   230
Woodcut: Master.

1. Or: If you would bowl you must pay the fee.

2. Esther 3: 2 ff.

69. DOING EVIL AND NOT BEING ON GUARD (BOS DUN UND NIT WARTEN)   232
Woodcut: Master.

1. Judg. 1: 6.

2. Ovid *Trist*. iii. 11. 39 ff., and *Ars Amat*. i. 653.

3. Cf. Ovid *Ars Amat*. i. 645 for Busiris. Diomede of Thrace is meant, who fed human beings to his horses. For Phalaris see the references under Berillus above.

4. Esther 7: 10.

5. Proverbial: *Fides nimia equum abegit*.

6. Prov. 23: 6 and 7.

70. NOT PROVIDING IN TIME (NIT FURSEHEN BY ZYT)   234
Woodcut: Master.

1. Perhaps Brant's idea of hibernation.

2. Prov. 10: 5.

3. Prov. 20: 4. This applies more to the climate of Palestine than to that of Germany.

4. Prov. 6: 6–8.

71. QUARRELING AND GOING TO COURT (ZANCKEN UND ZU GERICHT GON)   236
Woodcut: Master.

1. In Brant's letter of dedication to the *Panormia* (1499) of Ivo of Chartres, he complains in a similar vein.

2. *Petterle* might also stand for "legal blank"—*in petitorio*.

72. OF COARSE FOOLS (VON GROBEN NARREN) 238
Woodcut: Master.

1. The sow-bell is a symbol for billingsgate. So far as we know, the word *Grobian*, "ruffian," is used for the first time here in literature.

2. *Wie wol der gürtel hat kein glimpf*, lit.: "although the belt (i. e. the monk's cord) has no pendant" (or: no decency). The word *glimpf* has both meanings.

3. In the original she sings the "Moringer" song, a folksong. Brant interprets it as a sow's song because the word *mor* also means "sow." The pun is not apt because the "Moringer" song is not indecent.

4. A notorious priest under Otto the Jovial who played his pranks in and near Vienna in the fourteenth century. His escapades are narrated in the *Narrenbuch*.

5. A prankster featured in the late medieval epic, *Der grosse Rosengarten*.

6. As described in the third book of Persius.

7. See chap. 14, line 1, p. 92.

8. A pun is involved, *filz*, "felt," also meaning a rude peasant.

9. Corrupted French for "faites grande chère et belle chère"— eat, drink, and be merry.

10. Cf. chap. 11, lines 7 ff, p. 85, line 2.

73. OF BECOMING A PRIEST (VON GEYSTLICH WERDEN) 242
Woodcut: Same as No. 27.

1. That is, notoriously clumsy.

2. These lines remind us of Luther's sentiments.

3. Exod. 19: 13.   4. II Sam. 6: 7.   5. Num. 16.

74. OF USELESS HUNTING (VON UNNUTZEM JAGEN) 246
Woodcut: Same as No. 18.

1. Gen. 10: 9.   2. Gen. 25: 27.

3. Hubertus and Eustachius are patron saints of hunters.

75. OF BAD MARKSMEN (VON BOSEN SCHUTZEN) 248
Woodcut: Inferior artist.

1. Usually the first prize.

2. He will go home empty-handed.   3. I Sam. 20: 36.

4. Servius *Ad Aen*. iii. 402. See also Archer Taylor, *Problems in Literary History*, p. 71.

76. OF GREAT BOASTING (VON GROSSEM RUEMEN)   251
    Woodcut: Inferior artist.
    1. A boasting old nobleman; see line 20.
    2. That is, as a humble barrel maker.
    3. The people of Mainz had a reputation as prevaricators.
    4. A Swiss city in the canton of Bern (German: Pruntrut). In
    the Burgundian War this town fought on the Burgundian side
    against Basel. The incident is said to have occurred in the
    battle of Murten (1476).
    5. These lines give an ironical description of an imaginary coat-
    of-arms of a would-be nobleman.
    6. A suburb of Strassburg, selected here possibly because of
    the association of *benne*, a peasant's cart, or because it typifies
    a "backwoods" town.
    7. A notorious amusement resort near Strassburg.
    8. *Achten*. It means not "respect," but "censure" (MHG
    âhten, achten).
    9. This is one of the keynotes of German literature, chiefly
    the creation of the middle classes, from Brant's time to the
    present.
    10. Some of the sources for Roman and canon law.
    11. The bagpipe, as usual the fool's instrument.
    12. He is a favorite character of Brant. His name, banner, and
    picture appear also in the woodcuts of the Prologue, repeated
    in the cut to chap. 108. Perhaps Brant identifies himself with
    the castigating doctor. See Zeydel in *Modern Language Notes*,
    LVIII, 340 ff.

77. OF GAMBLERS (VON SPYLERN)   255
    Woodcut: Perhaps Master.
    1. Personified hatred. See No. 53.
    2. In the poem *De Ludo*, formerly ascribed to Vergil.
    3. The original Latin is: "Initio furiis ego sum tribus addita
    quarta" (I, gambling, have been added as the fourth to the
    three Furies). Brant's rendering of this is quaint.

78. OF OPPRESSED FOOLS (VON GDRUCKTEN NARREN)   259
    Woodcut: Inferior artist.
    1. Cf. above, chap. 33, line 71, p. 139, line 3.

79. KNIGHTS AND CLERKS (RUTER UND SCHRIBER)   261
Woodcut: Master.

   1. The original: He must have eaten the liver (*die leber gessen*), i. e., be the scapegoat.

   2. A fee was paid to the lord for safe passage through his domain. This was lucrative. Here Brant is outspoken in his criticism of the authorities for winking at a flagrant abuse.

80. FOOLISH NEWS (NARREHTE BOTTSCHAFFT)   263
Woodcut: Inferior artist. Note the Basel coat-of-arms.

   1. The meaning of these obscure lines seems to be: Holds the envelope of the letter cautiously in his mouth so that the seal will not break.

   2. Simrock in his translation (p. xiii) calls attention to the tradition that the most famous of the processional carnival "ships" started its voyage over land from Aachen (Aix la Chapelle). Archer Taylor, in the *Journal of American Folk Lore*, XLVII, 11, believes the phrase in the text (*hie zwüschen Ach*) means "nowhere." See also Taylor in *Studies in Honor of John Albrecht Walz*, Lancaster, 1941, p. 29.

   3. Cf. Prov. 25: 13.

81. OF COOKS AND WAITERS (VON KOCHEN UND KELLER)   265
Woodcut: Master.

   1. The butlers, etc., are speaking.

   2. A mixture of vinegar and honey—a cooling drink.

   3. Gen. 40.

   4. II Kings 25: 8. Neither biblical reference is appropriate.

82. OF PEASANTS' SQUANDERING (VON BURSCHEM UFFGANG)   268
Woodcut: Master. "Er muss dryn" means "It must go in."

   1. *Bannen und verlüten.* One could be excommunicated because of debts.

   2. *Dri spitz.* The words are also used to refer to a mantrap. The proverbial expression is supposed to mean: "The impossible is attempted nowadays." The illustration, however, shows not a *dri spitz* in the literal sense, but a *vier spitz*.

83. CONTEMPT OF POVERTY (VON VERACHTUNG ARMUT)   271
Woodcut: Same as No. 3.

   1. I Kings 21.

   2. Horace *Odes* i. 22. 9, and Juvenal *Satires* x. 22.

3. M. Curius Dentatus, ob. B.C. 270, conqueror of the Samnites and of Pyrrhus.

4. Mark 10: 24, and Matt. 5: 3.   5. Prov. 21: 6.

6. Prov. 22: 16.   7. Prov. 23: 5.

84. OF PERSISTING IN THE GOOD (VON BEHARREN IN GUTEM)   276
Woodcut: Same as No. 8.

1. Luke 9: 62.   2. Exod. 16: 3.

3. That is, food spewed up and eaten again. Cf. Prov. 26: 11, and II Pet. 2: 22.

4. Rev. 3: 15 ff.   5. Gen. 19: 26.

85. NOT PROVIDING FOR DEATH (NIT FURSEHEN DEN DOT)   278
Woodcut: Master. "Du blibst" means "you stay."

1. Wine drunk as a solemn confirmation of a business deal or contract, here referring to man's contract with Death.

2. Horace *Odes* i. 4. 13.

3. The spirit of the passage, typical of the late Middle Ages, reminds one of the colloquy *Der Ackermann aus Böhmen.*

4. Two popular dances.

5. Probably Diodorus is Brant's source.

6. Herodotus ii. 175 ff. and iii. 10.

7. According to Diodorus, Strabo, and Pliny.

86. OF CONTEMPT OF GOD (VON VERACHTUNG GOTTES)   284
Woodcut: Inferior artist.

1. Cf. chap. 23 above.   2. Gal. 6: 7.   3. II Kings 20.

4. Dan. 5.   5. *Mene tekel upharsin.*

6. Nebuchadnezzar. Dan. 4.

87. OF BLASPHEMING GOD (VON GOTTESLESTERN)   287
Woodcut: Master.

1. Parts of the body of Christ by which it was not uncommon to swear.

2. Lev. 24: 16. 3. II Kings 19.   4. Ovid *Metam.* i. 198.

5. Vergil *Aen.* vii. 648.

6. II Macc. 9: 5 ff. Charles, *Apocrypha,* p. 144.

88. OF TORTURE AND PUNISHMENT BY GOD (VON PLAG UND STROF GOTS)   289
Woodcut: Master.

1. Eccles. 34: 28. Charles, *Apocrypha,* p. 436.

2. Ezek. 14: 13.

89. OF FOOLISH TRADING (VON DORECHTEM WECHSEL)   291
Woodcut: Master.
   1. Cf. chap. 66, line 51, p. 222, line 15.

90. HONOR FATHER AND MOTHER (ERE VATTER UND MUTTER)   293
Woodcut: Master.
   1. Prov. 20: 20.   2. II Sam. 15: 18.   3. Gen. 9: 20 ff.
   4. Is this based upon a misinterpretation of Daniel, 4 and 5, or did Brant have some other source? Beltheshazzar is meant.
   5. II Chron. 32: 21.
   6. Tob. 4: 3. Charles, *Apocrypha*, p. 211.   7. I Kings, 2: 19.
   8. Jer. 35: 2. They were praised by God through the prophets.
   9. Exod. 20: 12.

91. OF PRATTLING IN CHURCH (VON SCHWETZEN IM CHOR)   295
Woodcut: Master.
   1. A comical figure on the organ pipes of the Strassburg Cathedral; it expanded and contracted its features and raised its arms comically while the organ played. Sometimes a priest, too, would ascend and join in the antics.

92. PRESUMPTUOUSNESS OF PRIDE (UBERHEBUNG DER HOCHFART) 297
Woodcut: Master.
   1. C. Schmidt, *Histoire littéraire de l'Alsace*, I, 300, has a plausible explanation. He says it refers to Pierre de Coignet or Coingnet, a grotesque figure that the clergy of Paris placed in the Cathedral of Notre-Dame to mock Pierre de Cugnières, who in 1329 under Philippe VI had sided with the laity against the hierarchy. A German alluding to the Parisian localism might easily convince his fellow-countrymen that he had actually studied in Paris.
   2. This was indeed the worst vice of the Germans. Literature is full of references to it.
   3. The young owl was used as a decoy in fowling. The stick (*klob*) is a split slab of wood, identical with the devil's trap mentioned above in the introduction to the chapter and seen in the cut.
   4. Num. 22: 13.   5. Jth. 10. Charles, *Apocrypha*, p. 259.
   6. II Kings 9: 30.
   7. Eccles. 9: 8. Charles, *Apocrypha*, p. 346.
   8. II Sam. 11. Bath-Sheba is meant.

9. Gen. 34: 1. But she went out to see the daughters of the land, not the men!

10. Wisd. of Sol. 5, 8, and 9. Charles, *Apocrypha*, p. 542.

11. Gen. 16: 4–6.   12. Exod. 4: 21, and 5: 2.

13. Num. 16. The example of Korah is a favorite with Brant.

14. That is, the tower of Babel. See Gen. 11.

15. II Sam. 24.

93. USURY AND PROFITEERING (WUCHER UND FURKOUFF)   302
Woodcut: Master.

1. Cf. chap. 76, line 11, p. 252, line 6.

94. OF HOPE OF GETTING LEGACIES (VON HOFFNUNG UFF ERBEN)   304
Woodcut: Master.

1. Cf. chap. 85, line 62, p. 280, line 5 from bottom.

2. An Italian legal scholar of the twelfth century, who survived his sons. But a different story is told of him. He had claimed that a husband surviving his wife must restore the dowry to her family. His own wife died and he promptly followed his own teaching. Zarncke, p. 437.

3. II Sam. 15 and 18.

4. The reference is to the birth of Isaac.

5. Luke 2: 26.

95. OF BEING MISLED ON HOLIDAYS (VON VERFURUNG AM FYRTAG) 306
Woodcut: Master.

1. Cf. chap. 28, line 6, and 94, line 12 (p. 127, line 1; 305, line 7).

2. Pointed shoes were popular, the points being stuffed with rags.

3. The text has *frytag* (Friday) instead of *fyrtag* (holiday). If this is not a misprint, the reference is to Friday as a day of abstinence.

4. Brant uses the term *hümpeler*. Cf. Luther's translation of Prov. 26: 10.

5. Num. 15: 32.

6. II Macc. 2: 16 ff. Charles, *Apocrypha*, p. 134.

7. Exod. 16: 22 ff.

96. GIVING AND REGRETTING (SCHENCKEN UND BERUWEN)   309
Woodcut: Master.

97. OF INDOLENCE AND SLOTH (VON TRAGKEIT UND FULHEIT) 311
Woodcut: Inferior artist.
1. Prov. 10: 26.
2. For the word *winterbutz*, cf. chap. 6, line 62; p. 74, line 26.
3. Num. 13: 14.   4. II Sam. 11.
5. For this and the following lines cf. Prov. 26: 13 f.

98. OF OUTLANDISH FOOLS (VON USLENDIGEN NARREN) 313
Woodcut: Inferior artist.
1. Prague, the seat of many heretics and unorthodox sects.
2. Probably witches, magicians, and the like. But Geiler calls them whores.

99. OF THE DECLINE OF FAITH (VON ABGANG DES GLOUBEN) 315
Woodcut: Inferior artist.
1. This chapter is probably written with more feeling than any other in the entire work, for it deals with a subject close to Brant's heart.
2. Constantinople and Trebizond.
3. In *De origine et conversatione bonorum regum et laude civitatis Hierosolymae* Brant deals more fully with their loss to Christendom.
4. Bulgarians.   5. Illyrians.
6. To which eastern European race this refers is not clear.
7. Taurians, inhabitants of the Crimea.
8. Negroponte, which fell in 1471. It is mentioned in Brant's *De origine*.
9. Pera, a suburb of Constantinople.
10. Kaffa, a Genoese city on the Black Sea, fell to the Turks by treachery. Cf. *De origine*.
11. Otranto, a seaport town which fell in 1481. Cf. *De origine*.
12. That is, Sicily.   13. That is, the papacy at Rome.
14. Horace *Epistles* i. 18. 84.
15. Historians of the time still maintained the fiction of an uninterrupted series of emperors since Julius Caesar.
16. The reference is probably to the so-called Capitulations, whereby candidates for imperial or ecclesiastical election agreed not to make changes after election, so that those electing them might keep their booty.
17. A proverb. Quoted by Bobertag from Agricola: "Wañ eyn

studt zergehen sol, so beyszt ein pferdt dem andern den schwantz ab."

18. Maximilian had been elected Roman king but not yet anointed emperor by the Pope.

19. That is, Palestine. Maximilian actually hoped to recapture it. This is one of Brant's favorite themes in his German and Latin worldly works.

20. Cf. chap. 16, line 57, p. 98, line 21.

21. Matt. 3: 10.

100. OF STROKING THE FALLOW STALLION (VON FALBEN
HENGST STRICHEN)   323
Woodcut: Master.

1. One explanation is: Fallow stallions were unpopular because of their color, and stroking one was a mark of insincerity and fawning flattery. Another: Since lords sometimes had horses of that color, stroking one would be equivalent to flattering its master.

2. Picking feathers off the master's coat and "stroking his comb" (*klubt federn, stricht kriden*) are marks of servile flattery.

3. "Owl" is used in this expression as a contemptuous designation for "hunting bird." It is merely another indirect reference to flattery.

4. Blowing flour from one's mouth is another expression for flattery. The meaning is: You cannot blow and still keep your mouth full of flour.

5. That is, mingle the truth (wool) and falsehood (hair).

101. OF BLOWING INTO EARS (VON OREN BLOSEN)   325
Woodcut: Master.

1. Esther 3.   2. II Sam. 16: 1 ff., and 19: 24 ff.

3. Alexander Balas is meant (ca. B.C. 150). Cf. I Macc. 10: 60 ff. Charles, *Apocrypha*, p. 104.

102. OF FALSITY AND DECEPTION (VON FALSCH UND BESCHISS)   327
Woodcut: Master.

1. The author of the anonymous *Der neuen Welt Gattung, Schlag und Eygenschafft* (1539) made use of this entire chapter without giving credit to Brant. Jacob Cammerlander

in his edition of the *Narrenschiff* (Strassburg, 1540) publishes the poem in place of chap. 102.

2. Cf. Zarncke, p. 446.

3. Mannikins or figurines set on the counter to distract the customer's attention (*was narren uf dem laden stan*).

4. Or Beghines, sisters not bound by perpetual vows, but established for devotion and charity. They enjoyed a bad reputation as beggars, intriguers, and matchmakers.

5. Alchemists were called *Unkenbrenner*, or toad-burners. They were supposed to use the ashes of toads and basilisks.

6. The word is *guckuss*. There may be a pun involved. The cuckoo might refer to the foolishness of the alchemist, to the fact that he, like the cuckoo, lays his eggs in others' nests to be hatched, and the work *gucken*, "to look" or "to peep," may also be in Brant's mind.

103. OF THE ANTICHRIST (VOM ENDKRIST)   331
Woodcut: Master.

1. With the exception of the Prologue and chap. 48, this is the only chapter in the first edition that has no triplet or quatrain as a motto. For some of the imagery Brant may have used the anonymous sermon which was discussed in the Introduction, pp. 13–14.

2. That is, the theological literature is vilified. Brant confuses his symbols in this chapter more than usually.

3. That is, the ship of true faith.

4. Ezek. 2: 6.   5. Cf. Ezek. 13 and 14.

6. That is, make exact pirated reprints of already existing books.

7. In some of the later editions an interpolation of eighteen lines at this point puts in a good word for the printers as purveyors of knowledge.

8. *Schluderaffen>schluraffen*, literally "lazy apes," then inhabitants of the fabled land of *Schlaraffia*, the land of milk and honey and the paradise for indolent carousers and gluttons. See chap. 108 below. The concept may be traced in some of its aspects to Lucian. The Goliards took it up. In medieval France the land was known as *Coquaigne*, in England

Cocaygne or *Cockayne*. It also occurs in Holland and became very popular in Germany in the sixteenth century.

9. Aix-la-Chapelle, or Aachen (Brant says *Ach*), selected as a distant but famous place of pilgrimage. See note 2 on chap. 80, line 24, p. 382.

10. Num. 11.

11. The abuses of absolution, becoming more marked at this time, were ignored by Brant and Geiler.

104. CONCEALING TRUTH (WORHEYT VERSCHWIGEN)   337
Woodcut: Master.

1. Cf. chap. 69, line 16, p. 233, line 11. Berillus was roasted in the ox of Phalaris.

2. Jonah 1: 3 ff.   3. II Kings 2.   4. Dan. 5: 17.

5. Num. 22: 7 and 19 ff.

6. Cf. above, p. 153, line 15, and p. 214, line 18.

7. Indicating harshness.   8. Indicating gentleness.

105. PREVENTION OF THE GOOD (HYNDERNYS DES GUTTEN)   340
Woodcut: Same as No. 42.

1. In 1487 Brant's mentor and friend a Lapide had joined this order and retired from the world, probably with Brant's warm approval. One of Brant's Latin poems deals with the same form of hypocritical ridicule of asceticism. See Zeydel in *Modern Language Quarterly*, IV, 209 ff.

2. When a Lapide took orders (see previous note) he was chided by Junker Brandolf von Stein, who said he would have done better by preaching. A Lapide is said to have replied: "Wann er zwo seelen hätte, wollte er gnug die eine an gut Gesellen gewagt han"—"if he had two souls he would gladly have risked giving one to jolly fellows" (see W. Vischer, *Geschichte der Universität Basel von 1460–1529*, Basel, 1860, p. 165).

106. REFRAINING FROM GOOD WORKS (ABLOSSUNG GUTTER WERCK)   343
Woodcut: Master.

1. Cf. Matt. 25.   2. Prov. 30: 24–28.

3. The reference is to Prov. 25: 16. But what is meant by sharp (pungent?) combs—*wafen scharff*—is not clear.

4. Ps. 49: 11 and 12.

107. OF REWARD FOR WISDOM (VON LON DER WISHEIT) 345
Woodcut: Master.
1. I Cor. 3: 19.
2. Xenophon *Memorabilia* ii. 1. 21 ff. In Strassburg Brant
later had this parable depicted in the form of a drama.
3. Luke 18: 16–17, and Matt. 11: 25.
4. A Greek bucolic poet, B. C. 120.

108. THE SCHLURAFFEN SHIP (DAS SCHLURAFFEN SCHIFF) 349
Woodcut: Same as the third cut of the Prologue.
1. Cf. note 8 on chap. 103, line 118, where we have simply
translated the term as "apes." Cf. also Introduction, pp. 9, 15.
2. Monte Fiascone, a town between Siena and Rome, famous
for its good wine and therefore a paradise for carousers and
tipplers. Perhaps chosen here because it suggests *Flasche*,
"flask."
3. See note 1 to chap. 91. Much of this chapter is used by
Johann Römoldt in his *Laster der Hoffart* (Vice of Pride). It
is placed in the mouth of Heinz Ohnetrost (Disconsolate
Henry).
4. Especially those seeking prebends in Rome.
5. The cliffs mentioned in the *Odyssey* xii. 61 ff., and xxiii.
327, as well as in Ovid *Metam.* xv. 337. Brant's knowledge of
the wanderings of Odysseus is not derived from Homer
directly, but from compendia of his own time. He hardly read
Greek.
6. The king of the Laestrygoni, who ate human flesh. Cf.
Odyssey x. 80 ff.
7. Here Brant narrates not according to Homer, but according to the later story, whereby Odysseus was slain by the son
whom Circe bore him.
8. The banner in the woodcut indicates the first two words
of this, the fools' theme song: *Gaudeamus omnes.*
9. Geiler delivered four sermons on this chapter.

109. CONTEMPT OF MISFORTUNE (VERACHTUNG UNGEFELLES) 355
Woodcut: Master.
1. Cf. chap. 56, lines 55–56, p. 192, line 19.

110. SLANDER OF THE GOOD (HYNDERRED DES GUTEN) 357
Woodcut: Master.

1. This means to attempt something impossible, which will eventually harm the person who tries it. The idea is from a fable in which the mice deliberate about hanging a bell on a cat.

2. In view of the great success of the work, Brant's scruples are amusing and reveal great modesty. At this point modern editions interpolate two chapters (110a, Von disches unzucht —Ill Breeding at Table, and 110b, Von fasnacht narren— Of Shrovetide Fools) which are not in the first edition of 1494, but were inserted by Brant, probably as an afterthought, in the second edition of 1495. Geiler frequently used chap. 110a, which deals with a burning problem of the day.

111. APOLOGY OF THE POET (ENTSCHULDIGUNG DES DICHTERS)   359
Woodcut: Master.

1. In the unauthorized Augsburg edition of 1498 there is an interpolation on scribbling lovers' names and symbols on walls. Cf. chap. 15 above.

2. Ps. 37: 35–36.

112. THE WISE MAN (DER WIS MAN)   363
Woodcut: Same as No. 22.

1. That is, the poem *Vir bonus*, then ascribed to Vergil.

2. The constellation.

INDEX

Abraham a Santa Clara, 33, 34
Abus du monde, Les (Gringoire), 36
Acht Schalkheiten, Die, 9
Adonville, Jacques d', 36, 37, 40
Adultery, 136, 372
Advice, good: not following, 78, 368
Affe, name for fools, 9, 17*n*
A Lapide, Johannes, 2, 4
Alciati, emblem literature, 41
Amenities of Literature (Disraeli), excerpt, 18
Amours, 88, 369
Anatomy of Melancholy (Burton), 42
An den christlichen Adel deutscher Nation (Luther), 1
Anger, ready, 142, 372
Antichrist, 331, 388
Apology of the poet, 359, 391
Armin, Robert, 42
Artists, *see* Woodcuts
Attendorn, publisher, 12
Awdelay, John, 41

Badius Ascensius, Iodocus, 28, 29*n*, 35, 43
Bad manners, 80, 368
Bad women, 212, 377
Balsac (Barsat, Balsat), Robert de, works: their influence, 35-37, 40
Barclay, Alexander, *The Shyp of folys* . . . , 28; texts used: style, 29; reprint and selections from, 30; works influenced by, 39, 40, 41, 42
Basel, importance of, 2; Brant's years in, 2-6
Basel, University of, 2
Beggars, 208, 377
Benefices, too many, 130, 371
Bergmann von Olpe, Johann, and his printing establishment, 5; magnificent first edition of *Narrenschiff*, 5, 21; woodcuts made in shop of, 10, 20, 367-91
Bescheidenheit (Freidank), 5
Bible, use as authority: by Brant, 16; by Erasmus, 43, 44

Blasphemy, 287, 383
Blauwe schute, Die (Oestvoren), 12
Blowing into ears, 325, 387
Boasting, great, 251, 381
Bobertag, Franz, edition of the *Narrenschiff*, 19, 23
Boke of Three Fooles (Skelton), 40
Books, useless, 62, 367
Borrowing too much, 118, 371
Bouchet, Jean, 38
Bowge of Court, The (Skelton), 40
Brandes, Herman, 27
Brant, Sebastian, momentous events of age in which he lived, 1; parents, dates of birth and death, 2; education, 2 f.; wife, 3; legal profession, 3; early literary and publishing work, 3-6; his pamphlet *De origine et conversatione bonorum regum et laude civitatis Hierosolymae*, 3; Latin poems issued as *Varia carmina*, 4; devotion to Holy Roman Emperor, 4, 5, 6, 7; distinguished role in public life, 6; friendship with Erasmus, 6, 7, 43; religious convictions and stern morality, 6, 7, 8; other characteristics, 7; Dürer's portrait of, 7, 20; philosophy: originality not his forte, 8; derivation of his allegorical idea of a ship, 11 ff.; authorities required for every point made: those most often used, 16; satire, 17, 41; gift in use of words, 17; individuality shown in content and style of *Narrenschiff*, 18; what role in preparation of woodcuts? 20; Strobel's biographical sketch of, 23; Locher's Latin version made in collaboration with, 24, 26; a scholasticist at the threshold of humanism, 43; Latin poem on work of Erasmus, 45; *see also Narrenschiff*
Burckhardt, Daniel, 20
Burg, Elisabeth, married Brant, 3
Burton, Robert, 42

Cammerlander, Jacob, 22
Care, too much, 116, 371
Carnival, link with fools' ship, 11
Carthusian monks, 14, 32
Catholicon des maladvisez, Le . . . (Desmoulin), 36
Cawood, edition of the *Narrenschiff*, 29
Champier, Symphorien, 35, 38
Chance, 146, 373
Charles V, 7
Chiding and erring oneself, 110, 370
Children, on the teaching of, 72, 368
Church, noise in, 162, 295, 374, 384
Classical writers, 1; Brant's use of, 16
Clerks and knights, 261, 382
Coarse fools, 238, 380
Cock Lorell's Bote, 39
Columbus, Christopher, 1, 2, 15, 378
Colyn Cloute (Skelton), 40
Complacency, 144, 202, 372, 376
Concealing truth, 337, 389
Contempt of holy writ, 84, 369; of eternal joy, 160, 373; of poverty, 271, 382; of God, 284, 383; of misfortune, 355, 390
Cooks and waiters, 265, 382
Copland, Robert, 37, 40, 41
Cornell University Library, 4*n*, 9*n*, 31
Councilors, good, 64, 367
Court, quarreling and going to, 236, 379
Courting misfortune, 164, 374

Dancing, 204, 376
Death, not providing for, 278, 383
Deception and falsity, 327, 387
Decline of the faith, 315, 386
Dekker, Thomas, 39, 42
Delay, seeking, 132, 372
De origine et conversatione bonorum regum et laude civitatis Hierosolymae (Brant), 3
Desmoulin, edition of the *Narrenschiff*, 36, 37
Dialogi duo de poetis nostrorum temporum (Giraldi), 38
Discord, causing, 76, 368
Disraeli, Isaac, quoted, 18

Disz ist ein hubsche predig gethon uff S. Ursula tag . . . , 13, 14
Doctoratus in stultitia (Hemmerlin), 9
Dringenberg, 2
Droit Chemin, Le (Balsac), 35-37, 40
Drouyn, Jehan, 27, 30, 35
Dürer, Albrecht, portrait of Brant, 7, 20; woodcuts ascribed to, 20
Dutch version: of Brant's work, 31; of Balsac's, 37

Eck, J. M. von, 1
Emblems, 41
England, antecedents of Brant, 9; chief versions of his work, 28-30 (*see also* Barclay, A.); his influence upon the literature, 32, 38-43; its importance and nature, 39
English Versions of the Ship of Fools, The (Pompen), 13*n*, 26, 37*n*
Envy and hatred, 184, 375
Epistolae obscurorum vivorum, 33
Erasmus, Desiderius, 2, 8, 42; acquaintance with Brant, 6, 7, 43; his *Moriae encomium* compared with the *Narrenschiff*, 18, 43-45; the most famous book on folly, 43
Esel, name for fools, 9, 17*n*
Eternal joy, contempt of, 160, 373
Evil, doing: and not being on guard, 232, 379
Experience of all lands, 220, 378

Fabliaux de Coquaigne, 9
Facetus, 6
Faith, decline of the, 315, 386
Falsity and deception, 327, 387
"Fastnachtspiele," 9
Father and mother, honoring, 293, 384
Feasting, gluttony and, 96, 370
Finding treasures, 108, 370
Fischart, Johann, 33, 34, 42
Flemish version, 28, 31*n*
Flitner, J., 22
Folly, sins of the day as exemplifications of, 17; most famous book on, 43
Foole's Bolt Is Sone Shot, A (Rowlands), 42

Foolish news, 263, 382
Foolish plans, 94, 370
Foolish trading, 291, 384
Fool, on not wishing to be a, 226, 379
Fools, distinguished from wise men in literatures, 8; names for, 9, 17n, 33; derivation of the allegorical idea of a ship of, 11-15; old device replaced by psychological approach, 42; old, 70, 368; heedless, 86, 369; unchanging, 140, 372; taking offense at, 154, 373; power of, 166, 374; coarse, 238, 380; oppressed, 259, 381; outlandish, 313, 386; see also Ship
Forgetting oneself, 198, 376
France, translations or paraphrases of Brant's work, 27; his influence on the literature, 35-38; and nature of its service, 39
Fraternity of Vagabonds (Awdelay), 41
Fraustadt, F., 29
Freidank, Bescheidenheit, 5, 16
Freystadt, edition of Narrenschiff, 22
Friar Bacon (Greene), 42
Friedländer, Max, 20
Friendship, 82, 369
Furter, Michael, 5

Gaguinus, Robert, 29n
Gallus, Jodocus, 12, 13, 14
Gamblers, 255, 381
Gäuchmatt (Murner), 6, 33
Geiler, Schiff der Penitentz und Busswirkung, 14, 15, 33
Gengenbach, Pamphilus, 33, 34
German literature, antecedents of Brant, 8; his influence upon, 32-35; Narr as a type, 33, 34
German society, Narrenschiff a telling picture of infirmities of, 18
German translations: Low Saxon, 26; modern, 31
Ghelen, Jan van, 31
Ghetelen, Hans van, 26
Giélée, Renart le Nouvel, 12
Giraldi, Lilo, 38
Giving and regretting, 309, 385
Gluttony and feasting, 96, 370

God, insolence toward, 92, 370; speaking against, 126, 371; predestination of, 194, 376; contempt of, 284, 383; blaspheming, 287, 383; torture and punishment by, 289, 383
Goedeke, Karl, 23, 31
Good, of persisting in, 276, 383
Good, prevention of, 340, 389; slander of, 357, 390
Good advice, not following, 78, 368
Good councilors, 64, 367
Good works, refraining from, 343, 389
Gossip, 325, 387
Gouch, name for fools, 9, 17n
Greed, 66, 367
Greek classical writers, 1; Brant's use of, 16
Greene, Robert, 42
Grieninger (Grüninger?), Johann, 22, 32
Grimm, Jakob, 23n
Grimm, Wilhelm, 6
Gringoire, 36, 37
Gülfferich, Hermann, 22
Gul's Hornbooke (Dekker), 42
Gyl of Brentford's Testament (Copland), 41

Han, Weygand, 22
Hasen Jacht, 22
Hasleben, edition of Narrenschiff, 22
Hatred and envy, 184, 375
Hawthorn, Julian, The Masterpieces and the History of Literature, 30
Heedless fools, 86, 369
Hemmerlin, Felix, 9
Herford, C. H., 10, 18, 32
Holbein, Hans, 43, 44
Holidays, on being misled on, 306, 385
Holy Roman Empire, 4, 7
Holy writ, contempt of, 84, 369
Höniger, Nicolaus, 22, 23
Horseload of Fools (Tarlton), 41
Humanism, era preceding, 1; Basel the center of, 2; Brant's unwitting encouragement of, 8; Erasmus outstanding, 43
Humor, Brant's, 18, 34

Hunting, useless, 246, 380
Hüpfuff, Matthys, 22
Hutten, Ulrich von, 8, 33
Hye Way to the Spyttel House
(Copland), 37, 40

Idle talk, 104, 370
Indolence and sloth, 311, 386
Ingratitude, 200, 376
Innovations, 68, 368
Insolence toward God, 92, 370
Ireland, W. H., 42
Italy, Brant's slight influence in, 38

Jamieson, T. H., 30, 40, 42
Jest books, 6, 18*n*
Joke, not taking a, 230, 379
Journeyman's ship, 172, 374
Joy, eternal: contempt of, 160, 373
Judgment of others, 128, 371
Junghans, H. A., 31

Kaisersberg, Geiler von, 19, 32
Karlstadt, A. R. B., 1
Kloster (Scheible), 23
Knights and clerks, 261, 382
Koegler, H., 20, 24

Lamparter, Nicolaus, 21, 22
Land of Cockayne, 9
Latin versions of the *Narrenschiff*,
24-26, 28; *see also* Locher, Jacob
Latin writers, Brant's use of, 16
La Tour-Landry, Chevalier de, 5
Lea, Henry Charles, 19
Le Dru, P., 38
Legacies, hope of getting, 304, 385
Leoni, Tomaso, 9
Lessing, G. E., 14
Liber vagatorum (Gengenbach), 34
Literature, *Narrenschiff's* far-reach-
ing influence upon, 31-45; English,
32, 38-43; German, 32-35; French,
35-38; Dutch, 37, 43-45; Italian, 38
Litigation, 236, 379
Locher, Jacob (Philomusus Suevus),
33; Latin translation of *Narren-
schiff*, 15, 16, 24-26, 32, 41; made in
collaboration with Brant, 24, 26; its
importance: editions and reprints,
25; arrangement and omissions,

25 f.; translations based upon, 27,
28, 29, 31
Low Saxon translation, 26
Lucian, 9, 45
Luck, vaunting, 114, 371
Luther, Martin, 1, 7, 8
Lydgate, John, 9, 10, 12*n*, 38, 39, 41

Manners, bad, 80, 368
Marchand, G., 28
Marksmen, bad, 248, 380
Marnef, publisher, 25, 28
Marrying for the sake of goods, 182,
375
Masters, serving two, 102, 370
Maximilian, Emperor, 4, 5, 6
Medicine, foolish, 188, 375
Messengers, 263, 382
Meusebach collection, 21
Meyer, Martin, letter to Sylvius, 1
Misfortune, contempt of, 355, 390;
courting, 164, 374
. . . *Modern Ship of Fools, The*
(Ireland), 42
*Monopolium et societas vulgo des
Liechtschiffs* (Gallus), 12, 13
Moore, W. G., 37, 40
More, Sir Thomas, 9, 39*n*
Moretus, 6
Moriae encomium, 18, 43-45; *see*
Erasmus
Moyens d'éviter merencolie, Les . . .
(Adonville), 36, 40
Murner, Thomas, 6, 15, 19*n*, 22; in-
fluence of *Narrenschiff* in works
of, 33

Narr, name for fools, 9, 15, 17*n*; as
a type: popular terms beginning
with, 33; life of, and changes in,
type, 34
Narrenbeschwörung (Murner), 33
Narrenschiff (Brant), Bergmann's
edition a magnificent piece of
bookmaking: one of the truly remarkable books of the age, 5; antecedents and genesis, 8-15; a compilation, 8, 15; how planned and
made-up, 10 f.; contents and style,
10, 15-19; woodcuts, 10, 17, 19-
21, 24, 32, 33, 40, 41, 44, 367-91;

Prologue, 11, 14, 20, 367 (*text*, 57-61); best chapters: subjects of its preachment, 18; *Moriae encomium* of Erasmus compared with, 18, 43-45; influence upon course of historical events, 19; editions and reprints, 21-24; a secular, or layman's, Bible, 24, 32; translations and adaptations, 24-31; Latin, 24-26, 28 (*see also under* Locher, J.); Low German, 26; French, 27; Flemish, 28, 31*n*; English, 28-30; Dutch, 28, 31; modern German, 31; far-reaching influence as a force in literature, 31-45; in England, 32, 38-43; Germany, 32-35; France, 35-38; Italy, 38; commentary, 367-91

Narren schyp, Dat (Ghetelen?), 26

Nash, Thomas, 42

Navicula seu speculum fatuorum praestantissimi sacrarum . . . (Kaisersberg), 32

Nef des dames vertueuses, La (Champier), 38

Nef des princes et des battailes, La . . . (Balsac), 35

Nest of Ninnies (Armin), 42

Neues Narrenschiff (Weickert), 35

Noise in church, 162, 295, 374, 384

Oestvoren, Jacob van, 12

Oneself, chiding and erring, 110, 370; forgetting, 198, 376

Open plans, 152, 373

Order of Fools (Lydgate), 9, 10

Orders of Knaves, 40

Parents, bad example of, 176, 374

Pasquin, 45

Patients who do not obey, 148, 373

Pauli, Johann, 32

Peasants' squandering, 268, 382

Persisting in the good, 276, 383

Petri, Sebastian H., 22

Philomusus Suevus, *see* Locher, Jacob

Picker, Barbara, education of, and influence over, Brant, 2

Plans, foolish, 94, 370; open, 152, 373

Pleasure, sensual, 178, 374

Pluemen der Tugend (Vintler), 9

Poet, apology of the, 359, 391

Poetry, new German type, 4; Brant's verse and translations, 4 f.

Pompen, Aurelius, 13*n*, 26, 28, 29, 37*n*

Poverty, contempt of, 271, 382

Power, end of, 190, 376

Prattling in church, 295, 384

Predestination of God, 194, 376

Pride, presumptuousness of, 297, 384

Priest, becoming a, 242, 380

Printer-publishers, Brant's work with, 3, 5; Bergmann's press and bookmaking, 5; his woodcuts, 10, 20, 367-91

Profiteering and usury, 302, 385

Prologue, 11, 14, 20, 367; *text*, 57-61

Providing in time, not, 234, 379

Punishment, impatience of, 186, 375

Pynson, Richard, 29

Quarreling and going to court, 236, 379

Quartern of Serving Men (Awdelay), 41

Rabelais, 37

Raben, Georg, 22

Rechten weg nae t Gaesthuys . . . Den, 37

Reformation, era preceding, 1; floods of reading matter: influence upon *Narrenschiff*, 23

Regnars, Les . . . , 38

Regretz et peines des mal advisez (Adonville), 36

Reinke de Vos, 27

Renart le Nouvel (Giélée), 12

Reuchlin, Johann, 3, 8

Riches, useless, 100, 370

Ridpath, J. C., *Library of Universal Literature*, 30

Rihel, edition of the *Narrenschiff*, 22

Ritter vom Turn (Stein), 5

Rivière, Pierre, 27, 28, 29, 41

Rowlands, Samuel, 39, 42

Sachs, Hans, 33

St. Ursulä Schifflein (Carthusian monks), 14, 32

Salvation, on the road of, 170, 374

Satire, of Brant, 17, 41; moral, supplanted by modern, 41

Scheible, J., 23
Schelmenzunft (Murner), 33
Schif der flust, Das (Teichner), 12
Schiff der Penitentz . . . (Geiler), 14
Schlaraffenland, 9
Schluraffen ship, 349, 390
Schröder, Carl, 27
Schultz, Franz, edition, 20, 21, 23; its great value, 24
Scorners, 158, 373
Secrets, keeping, 180, 375
Self-complacency, 202, 376
Sensual pleasure, 178, 374
Sensuit le droit chemin de l'hôpital . . . (Balsac), 35
Serenading at night, 206, 377
Sermons of Kaisersberg on the Narrenschiff, 19, 32
Serving two masters, 370
Ship, allegory of, in Brant's work, 11; derivation of the idea, 11-15; fiction of, stressed in Locher's Latin version, 26; notion died out in Germany, 34; see also Fools
Ship, journeyman's, 172, 374
Ship, Schluraffen, 349, 390
Ship of Fools Fully Fraught, The . . . , 42
Shyp of folys, The . . . (Barclay), 28-30, 41, 42
Shyppe of Fooles, The (Watson), 30
Simrock, Karl, 19, 31
Sixteen Knaves . . . (Rowlands), 42
Skelton, John, 39, 40
Slander of the good, 357, 390
Sottie, la, 9n
Spamer, Adolf, 13
Speculum stultorum (Wireker), 9, 10
Springer, Jaro, 20
Squandering, peasants', 268, 382
Stallion, fallow: stroking the, 323, 387
Stars, attention to, 216, 378
Stein, Johann H. von, 2
Stein, Marquart vom, 5
Strassburg, Brant's distinguished role in life of, 6
Strobel, Adam Walther, 23, 35
Studying, useless, 124, 371

Stultiferae naves sensus animosque trahentes mortis in exitium (Badius), 28, 35n
Summer's Last Will and Testament (Nash), 42

Talk, idle, 104, 370; paying no heed to, 156, 373
Tarlton, jester, 39, 41
Teaching of children, 72, 368
Teaching wisdom, 112, 371
Teichner (Heinrich), 12
Theatre for Voluptuous Worldlings (Van der Noot), 41
Tore, name for fools, 9, 17n
Torture and punishment by God, 289, 383
Trading, foolish, 291, 384
Travel, 220, 378
Treasures, finding, 108, 370
Tritheim, J., 33
Truth, concealing, 337, 389
Twenty-five Orders of Fools, The, 41

Ursula, St., ship of, 13 f., 32
Useless books, 62, 367
Usury and profiteering, 302, 385

Van der Noot, 41
Van det edele lant van Cockaenghen, 9
Van Praet, 28, 31n
Varia carmina (Brant), 4
Vérard, A., 38
Vintler, Hans, 9
Vir bonus, 16
"Volksfeste," 34
Von dem grossen Lutherischen Narren (Murner), 33

Waiters and cooks, 265, 382
Waldseemüller, Martin, 1
Warner's Library of the World's Best Literature, 30
Watson, Henry, 30, 39, 40, 41
Weickert, Felix, 35
Weiditz, Hans, 41n
Weimar Society of Bibliophiles, 24
Weisbach, W., 20

Wimpheling, Jacob, 6, 12, 13, 28, 33, 35

Wireker, Nigel, 9, 10, 12n, 38, 39

Wisdom, reward for, 345, 390; teaching, 112, 371

Wise man, 363, 391

Wishing, useless, 120, 371

Wives, guarding, 134, 372

Wölfflin, F., 20

Women, bad, 212, 377

Women, good: Brant's respect for, 2

Woodcuts, 10, 17, 19-21; reproductions, 19, 24, 32, 33, 40; some ascribed to Dürer, 20; the artists, 20, 41n; artistry, 21; editions and reprints without cuts, 22; best extant discussion of, 24; based on proverbs, were genuine emblems, 41; Holbein's cuts reminiscent of *Narrenschiff's*, 44; attributions and descriptions, 367-91

Worde, Wynkyn de, 30

Zachoni, publisher, 25

Zarncke, F., 9n, 12n, 31, 34; monumental edition of the *Narrenschiff*, 19, 23; its value, 24

Zetter, Jakob de, 22

Zur Vorgeschichte des Narrenschiffes (Zarncke), 9n

Zwingli, Huldreich, 1, 7, 8

A CATALOGUE OF SELECTED DOVER BOOKS
IN ALL FIELDS OF INTEREST

A CATALOGUE OF SELECTED DOVER BOOKS
IN ALL FIELDS OF INTEREST

WHAT IS SCIENCE?, *N. Campbell*
The role of experiment and measurement, the function of mathematics, the nature of scientific laws, the difference between laws and theories, the limitations of science, and many similarly provocative topics are treated clearly and without technicalities by an eminent scientist. "Still an excellent introduction to scientific philosophy," H. Margenau in *Physics Today*. "A first-rate primer . . . deserves a wide audience," *Scientific American*. 192pp. 5⅜ x 8.
60043-2 Paperbound $1.25

THE NATURE OF LIGHT AND COLOUR IN THE OPEN AIR, *M. Minnaert*
Why are shadows sometimes blue, sometimes green, or other colors depending on the light and surroundings? What causes mirages? Why do multiple suns and moons appear in the sky? Professor Minnaert explains these unusual phenomena and hundreds of others in simple, easy-to-understand terms based on optical laws and the properties of light and color. No mathematics is required but artists, scientists, students, and everyone fascinated by these "tricks" of nature will find thousands of useful and amazing pieces of information. Hundreds of observational experiments are suggested which require no special equipment. 200 illustrations; 42 photos. xvi + 362pp. 5⅜ x 8.
20196-1 Paperbound $2.00

THE STRANGE STORY OF THE QUANTUM, AN ACCOUNT FOR THE GENERAL READER OF THE GROWTH OF IDEAS UNDERLYING OUR PRESENT ATOMIC KNOWLEDGE, *B. Hoffmann*
Presents lucidly and expertly, with barest amount of mathematics, the problems and theories which led to modern quantum physics. Dr. Hoffmann begins with the closing years of the 19th century, when certain trifling discrepancies were noticed, and with illuminating analogies and examples takes you through the brilliant concepts of Planck, Einstein, Pauli, Broglie, Bohr, Schroedinger, Heisenberg, Dirac, Sommerfeld, Feynman, etc. This edition includes a new, long postscript carrying the story through 1958. "Of the books attempting an account of the history and contents of our modern atomic physics which have come to my attention, this is the best," H. Margenau, Yale University, in *American Journal of Physics*. 32 tables and line illustrations. Index. 275pp. 5⅜ x 8.
20518-5 Paperbound $2.00

GREAT IDEAS OF MODERN MATHEMATICS: THEIR NATURE AND USE, *Jagjit Singh*
Reader with only high school math will understand main mathematical ideas of modern physics, astronomy, genetics, psychology, evolution, etc. better than many who use them as tools, but comprehend little of their basic structure. Author uses his wide knowledge of non-mathematical fields in brilliant exposition of differential equations, matrices, group theory, logic, statistics, problems of mathematical foundations, imaginary numbers, vectors, etc. Original publication. 2 appendixes. 2 indexes. 65 ills. 322pp. 5⅜ x 8.
20587-8 Paperbound $2.25

PRINCIPLES OF ART HISTORY,
H. Wölfflin
Analyzing such terms as "baroque," "classic," "neoclassic," "primitive,"
"picturesque," and 164 different works by artists like Botticelli, van Cleve,
Dürer, Hobbema, Holbein, Hals, Rembrandt, Titian, Brueghel, Vermeer, and
many others, the author establishes the classifications of art history and style
on a firm, concrete basis. This classic of art criticism shows what really
occurred between the 14th-century primitives and the sophistication of the
18th century in terms of basic attitudes and philosophies. "A remarkable
lesson in the art of seeing," *Sat. Rev. of Literature.* Translated from the 7th
German edition. 150 illustrations. 254pp. 6⅛ x 9¼. 20276-3 Paperbound $2.25

PRIMITIVE ART,
Franz Boas
This authoritative and exhaustive work by a great American anthropologist
covers the entire gamut of primitive art. Pottery, leatherwork, metal work,
stone work, wood, basketry, are treated in detail. Theories of primitive art,
historical depth in art history, technical virtuosity, unconscious levels of pat-
terning, symbolism, styles, literature, music, dance, etc. A must book for the
interested layman, the anthropologist, artist, handicrafter (hundreds of unusual motifs), and the historian. Over 900 illustrations (50 ceramic vessels,
12 totem poles, etc.). 376pp. 5⅜ x 8.   20025-6 Paperbound $2.50

THE GENTLEMAN AND CABINET MAKER'S DIRECTOR,
Thomas Chippendale
A reprint of the 1762 catalogue of furniture designs that went on to influence
generations of English and Colonial and Early Republic American furniture
makers. The 200 plates, most of them full-page sized, show Chippendale's
designs for French (Louis XV), Gothic, and Chinese-manner chairs, sofas,
canopy and dome beds, cornices, chamber organs, cabinets, shaving tables,
commodes, picture frames, frets, candle stands, chimney pieces, decorations, etc.
The drawings are all elegant and highly detailed; many include construction
diagrams and elevations. A supplement of 24 photographs shows surviving
pieces of original and Chippendale-style pieces of furniture. Brief biography
of Chippendale by N. I. Bienenstock, editor of *Furniture World.* Reproduced
from the 1762 edition. 200 plates, plus 19 photographic plates. vi + 249pp.
9⅛ x 12¼.   21601-2 Paperbound $3.50

AMERICAN ANTIQUE FURNITURE: A BOOK FOR AMATEURS,
Edgar G. Miller, Jr.
Standard introduction and practical guide to identification of valuable
American antique furniture. 2115 illustrations, mostly photographs taken by
the author in 148 private homes, are arranged in chronological order in exten-
sive chapters on chairs, sofas, chests, desks, bedsteads, mirrors, tables, clocks,
and other articles. Focus is on furniture accessible to the collector, including
simpler pieces and a larger than usual coverage of Empire style. Introductory
chapters identify structural elements, characteristics of various styles, how to
avoid fakes, etc. "We are frequently asked to name some book on American
furniture that will meet the requirements of the novice collector, the beginning dealer, and . . . the general public. . . . We believe Mr. Miller's two
volumes more completely satisfy this specification than any other work,"
Antiques. Appendix. Index. Total of vi + 1106pp. 7⅞ x 10¾.
                            21599-7, 21600-4 Two volume set, paperbound $7.50

THE BAD CHILD'S BOOK OF BEASTS, MORE BEASTS FOR WORSE CHILDREN, and A MORAL ALPHABET, *H. Belloc*
Hardly and anthology of humorous verse has appeared in the last 50 years without at least a couple of these famous nonsense verses. But one must see the entire volumes — with all the delightful original illustrations by Sir Basil Blackwood — to appreciate fully Belloc's charming and witty verses that play so subacidly on the platitudes of life and morals that beset his day — and ours. A great humor classic. Three books in one. Total of 157pp. 5⅜ x 8. .
20749-8 Paperbound $1.00

THE DEVIL'S DICTIONARY, *Ambrose Bierce*
Sardonic and irreverent barbs puncturing the pomposities and absurdities of American politics, business, religion, literature, and arts, by the country's greatest satirist in the classic tradition. Epigrammatic as Shaw, piercing as Swift, American as Mark Twain, Will Rogers, and Fred Allen, Bierce will always remain the favorite of a small coterie of enthusiasts, and of writers and speakers whom he supplies with "some of the most gorgeous witticisms of the English language" (H. L. Mencken). Over 1000 entries in alphabetical order. 144pp. 5⅜ x 8. 20487-1 Paperbound $1.00

THE COMPLETE NONSENSE OF EDWARD LEAR.
This is the only complete edition of this master of gentle madness available at a popular price. *A Book of Nonsense, Nonsense Songs, More Nonsense Songs and Stories* in their entirety with all the old favorites that have delighted children and adults for years. The Dong With A Luminous Nose, The Jumblies, The Owl and the Pussycat, and hundreds of other bits of wonderful nonsense: 214 limericks, 3 sets of Nonsense Botany, 5 Nonsense Alphabets, 546 drawings by Lear himself, and much more. 320pp. 5⅜ x 8. 20167-8 Paperbound $1.75

THE WIT AND HUMOR OF OSCAR WILDE, *ed. by Alvin Redman*
Wilde at his most brilliant, in 1000 epigrams exposing weaknesses and hypocrisies of "civilized" society. Divided into 49 categories—sin, wealth, women, America, etc.—to aid writers, speakers. Includes excerpts from his trials, books, plays, criticism. Formerly "The Epigrams of Oscar Wilde." Introduction by Vyvyan Holland, Wilde's only living son. Introductory essay by editor. 260pp. 5⅜ x 8. 20602-5 Paperbound $1.50

A CHILD'S PRIMER OF NATURAL HISTORY, *Oliver Herford*
Scarcely an anthology of whimsy and humor has appeared in the last 50 years without a contribution from Oliver Herford. Yet the works from which these examples are drawn have been almost impossible to obtain! Here at last are Herford's improbable definitions of a menagerie of familiar and weird animals, each verse illustrated by the author's own drawings. 24 drawings in 2 colors; 24 additional drawings. vii + 95pp. 6½ x 6. 21647-0 Paperbound $1.00

THE BROWNIES: THEIR BOOK, *Palmer Cox*
The book that made the Brownies a household word. Generations of readers have enjoyed the antics, predicaments and adventures of these jovial sprites, who emerge from the forest at night to play or to come to the aid of a deserving human. Delightful illustrations by the author decorate nearly every page. 24 short verse tales with 266 illustrations. 155pp. 6⅝ x 9¼.
21265-3 Paperbound $1.50

FAIRY TALE COLLECTIONS, *edited by Andrew Lang*
Andrew Lang's fairy tale collections make up the richest shelf-full of traditional children's stories anywhere available. Lang supervised the translation of stories from all over the world—familiar European tales collected by Grimm, animal stories from Negro Africa, myths of primitive Australia, stories from Russia, Hungary, Iceland, Japan, and many other countries. Lang's selection of translations are unusually high; many authorities consider that the most familiar tales find their best versions in these volumes. All collections are richly decorated and illustrated by H. J. Ford and other artists.

THE BLUE FAIRY BOOK. 37 stories. 138 illustrations. ix + 390pp. 5⅜ x 8½.
21437-0 Paperbound $1.95

THE GREEN FAIRY BOOK. 42 stories. 100 illustrations. xiii + 366pp. 5⅜ x 8½.
21439-7 Paperbound $1.75

THE BROWN FAIRY BOOK. 32 stories. 50 illustrations, 8 in color. xii + 350pp. 5⅜ x 8½.
21438-9 Paperbound $1.95

THE BEST TALES OF HOFFMANN, *edited by E. F. Bleiler*
10 stories by E. T. A. Hoffmann, one of the greatest of all writers of fantasy. The tales include "The Golden Flower Pot," "Automata," "A New Year's Eve Adventure," "Nutcracker and the King of Mice," "Sand-Man," and others. Vigorous characterizations of highly eccentric personalities, remarkably imaginative situations, and intensely fast pacing has made these tales popular all over the world for 150 years. Editor's introduction. 7 drawings by Hoffmann. xxxiii + 419pp. 5⅜ x 8½.
21793-0 Paperbound $2.25

GHOST AND HORROR STORIES OF AMBROSE BIERCE,
edited by E. F. Bleiler
Morbid, eerie, horrifying tales of possessed poets, shabby aristocrats, revived corpses, and haunted malefactors. Widely acknowledged as the best of their kind between Poe and the moderns, reflecting their author's inner torment and bitter view of life. Includes "Damned Thing," "The Middle Toe of the Right Foot," "The Eyes of the Panther," "Visions of the Night," "Moxon's Master," and over a dozen others. Editor's introduction. xxii + 199pp. 5⅜ x 8½.
20767-6 Paperbound $1.50

THREE GOTHIC NOVELS, *edited by E. F. Bleiler*
Originators of the still popular Gothic novel form, influential in ushering in early 19th-century Romanticism. Horace Walpole's *Castle of Otranto*, William Beckford's *Vathek*, John Polidori's *The Vampyre*, and a *Fragment* by Lord Byron are enjoyable as exciting reading or as documents in the history of English literature. Editor's introduction. xi + 291pp. 5⅜ x 8½.
21232-7 Paperbound $2.00

BEST GHOST STORIES OF LEFANU, *edited by E. F. Bleiler*
Though admired by such critics as V. S. Pritchett, Charles Dickens and Henry James, ghost stories by the Irish novelist Joseph Sheridan LeFanu have never become as widely known as his detective fiction. About half of the 16 stories in this collection have never before been available in America. Collection includes "Carmilla" (perhaps the best vampire story ever written), "The Haunted Baronet," "The Fortunes of Sir Robert Ardagh," and the classic "Green Tea." Editor's introduction. 7 contemporary illustrations. Portrait of LeFanu. xii + 467pp. 5⅜ x 8.
20415-4 Paperbound $2.50

THE PRINCIPLES OF PSYCHOLOGY,
William James
The full long-course, unabridged, of one of the great classics of Western literature and science. Wonderfully lucid descriptions of human mental activity, the stream of thought, consciousness, time perception, memory, imagination, emotions, reason, abnormal phenomena, and similar topics. Original contributions are integrated with the work of such men as Berkeley, Binet, Mills, Darwin, Hume, Kant, Royce, Schopenhauer, Spinoza, Locke, Descartes, Galton, Wundt, Lotze, Herbart, Fechner, and scores of others. All contrasting interpretations of mental phenomena are examined in detail—introspective analysis, philosophical interpretation, and experimental research. "A classic," *Journal of Consulting Psychology.* "The main lines are as valid as ever," *Psychoanalytical Quarterly.* "Standard reading . . . a classic of interpretation," *Psychiatric Quarterly.* 94 illustrations. 1408pp. 5⅜ x 8.
20381-6, 20382-4 Two volume set, paperbound $6.00

VISUAL ILLUSIONS: THEIR CAUSES, CHARACTERISTICS AND APPLICATIONS,
M. Luckiesh
"Seeing is deceiving," asserts the author of this introduction to virtually every type of optical illusion known. The text both describes and explains the principles involved in color illusions, figure-ground, distance illusions, etc. 100 photographs, drawings and diagrams prove how easy it is to fool the sense: circles that aren't round, parallel lines that seem to bend, stationary figures that seem to move as you stare at them — illustration after illustration strains our credulity at what we see. Fascinating book from many points of view, from applications for artists, in camouflage, etc. to the psychology of vision. New introduction by William Ittleson, Dept. of Psychology, Queens College. Index. Bibliography. xxi + 252pp. 5⅜ x 8½.
21530-X Paperbound $1.50

FADS AND FALLACIES IN THE NAME OF SCIENCE,
Martin Gardner
This is the standard account of various cults, quack systems, and delusions which have masqueraded as science: hollow earth fanatics. Reich and orgone sex energy, dianetics, Atlantis, multiple moons, Forteanism, flying saucers, medical fallacies like iridiagnosis, zone therapy, etc. A new chapter has been added on Bridey Murphy, psionics, and other recent manifestations in this field. This is a fair, reasoned appraisal of eccentric theory which provides excellent inoculation against cleverly masked nonsense. "Should be read by everyone, scientist and non-scientist alike," R. T. Birge, Prof. Emeritus of Physics, Univ. of California; Former President, American Physical Society. Index. x + 365pp. 5⅜ x 8.
20394-8 Paperbound $2.00

ILLUSIONS AND DELUSIONS OF THE SUPERNATURAL AND THE OCCULT,
D. H. Rawcliffe
Holds up to rational examination hundreds of persistent delusions including crystal gazing, automatic writing, table turning, mediumistic trances, mental healing, stigmata, lycanthropy, live burial, the Indian Rope Trick, spiritualism, dowsing, telepathy, clairvoyance, ghosts, ESP, etc. The author explains and exposes the mental and physical deceptions involved, making this not only an exposé of supernatural phenomena, but a valuable exposition of characteristic types of abnormal psychology. Originally titled "The Psychology of the Occult." 14 illustrations. Index. 551pp. 5⅜ x 8. 20503-7 Paperbound $3.50

THE WONDERFUL WIZARD OF OZ, *L. F. Baum*
All the original W. W. Denslow illustrations in full color—as much a part of "The Wizard" as Tenniel's drawings are of "Alice in Wonderland." "The Wizard" is still America's best-loved fairy tale, in which, as the author expresses it, "The wonderment and joy are retained and the heartaches and nightmares left out." Now today's young readers can enjoy every word and wonderful picture of the original book. New introduction by Martin Gardner. A Baum bibliography. 23 full-page color plates. viii + 268pp. 5⅜ x 8.
20691-2 Paperbound $1.95

THE MARVELOUS LAND OF OZ, *L. F. Baum*
This is the equally enchanting sequel to the "Wizard," continuing the adventures of the Scarecrow and the Tin Woodman. The hero this time is a little boy named Tip, and all the delightful Oz magic is still present. This is the Oz book with the Animated Saw-Horse, the Woggle-Bug, and Jack Pumpkinhead. All the original John R. Neill illustrations, 10 in full color. 287pp. 5⅜ x 8.
20692-0 Paperbound $1.75

ALICE'S ADVENTURES UNDER GROUND, *Lewis Carroll*
The original *Alice in Wonderland*, hand-lettered and illustrated by Carroll himself, and originally presented as a Christmas gift to a child-friend. Adults as well as children will enjoy this charming volume, reproduced faithfully in this Dover edition. While the story is essentially the same, there are slight changes, and Carroll's spritely drawings present an intriguing alternative to the famous Tenniel illustrations. One of the most popular books in Dover's catalogue. Introduction by Martin Gardner. 38 illustrations. 128pp. 5⅜ x 8½.
21482-6 Paperbound $1.00

THE NURSERY "ALICE," *Lewis Carroll*
While most of us consider *Alice in Wonderland* a story for children of all ages, Carroll himself felt it was beyond younger children. He therefore provided this simplified version, illustrated with the famous Tenniel drawings enlarged and colored in delicate tints, for children aged "from Nought to Five." Dover's edition of this now rare classic is a faithful copy of the 1889 printing, including 20 illustrations by Tenniel, and front and back covers reproduced in full color. Introduction by Martin Gardner. xxiii + 67pp. 6⅛ x 9¼.
21610-1 Paperbound $1.75

THE STORY OF KING ARTHUR AND HIS KNIGHTS, *Howard Pyle*
A fast-paced, exciting retelling of the best known Arthurian legends for young readers by one of America's best story tellers and illustrators. The sword Excalibur, wooing of Guinevere, Merlin and his downfall, adventures of Sir Pellias and Gawaine, and others. The pen and ink illustrations are vividly imagined and wonderfully drawn. 41 illustrations. xviii + 313pp. 6⅛ x 9¼.
21445-1 Paperbound $2.00

Prices subject to change without notice.

Available at your book dealer or write for free catalogue to Dept. Adsci, Dover Publications, Inc., 180 Varick St., N.Y., N.Y. 10014. Dover publishes more than 150 books each year on science, elementary and advanced mathematics, biology, music, art, literary history, social sciences and other areas.

22. Teachings of Wisdom
63. Of Beggars
27. Of Useless Studying
26. Of Useless Wishing